J. L. AUSTIN
A Critique of Ordinary Language Philosophy

The Author:

KEITH GRAHAM

Keith Graham is Lecturer in Philosophy at the University of Bristol. He was educated at University College, London (First Class Honours) and University College, Oxford, where he took his B.Phil. in 1970. His philosophical articles have appeared in *Ratio, Inquiry, Analysis,* and in the *Proceedings of the Aristotelian Society.*

J.L. Austin

A Critique of Ordinary Language Philosophy

KEITH GRAHAM

Department of Philosophy, University of Bristol

HUMANITIES PRESS · NEW JERSEY

This edition first published in USA by
HUMANITIES PRESS INC.
Atlantic Highlands, New Jersey 07716

© Keith Graham 1977

Library of Congress Cataloging in Publication Data

Graham, Keith.
    J.L. Austin : a critique of ordinary language
philosophy
    Bibliography: p.
    Includes index.
        1. Austin, John Langshaw, 1911–1960.
2. Languages–Philosophy. 3. Philosophy.
I. Title.
P85.A8G7   192   77–22624
ISBN 0–391–00747–5

Typeset by Computacomp (UK) Ltd.,
Fort William, Scotland
and printed in England by
Redwood Burn Ltd., Trowbridge & Esher

'Philosophy recovers itself when it ceases to be a device for dealing with the problems of philosophers, and becomes a method, cultivated by philosophers, for dealing with the problems of men.'
JOHN DEWEY

'Conceptual investigations are seldom or never separable from either substantive ones or from evaluation.'
ERNEST GELLNER

Acknowledgments

Quotations from the following works of J. L. Austin are made by permission of the Oxford University Press, Oxford: *Philosophical Papers*, edited by J. O. Urmson and G. J. Warnock, second edition, © Oxford University Press 1970; *How To Do Things With Words*, edited by J. O. Urmson, © Oxford University Press 1962; *Sense and Sensibilia*, edited by G. J. Warnock, © Oxford University Press 1962.

Contents

Preface

I should like to thank Peter Alexander, Ed Brandon (who also proof-read), Hugh Flinn, David Hirschmann, Paul Snowdon, Bill Valinas and Christopher Williams for helpful comments. I owe an especially large debt of gratitude to Adrian Ashley for stimulating and illuminating conversations on the entire manuscript, and for forcing me to clarify my thoughts.

I dedicate this book to my parents, who made generous sacrifices over many years in order to give their children an education.

Abbreviations of Austin's Works

PP *Philosophical Papers*
W   *How To Do Things With Words*
SS *Sense and Sensibilia*
CR *Cahiers de Royaumont* No. IV (containing Austin's 'Performatif-Constatif', with discussion), Les Editions de Minuit, 1962

I

Introduction

1. Aims of the book

This is a book about one man. It is also a book about
an entire movement in philosophy which has been
dominant for the last thirty years. With the arguable
exception of Ludwig Wittgenstein, no one has had a
greater influence on philosophy during this period, at
least in the English-speaking world, than J. L. Austin.
This is a fact which stands in need of explanation.
Austin published only seven papers in his own lifetime,
and in contrast to Wittgenstein his posthumous output
adds up to only three small volumes. Moreover,
although the number of books and papers published
by others under Austin's influence must be legion,
comprehensive discussions directly about his
philosophy as a whole are rare. One of my aims in this
book is to make good this deficiency, to expound the
main doctrines of Austin's philosophy, in order to
show what it is which has had such an influence.
Accordingly, although I do not deal with everything
which he wrote, I do consider all those works which
have produced noteworthy acceptance or reaction in
other philosophers. This includes much of the
posthumous work. Austin died prematurely, and it
may be that his contribution and his effect on others
would have been different if he had not. Be that as it
may, it is the actual historical influence which is my
concern.

Exposition is not my only aim, however. With the
signal and significant exception of his theories about
the nature of language, which I try to show are
suggestive and fruitful, I believe that Austin's

1

philosophy is stultifying and exercises an influence for the bad on those who come into contact with it. I have therefore attempted to say not only what his philosophy is but also what is wrong with it. In doing so, I have kept three types of reader in mind: the elusive educated layman, who may want to know something of what goes on in contemporary philosophy; students of the subject who, sometimes to their cost, find out; and fellow professional philosophers. Technical terminology has been unavoidable in places, but I have kept it to a minimum and I have tried to keep clarity of expression high on my list of priorities. Much lower on the list have been points of comparatively fine detail — what Austin himself would regard as the essence of the subject. I have no doubt that somewhere I have said 'sentence' when I should have said 'statement', or 'fact' when I should have said 'state of affairs'. And I do not much care, provided the broad lines of my argument stand examination.

One possible reaction might be to suppose that a critique of Austin holds merely historical interest, on the grounds that his influence has waned. There could be no more dangerous mistake (though it is one which I have heard people make). Some recent examples from my own experience may be relevant. The question whether a person can be in error about the nature of his own desires is a serious and important one. I have heard two philosophers attempt to resolve it by pitting against each other the idioms 'I didn't want it *all along*' and 'I didn't want it *after all*' (their verbal italics), said in relation to a previously-ordered steak. In a discussion on the legitimacy of political authority I have heard a philosopher labour the point that I can order some coal but I cannot command it. And I have heard a philosopher ask (and get away with asking) as a *rhetorical* question, 'How could ordinary language possibly be wrong?' Each of these (by no means atypical) examples reflects the influence of one or more of the principles guiding Austin's own philosophy. The same, I believe, is true of many publications in leading philosophical journals (a claim which the reader may test after reading this book). And, most seriously of all, the same is true of the philosophy being taught today in many universities and colleges in Britain and America. If anything, I should say that Austin's influence is on the increase: his work receives increasing attention outside the English-speaking world in such places as Germany and Scandinavia, and his ideas have begun to be taken up in other disciplines, such as legal theory and social psychology.

Finally, I should say a word about the nature of my exposition. It is not a genetic or functional account: I do not attempt to trace the historical influences on Austin or lay bare the interests which his kind of philosophy serves. These are important tasks which I leave to those better qualified to pursue. What I have given is a *critical* account, an account which involves assessing the plausibility and validity of Austin's philosophy considered on its own feet, without regard to its origins or its extraneous effects. I have also tried to give, around the edges of my arguments, some clear indications of an alternative and preferable procedure to Austin's.

2. Brief historical background

Although it is the content of Austin's philosophy which I shall examine, so that what follows is critical philosophy rather than history of ideas, nevertheless that content itself can only be fully understood by locating it in an historical context. I shall therefore now describe Austin's place in the recent developments of his subject.

The widest tradition to which he belongs is *empiricism*, where the term is used not to denote any particular doctrines, nor even to describe only a philosophical tradition, but rather to indicate a certain approach or attitude of mind. Deeply rooted in the English intellectual tradition is a feeling for concreteness and particularity, a mistrust of abstract, high-flown generalisations and an insistence that even speculative thought should be anchored in the concreteness of tangible, everyday experience. (A colleague responded to this claim by saying, 'Well, could you give me an example?') This is an attitude which contrasts with some, though by no means all, European intellectual traditions. It is by virtue of sharing this temperament, rather than holding any particular doctrine, that Austin deserves to be called an empiricist. Now this tradition is valuable: it encourages rigorous standards of clarity and precision, which is valuable both because clear thought is better in itself than unclear thought and because error is more readily exposed in clear thought. It is a tradition which reinforces what Bertrand Russell once called a robust sense of reality. But as with people, so with intellectual traditions: their virtues are often those very same characteristics which constitute their vices. The empiricist attitude too easily lapses into a pedestrian philistinism, a refusal to see connexions or to consider general questions, and an obsession with small details. We shall see that Austin amply illustrates both sides of the empiricist attitude.

At the end of the nineteenth century there was an important turning point in philosophy (cf. Dummett 1973, Chapter 19), and it was one which provided a new expression of the empiricist temper. Since the time of Descartes the orientation of the subject had been towards epistemology. There were various facts or supposed facts about the nature of the world, the human mind and so on, and questions were raised in philosophy about the security of our *knowledge* in these matters. The basic questions were about what we know, and how. This orientation changes with the arrival of the German philosopher Gottlob Frege (a philosopher of decidedly empiricist cast of mind, whose book *The Foundations of Arithmetic* was translated into English by Austin). In effect, Frege pushes philosophical discussion a stage further back. For him the basic question is not 'How do we know these things?' but rather 'How are these things which we take ourselves to know to be construed? What is the meaning of the claims which people make about the nature of the world and of the human mind?' In short, the *meaning* and the *analysis* of thought come into the centre of the picture, a position which they still hold.

This new orientation is reflected in the work of two major British philosophers of the twentieth century, G. E. Moore and Bertrand Russell. The period preceding theirs had been uncharacteristically unempiricist, and in their different ways each was in reaction against the idealism of figures such as F. H. Bradley and T. H. Green. In Moore's case this took the form of reaffirming a number of commonsense convictions of a kind which the idealists had denied, as for example that there is a physical world external to the mind, containing a number of separate and discrete objects. What interest Moore has as a philosopher arises from his insistence that while the truth of such beliefs cannot sensibly be questioned, their analysis can. He therefore sees it as his task to analyse, that is to interpret and give meaning to, the language in which those beliefs are cast. Russell's concerns are only partially similar. He too wishes to insist on the reality and the diversity of the world, but he does not believe that it is possible to justify everything which is affirmed by common sense. Accordingly, taking the precise and unambiguous language of mathematics as his paradigm, he wishes to construct a language which properly reflects those features of the world which we are correct in supposing it to have.

With Moore and Russell language has entered explicitly on to the scene, but whereas with Moore the emphasis is on reaffirming the language of common sense, with Russell it is on reforming it. This difference becomes greatly magnified when we consider the approach to the subject which each has inspired in later philosophers. Associated with Russell there is what might be called a tradition of *alternative language philosophy*, consisting in attempts to validate some set of concepts as providing an acceptable means of looking at some part of the world, regardless of whether those concepts happen to coincide with those embodied in the language of common sense. The kind of philosophers who approach their subject in this way include Carnap, Tarski, Quine and Davidson. In contrast, Moore is directly responsible for *ordinary language philosophy*, as practised by such people as Ryle, Strawson, the later Wittgenstein and, unequivocally, Austin. Now to group these last-mentioned together under this label is of course to oversimplify, as indeed is the drawing of the historical family tree which I have indulged in. All the same, there really is a similarity of approach here which is worth calling attention to, whatever other differences there may be. What Austin and the others have in common is the premium which they all place on ordinary, everyday non-technical language, and a corresponding mistrust of philosophers, or anyone else, who may try to change it. My discussion will be concerned with Austin's specific version of this attitude. I believe that many of my criticisms would be equally applicable to the other philosophers mentioned, but I shall not offer any arguments for this.

Anyone who has a nodding acquaintance with contemporary philosophy knows that it is centrally concerned with language. What my historical sketch indicates, and what will become more apparent from subsequent, more detailed, argument, is that it is possible to be concerned with language in very different ways. Labels like 'linguistic analysis' and 'philosophy of language' are sometimes used to cover a number of distinct and diverse approaches to philosophy, and this is harmful and misleading. 'Philosophy of language' is the name not of one but of a group of related methods, and one thing I hope to show is that if Austin's method of dealing with philosophical problems is defective this is not because it involves looking at language, but rather because of the particular way in which he looks at it.

One further point. As well as relating to method, the

expression 'philosophy of language' also designates a
subject, a particular area of enquiry — philosophy of
language as opposed to philosophy of mind, science,
and so on. Austin also discusses language as a subject in
its own right, and has interesting and suggestive things
to say about it. There are many connexions between
his use of philosophy of language as a method and his
views on the philosophy of language as a subject. I shall
try to trace these, and show how they are responsible
for some of the errors into which he falls.

So far I have given a rough sketch of the framework
in which Austin is to be located. In the next chapter
I shall consider the particular principles and presuppositions governing his use of the philosophy of
language as a method. But before doing so, I shall have
to carry out two further tasks. I have described a
tradition with a particular approach, but it is necessary
to be more explicit about what it is an approach *to*.
That is, the nature of philosophical problems
themselves needs to be made clear. This is all the more
important since Austin's arguments are addressed
largely to fellow philosophers, and I wish to make
explicit how his discussions connect with the
philosophical questions which anyone at all might raise
simply by thinking about the more general features of
the world and our experience of it. The second task,
connected with this, will be to take the reader inside
the tradition stemming from Frege, which I have so far
described only from an external point of view. I believe
this tradition can provide a useful way of looking at
philosophical problems, one which will enable us at
once to understand Austin's own approach and to see
more clearly where it goes wrong. The principles I
advocate in the sections which follow will inform many
of my later criticisms of Austin.

II

Philosophy of Language as a Method

1. Introduction

Philosophical thinking can take a variety of forms and come from a variety of sources. I may begin to think philosophically by reflecting on certain facts about myself, or about other people, or about inanimate nature. I think of myself, for example, primarily as a physical being, someone with a body which is extended in space. But it is a traditional belief in my culture that I also have a soul, and that it is as a soul that I survive when my body has become lifeless and disintegrated. Is such a belief well-founded? How, in any case, is the soul to be described, and how should I understand its relation to my body?

I can ask these questions about another person as easily as about myself. But there are further questions which, in reflective moments, I may be disposed to ask about other people precisely because they are other than and separate from myself. In this spirit I may wonder just what it feels like to be someone else — say, what it felt like to be able to write a novel like *War and Peace*. Or I may wonder what it is like to have passionately strong convictions about some particular matter to which I myself am indifferent. Such speculation may stem from the suspicion that there is a dimension of the existence of other people which is hidden from me, and this suspicion may itself prompt further questions. Can I ever establish totally reliable connexions between the way other people outwardly behave and the happenings of their inner, mental life? For example, can I ever know for certain what motivates another person to act in a particular way? Of course, I have other people's testimony for what they are thinking and what reasons they have for doing things, but then I may begin to wonder if such testimony itself is ever totally to be relied upon.

This is the direction my thinking may take if I am initially struck by the innate mysteriousness of other people. On the other hand, I might feel that such doubts are unreal, and that it is simply a matter of investigating the various mechanisms and operations of the brain if I want to know what goes on in other people's minds. The question which then arises is how far I am prepared to spread the idea of intelligence, for there are machines which bear a resemblance to the brain both in structure and in operation. Are these machines to be credited with intelligence? Again, if I suppose that people's behaviour is accounted for in terms of neural and physical states, it may seem to follow from this that their every action must be predetermined and that the idea of people as autonomous agents is an illusion. But then, am I not myself such a person, so that I cannot deny free will to others without denying it to myself?

When I turn my attention to the inanimate world, similar doubts may assail me. I take the world to be a colourful place, for example, but the highly informative and systematic account of the world which modern physics is able to give seems to leave this feature of colourfulness out altogether. Am I therefore mistaken in what I normally believe here, and is colour something which exists only in the eye, or mind, of the beholder? And is this also true of some further features which I normally take the external world to possess on its own account?

My philosophising about the world may in this way take some doubt as its starting point, but that does not have to be so. Instead, I may take my usual knowledge of the world for granted and ask how that knowledge is to be characterised. Much of it is gained through sense perception: so is such perception best construed as some kind of direct contact between the world and me, or as the world's producing some kind of representation of itself in me, or what?

With certain provisos, questions of this kind are typical philosophical ones; that is, they are typical of the questions which philosophers, throughout the history of the subject, have tried to answer. The main proviso is this. I have deliberately presented the matter as though it is always the questions which give rise to the philosophy rather than philosophy itself giving rise to questions. The suggestion is that I begin with a kind of puzzlement about some aspect of the world and then attempt to philosophise, or turn to what philosophers have said, in order to reach some satisfactory solution. This is a reflection of Aristotle's view that philosophy begins in wonder, and that any philosophy worth its salt will ultimately have its roots in some independently existing problems. But such a claim needs to be tempered in two ways. First, the attempt to philosophise is bound to give rise to new problems as well as those which, so to speak, have a life of their own, for it will involve the forging of new ideas which may be in various ways problematic. Secondly, it is sadly not true that everyone is motivated to philosophise in the way Aristotle suggests, for reasons of curiosity about the nature of the world and its contents. G. E. Moore, for example, said he did not think the world or the sciences would ever have suggested any philosophical problems to him; it was what other philosophers had said about the world or the sciences which did that (Moore 1942, p. 14). We shall see that in this respect Austin is much closer to Moore than he is to Aristotle.

Some of the questions mentioned so far call for a yes/no answer, or a more qualified version of such an answer. It is unlikely that this can be satisfactorily given purely as a result of philosophical research, or indeed purely as a result of any other single kind of research. It would, after all, be a staggering coincidence if each of the profoundest questions raised by men could be allocated to one and only one academic discipline. The problem of personal survival is not only philosophical but biological, the problem of knowing another person's motives is not only philosophical but psychological, and so on. This is a point worth mentioning for two opposite reasons: because of the historical tendency of philosophers to arrogate to themselves the power to answer such questions entirely out of their own resources, and because of the contemporary tendency (perhaps a reaction to the grandiosity of the first claim) to disclaim that philosophers are professionally concerned with such profound questions at all. But the proper antidote to excessive ambitiousness is not to abandon such problems altogether; it is, rather, to insist on the fact that philosophy can contribute to certain aspects of complete solutions, even if it cannot offer complete solutions on its own. What this comes down to in practical terms is that work in the philosophy of X (e.g. the philosophy of science, or of law, or of the mind) will need to be informed by an awareness of what has been discovered in the relevant field X. We shall see several instances where Austin fails to take this point seriously enough.

Not all of the questions mentioned so far can be given yes/no answers. Whatever I am looking for when I raise a question like 'What is knowledge?' it will have to be something more complicated than that. It is indeed perhaps a feature of such questions that I may raise them without having any very clear idea what is to count as a solution to them. If so, this will have repercussions on one's view of philosophy and philosophical method. Let us call such questions 'analytical questions', recognising that at the moment this is no more than a label.

2. Aspects of philosophical problems
So far we have some questions, with nothing said about how they are to be answered. With these and similar questions in mind I shall now offer a particular

classification of different aspects which such philosophical problems can assume. This will not be some spuriously neutral God's eye view of the questions: it will be a classification broadly within the analytical tradition stemming from Frege which I outlined in Chapter I.

The different aspects of philosophical problems may be distinguished and explained as follows:

(A) Analytical questions: Some philosophical questions may best be viewed as arising in a situation where we all agree that there are things of a certain description and where we also agree which things merit the relevant description and which do not; but yet we suffer from a kind of puzzlement, which could be expressed by saying that we are unsure how to state the rationale or basis for our agreed decisions about how things are to be described. This is the best way of interpreting the question 'What is sense perception?' as it was raised earlier. We may agree that I am now seeing the paper I am writing on, that I am not seeing the Eiffel Tower, but what sort of thing is it that makes these true? Is the basis for the truth of my claim to be seeing the paper some relation between a subject and the world? If so, what is the nature of that relation? Or is it just some state of the subject? Or is there perhaps some reason to think that there is more than one kind of seeing?

The raising of this kind of question is as old as philosophy itself. Socrates raises it, for example, in Plato's dialogue *Meno* when he asks what virtue consists in. It can safely be assumed that he and his interlocutors would agree that justice and temperance are virtues whilst dishonesty is not, but the question Socrates wants answered is what it is about the first two which makes them entitled to the description 'virtue'. In such cases what is being sought is the principle governing the application of some concept which we are quite happy to go on applying as we do. This may seem to be no more than the replacement of the label 'analytic' with a longer one, but more will be said about this type of question in due course.

(B) Borderline questions: In contrast to these analytical questions, some of the questions mentioned earlier are prompted by the fact that we are not always so sure how to describe the world. Specifically, we may be unsure how to divide phenomena into those which do and those which do not merit a certain description. Thus, I recognise that my next-door neighbour is a person and that in consequence it is possible to enter into certain relations with him and have certain obligations towards him, and I recognise just as certainly that his car is not a person. But I may be far less certain what to say about a viable but unborn human foetus, or someone who has been in a coma for several years, or some concoction which a scientist of the future is able to produce from a test-tube. In the same way, I may be quite happy to assign the description 'rational' to my neighbour and withhold it from his car, but quite uncertain what to say in this respect about ants, bees and dolphins, which seem to meet some but not all of the requirements of rationality.

What happens here is that we are agreed about what are the central cases of phenomena falling under some concept such as rationality; but we are not sure how far the application of the concept does or should extend, and in consequence we have trouble with borderline cases.

(C) Comprehensive questions: Finally, we saw that sometimes questions are raised which are radically distinct from the two kinds so far categorised. There are occasions when perfectly general doubts assail us: despite usually describing certain things in a certain way, we begin to wonder if there really is anything of the given description. We wonder, for example, if anyone is ever really responsible for his actions, although normally we take it for granted that people often are. Or we wonder if the whole of life may not be a dream, despite our usual practice of distinguishing between waking and sleeping. In short, we come to

question in a comprehensive way whether some concept really has application at all.

This three-fold classification is, of course, immensely oversimplified. It is also an idealisation. I doubt that any analytical philosopher would conceive of philosophical questions in exactly this way, and some would raise many objections to it. Nevertheless, I hope the classification can illuminate such questions and Austin's approach to them. In the present and succeeding chapters, I shall frequently refer to analytical, borderline and comprehensive questions, problems, aspects, etc., depending on which of my headings they fall under.

3. Concepts

At this point someone may object that, far from being enlightening, my classification only obscures the nature of philosophical problems. The questions originally introduced were all, roughly, about some part of the world — people, minds, objects, etc. But now I have made it seem that they are questions not about these substantial entities but rather about concepts, whatever they are. Does this perhaps signal a move away from the concreteness of the original questions into a realm consisting of ideas and nothing else?

There is certainly a danger in replacing questions about 'so-and-so' with questions about 'the concept of so-and-so'. For one thing, as Austin points out, it may lead us mistakenly to suppose that concepts are articles of property, as if we could find out all about them by inspecting the furniture of our minds (PP, p. 41). But that is not a mistake which we are forced to make, and there are strong reasons in favour of shifting to talk of concepts. Sooner or later, once we have begun to raise philosophical questions, we are faced with a confrontation between our thoughts and the world, and we have to decide how adequate the former are for understanding the latter. Now there is one way of construing this confrontation which is tempting but which should be resisted. This is to suppose that our apprehension of the world, the way we think and talk about it, is a matter of our receiving a certain image of it, so that the adequacy of our apprehension is determined by the accuracy of the image. This is to be resisted for two reasons. First, talk here of receiving an image involves (except, arguably, in the case of sense perception) the use of a potentially misleading metaphor, as we shall see when we come to consider the problem of truth. But secondly, it also wrongly suggests that the influence is all one way, from the world to us. The world does not present itself to us ready-labelled, complete with an explanation of its various parts; on the contrary, it is necessary for us to order and categorise the data of our experience. This is where concepts come in, for our ordering of experience occurs through a series of filters, a network of particular ideas and ways of looking at things. What we then have to decide is whether particular ideas and ways of looking at things which we use in making judgments about the world are adequate, and if so, where they apply and for what reasons. As Austin puts it, with reference to the words which embody our concepts, it is necessary to 'prise them off the world, to hold them apart from and against it, so that we can realise their inadequacies and arbitrariness' (PP, p. 182). To put it bluntly, it is taking too naïve a view of philosophical questions to suppose that they can be settled simply by looking how the world is. We must also consider our own interpretation of the world.

How much freedom we have in choosing concepts to interpret the world with is a difficult and controversial question (which I intend to sidestep as far as possible). Some would argue that certain concepts and categories, certain ways of arranging our experiences, are essential if we are to make any coherent sense at all of such experiences; others would say that we have a completely free choice. My point here is the more limited one that we at least have to recognise the existence of the problem, and consider the contribution which *we* make in forming the judgments we do about the world. That there is such a problem should be made all the more evident by the fact that there already exist many different and rival ways of ordering experience. Notoriously, different languages embody different colour discriminations; in Russian, kinship relations are categorised differently from in English, so that the term 'brother-in-law' may be translated in one of four ways into Russian; the Romans categorised certain phenomena as falling under the concept of *pietas*, which we do not do; and we categorise certain phenomena as falling under the concept of personal moral responsibility, as the ancient Greeks did not. We can ask for a validation of any such concept, whether it be one from another culture, one current in our own, or one which is not in use but which is deliberately constructed and proposed for use as a new way of looking at the world.

When it is understood that there are these reasons for translating our original questions into questions about concepts, it should be clear that this does not imply a desertion of the real world for a world only of ideas. I have as yet said very little about how the validation of concepts is to be achieved, but if the whole point in examining them is to see how adequate they are for interpreting the world then it must obviously involve a joint consideration both of concepts and of the world (though not along the lines of the simple comparison suggested by the 'image' metaphor). The confrontation really must be a confrontation.

4. Priority of analytical questions

Before this two-way connexion between concepts and the world is spelled out further, I should make some more remarks about the classification introduced in section 2. Although it is intended to be fairly exhaustive, its divisions are not exclusive. The classification gives three aspects which philosophical problems may take, rather than three different types of problem. The significance of this is that a given problem, say that of free will, can assume different aspects at different times.

We can pick out two general ways in which a problem may change its aspect, and both serve to emphasise the priority which attaches to the analytical aspect. First, suppose that we begin with some comprehensive doubt, e.g. whether the concept of sexual perversion has any application or whether, on the contrary, there is no such thing as sexual perversion but only different sexual appetites and inclinations. Then one obvious way of attempting to settle this question is by seeing whether it is possible to formulate some consistent and acceptable principle for applying the concept in question. Similarly, if we have a problem about a borderline case, e.g. whether a twenty-six-week-old unborn foetus counts as a person, then we may attempt to resolve it by arriving at an explicit account of the conditions for applying that concept. In short, we may attempt to settle a borderline or comprehensive question by producing an analytical theory.

If this is correct then we may have to give priority to analysis, not necessarily because it holds most intrinsic interest for us, but rather because it will equip us best for dealing with other problems. Although this is a view which has gained prominence since Frege, the germ of it has always been present in philosophical enquiry, and once again it can be traced back to Plato. In the *Laches*, when it is asked whether a certain form of weapon-training will lead to fitness and courage, Socrates insists that before this the prior question must be answered what exactly courage is. And again in the *Meno* he insists that an adequate answer to the question whether someone can be taught to be virtuous requires first an explicit consideration of what virtue is.

When someone originally motivated by puzzlement about the world turns for help to philosophy, then the stress on an analytic approach which he finds, at least in the tradition to which Austin belongs, can easily lead to disappointment and despair. The analytical, as much as the conceptual, approach may seem to imply a withdrawal from the original problems. Thus, one may start with some pressing and often practical question, such as 'Will this weapon-training make men courageous?'. Socrates lays down the challenge to state what courage is, rejects various answers without stating explicitly what kind of answer would satisfy him, and the original question seems to be abandoned forever. In a contemporary context one might begin with the problem how one ought to conduct oneself in a certain situation and become bogged down in a discussion about the meaning of 'ought', resulting in a similar neglect of the original problem. Hence one may be led to the conclusion that analytical philosophy necessarily deals only with trivial academic questions, the answers to which (assuming any are arrived at) can make no difference either to the way we look at the world or to the way we behave in it.

Once again, the fear expressed in this criticism is a reasonable one; but it applies less to the analytical approach than it does to an abuse of that approach. Where there is genuine uncertainty about the application of a concept it seems obviously sensible to try to give an explicit account of where and why it should be applied. On the other hand, it is possible to abuse this device by making an on-the-spot demand for an analysis of a concept which is not problematic and whose extent and application can be taken for granted in the given context: almost any argument could be stopped dead in its tracks by asking its proponent, 'What exactly do you mean by "if"?' But such mischievous use of the analytical approach does not vitiate it as an approach, any more than the value of some life-saving surgical instrument could be doubted on the grounds that it was used by homicidal maniacs to slice off their neighbours' heads.

Moreover, even when analysis is pursued for its own sake it is not clear that it can be guaranteed immunity from further decisions about what we might think or say, and it is here that we see the second intermingling of the three aspects of philosophical enquiry. I may begin an analytical enquiry believing I know without any doubt which phenomena merit some description and which do not, and seeking only for an account why this is so. For example, I may be confident that I know perfectly well which actions are voluntary and which are not, and just want to know on what basis I pick out some as voluntary. But this initial conviction may become weakened in the course of my enquiry. Either I may come to feel doubts about whether certain types of action are voluntary or not, or (worse still) my search for a principle governing the application of the concept of voluntariness may lead me to the conclusion that no such acceptable principle can be found, that the concept of voluntariness is flawed in some way, that it has no application — in short, that there are no voluntary actions. This interdependence between the analysis of a concept and the way it is actually applied is something which Austin seems to recognise, at least in principle (cf. PP, p. 74); what I am emphasising here is the fluidity of the situation and the fact that my analysis may react back on the way I describe the world. I have not yet said anything about just how this may come about, but this will be remedied as the argument moves on, and its significance will become apparent when we consider Austin's discussions of particular philosophical problems.

5. Linguistic philosophy

The philosophical tradition to which Austin belongs is not only conceptual and analytic; it is also linguistic. The philosophy of language, construed as a method or a way of approaching philosophical problems, might be regarded as on a level with but distinct from a philosophy of, say, introspection, a 'phenomenological' approach. If our apprehension of the world is mediated by concepts which must be analysed before we can reach conclusions about the problems which interest us, then two natural ways of going about the task would be either to examine the contents of our consciousness when we think about some part of the world or to examine the content and structure of the language we use to talk about it. However, we should not be surprised if these two apparently distinct ways turn out not to be so distinct after all. On the one hand, if I am to report or discuss the results of my acts of introspection then I shall have to do so in language; and on the other hand, it may be that certain introspective judgments will have to be made in the course of relating language to the world. It is interesting to note in this connexion that Austin was tempted to call his own method 'linguistic phenomenology' (PP, p. 182).

There is, however, an additional reason for paying attention to language, besides the need to analyse different ways of looking at the world. I have criticised the idea that there is a straightforward match between the nature of the world and our judgments about it: it is equally naïve to assume a straightforward match between our thoughts about the world and the language in which we express them. The point can be brought out by means of an example. Consider the sentences

(1) Spinach is 20p per pound.
(2) Spinach is nice.

On the face of it (1) and (2) are identical in structure, each involving the assertion that spinach has a certain property — that of being a certain price and that of being nice. Yet it is very evident that despite this surface similarity, the type of message which each of them is used to convey is very different. When I utter (1) then I am doing what I seem to be doing, ascribing a certain property to an object which it either does or does not possess, regardless of any thoughts or attitudes I may have. On the other hand, when I utter (2) I am not ascribing that kind of property to an object at all. Contrary to what is suggested by the surface form of the sentence, what I am doing is describing or expressing a certain reaction which I have to an object. One way of putting this would be to say that I am recording a relation in which I stand to the object rather than a property which it has independently of me. The structure of (2) could accordingly be exhibited by reconstituting it as

(3) I like spinach.

Now in the example in question these points are very obvious — that is why it can be used as an example. But in other areas philosophical controversy abounds over whether a given style of language is or is not misleading. Consider, for example, the judgment

(4) That course of action is unjust.

This again has the same outward form as (1). Is that its real form, or is its real form, as with (2), something quite different? In other words, are justice and its opposite properties which actions possess independently of anyone's thoughts and attitudes? or does the justice or injustice of an action depend essentially on someone's feeling some way towards it? Here it is by no means obvious what is the correct answer, and depending on what we take it to be, we may go about making moral decisions in a different way and act differently in the world. The fact that language can mislead in this way — and in contexts where it is of practical importance not to be misled — produces the need for analysis, a careful and detailed explanation of just what is involved in various philosophically important types of statement.

6. Analysis

As we have seen, anyone who adopts an analytical approach in philosophy commits himself to the view that it is a useful or indispensible precondition of answering questions about, say, virtue or knowledge that we should give an explicit account, an analysis, of the ideas of virtue and knowledge. It would be ironical, and perhaps damaging to the plausibility of the analytical approach, if no such explicit account could be given of the idea of analysis itself. But can such an account be given? That is, is it possible to give some general specification which will make it clear what has to be done for an analysis to be successful? The father of this approach, Socrates, often rejected certain attempts on the grounds that they had failed to give an analysis: thus, he would complain that you do not give an analysis of virtue merely by naming examples, qualities which are virtues. He is less explicit about what kind of attempt would not constitute a failure. He does, it is true, occasionally give examples of a successful analysis, such as the analysis of the idea of quickness as 'the ability to achieve much in a short time'; but giving only examples in this way leaves the interlocutors with the need to 'catch on' to what is required in general. My impression is that many contemporary students are left just as much at sea, since they are given no clear guidance on the general criteria for a successful analysis. And how can one hope to achieve anything when one does not know in advance what is to count as having achieved it?

Yet we should perhaps not allow this question to pass as a rhetorical one. When someone sits down to write a novel or compose a symphony it is doubtful that he does so with advance standards which would allow him to predict a point at which he would be able to say, 'Now I have successfully completed the task'. If philosophy is like certain other artistic and intellectual endeavours in that it involves the attempt to look at things afresh, then ultimately it may also be like them in having no definite stopping-place. But only ultimately: even if an exhaustive account of the requirements of an analysis cannot be given, nevertheless in the short term it is possible to list certain requirements which will allow the procedure to begin.

First, and most obviously, if I am to analyse the concept of virtue or knowledge then I must give some kind of equivalence. If my analysis is linguistic it will take the form of analysing a typical statement in which the relevant concept is expressed, e.g. 'I know that so-

and-so'; and if it is motivated by an ordinary language approach I shall take as a datum the way people ordinarily use the concept of knowledge in their language. Thus, I have to *say in other words* what knowledge is. However, not just any other words will do, and it is often insisted that it is not sufficient to give a 'merely verbal' equivalence. Thus, suppose that for the analysis of

(A) I know that so-and-so

we were offered

(B) I am aware that so-and-so.

Then it would be objected that this is to give a synonym rather than an analysis of knowledge. An analysis would have to consist in terms far less closely connected with knowledge than this, which merely records a connexion which could be taken straight from a dictionary.

Apart from any unclarities already contained in this objection, it is likely to create confusion when it is coupled with an insistence that, on the other hand, any analysis must be given in terms which are very closely connected indeed with the concept to be analysed. This is the requirement which is sometimes expressed by saying that in giving an analysis we lay bare those features which are *essentially* connected with the concept to be analysed. To give an example, it may be that we apply the concept of rationality to X, Y and Z, and it may be that X, Y and Z are all two-legged; but I could not attempt to use the idea of two-leggedness in an analysis of rationality, because the connexion between these two things is merely accidental, not sufficiently close to count as an essential connexion. As it is often put, 'two-legged' is no part of the meaning of 'rational', or being two-legged is not something which is a property of rational creatures 'in all possible worlds'. Correspondingly, on the positive side, an adequate analysis will isolate and describe just those properties the idea of which is contained in the concept of rationality. When those properties have been specified in sufficiently independent terms, the test of the analysis will then consist in asking, 'Can we imagine a world in which there are creatures which possess those properties but not rationality (or vice versa)?' 'Is this what it means to be rational?'

But what is it to describe a concept in 'sufficiently independent terms', and what are we to make of the demand that there should both be and not be a close connexion between the concept to be analysed and the terms in which it is analysed? This apparently contradictory demand gives rise to a double-bind trap which will probably be recognised by anyone who has been a student of philosophy. It seems that anything one tries to say in philosophy will be vitiated either because it expresses a merely accidental or contingent connexion, and is therefore of no philosophical import, or because it expresses a necessary connexion and is therefore merely true by definition. When I was a student a tutor threw this dilemma into a sharp relief for a group of us by leaving us at the end of a discussion with the question, 'What is the difference between a trivial tautology and an interesting conceptual truth?' At the time it seemed that the question had merely been given as an exercise; in retrospect, I suspect that the tutor would have been as eager as any of us to be told the answer.

Moreover, there is an answer, though it is not the kind which satisfies anyone without a good deal of explanation, viz. 'It all depends on what you know already.' The requisite explanation begins with an insistence that we take seriously the implications of the suggested parallel between philosophy and art, the claim that in both we are often concerned with a re-presentation of something familiar in unfamiliar terms. What this implies is that there will be an area of philosophical theorising where degrees of success rather than straight success-or-failure is at stake. To be sure, I may be straightforwardly right or wrong in my attempt to reproduce what is involved in some concept (if I say that knowledge of something consists in standing six yards to the left of that thing, I am hopelessly wrong); but my attempt to reproduce what is involved in that concept *in novel terms* may be more or less achieved. This also explains the apparently contradictory demand that the terms of the analysis both be and not be closely connected with the concept being analysed. They must stand in the properly intimate relation to the concept if I am to reproduce its meaning, but it must not be too *obvious* that they stand in such a relation.

An important consequence of this interpretation of 'analysis' is that, beyond a certain point, the criteria for a successful analysis will be partly intuitive or psychological. A successful analysis will be one which links two sets of ideas in such a way that we can truthfully say of it, 'Yes, these ideas *are* inseparable, yet this is not a point which would otherwise have readily occurred to us.' This explains why the proposed analysis of knowledge as 'being aware' would be rejected — not because it is wrong to link the two, but because it is just too obviously right. In contrast, an example of a more successful analysis may be given from the contemporary literature. Mackie (1965) has suggested that what is often involved in the concept of one thing's causing another is the idea that the first occurred and was an *INUS-condition* of the second. 'INUS -condition' is an acronym, formed from the initial letters of the expression ' *i*nsufficient but *n*ecessary part of an *u*nnecessary but *s*ufficient condition'. Expressing this on the pattern of an equivalence between two types of statement, it is suggested that

(C) X caused Y

is to be analysed as

(D) X occurred and was an INUS-condition of Y.

Whatever else we may say of (C) and (D), we shall certainly not say that they are too obviously equivalent in the way that (A) and (B) were. On the contrary, we have to stop and think carefully in order to work out just what (D) means.[1] When we have done so, if we conclude (as I believe we should) that it accurately reproduces at least part of what is involved in the idea of causation in at least some of its uses, then we shall also conclude that the analysis is to that degree a successful one.

In this way we arrive at an example of the kind of analysis which is required, but not just an example which leaves people with the need to catch on to the requirements. We can point to those features of the analysis which make it a successful one. It accurately reproduces the logical implications of the concept to be analysed, and does so in an interestingly novel way. Degree of accuracy and degree of novelty determine the degree of successfulness of the analysis.

The presence of a psychological component amongst the criteria for a successful analysis may be helpful towards removing a kind of bafflement which may be produced in the context of the double-bind trap mentioned earlier. The attempt to condemn an analysis as 'merely true by definition' rather than 'merely contingent' is often accompanied by the argument that the analysis suffers from circularity. This is a very common type of argument in analytical philosophy, and in its general form it goes like this. 'Look, you offer an analysis of A in terms of B and C. But the ideas B and C themselves have to be explained in terms of A, which is the thing you are supposed to be explaining, not the thing you are supposed to be using to explain something else. Therefore, your analysis is circular.' No doubt actual arguments in actual situations are deployed with greater subtlety, but in my experience this is often their skeletal form. They occasion bafflement because an analysis is, after all, supposed to be an equivalence; and if one thing is equivalent to a second, how could the second fail to be equivalent to the first? To rearrange it so that it was *not* equivalent to the first would be to fail to give an analysis, and hence to fall for the second part of the double-bind.

What force there is in this form of argument can best be brought out by re-expressing it. If A is explained in terms of *B* and *C*, and it is *very obvious* that *B* and *C* are themselves to be explained in terms of *A*, then the complaint of circularity will have a point. However, if *B* and *C* can be linked to *A* through a whole series of intermediate ideas *D-Z*, then though some circularity may be involved it will be of an inescapable and unobjectionable kind. In short, there is something to be said for the view that all arguments of a certain type in philosophy are circular but that this does not matter as long as the circle is big enough.

I suggested earlier that any successful method of analysing concepts will involve paying attention not just to concepts but also the world, although we must abandon any simple idea of mapping a concept on to the world as one might check a brass-rubbing for accuracy by holding it against the brass. It may be as well to expand on this — otherwise, the remarks made here and earlier about analysis are likely to seem both oversimplified and misguided. In an attempt to forestall misunderstanding, therefore, I should enter two general qualifications to the account of analysis so far developed (the second of which has numerous ramifications).

First, when we are searching for a set of terms to express the principle governing the application of some concept, there is no advance guarantee that just one clear set of ideas will be available to cover all contexts in which that concept does have application. To use a piece of jargon due to Wittgenstein, it may be that there is only a 'family resemblance' amongst all those contexts which are cases of of someone's *knowing* something, for example, rather than one definite feature which they all have in common. This is a point with which Austin was equally familiar (PP, pp. 7off.). A slightly different possibility is that there should be *two* sets of ideas in terms of which the concept is to be explained, such that the concept is appropriate where either one of these two sets applies. It will not be easy to tell merely by attempting to analyse a concept whether there is a single principle governing its application, or a disjunctive principle, or no principle at all, for the failure in practice to find a principle of the simplest kind will not be proof that none exists. There are good heuristic reasons for attempting to formulate one, and these will be spelled out in connexion with meaning in Chapter IV.

The second general qualification is that the nature of the link between a judgment and that part of the world which it is about is far more complex than the link between a name and the object it names. This distinction in type between judgments and names is a commonplace in philosophy (though it was not always so), but it is very doubtful that all the consequences of the distinction have yet been drawn out. It is relevant to the present discussion because talk of the application of a concept is often the same as talk of the appropriateness of a certain judgment. Now there are various ways in which the judgment/situation relation can turn out to be more complex than the naming relation. The judgment may correlate, in some way peculiar to itself, with some feature of a situation but not any immediately discernible feature. So, for example, when someone is described as being responsible for an action he has performed, it is unlikely that the concept of responsibility correlates with any immediately discernible feature either of the agent or of his action. If we are seeking the principle of application for a concept of this kind, then what we might try to do is select some relatively superficial feature of the situation which does not itself give the grounds for applying the concept, but which can be taken as a reliable guide to the presence of a second, more recondite, feature which does give the grounds of application.

However, there is another kind of case which falls within the ambit of this second general qualification. We often employ concepts which correlate with features of the world neither in a simple nor in a complex way, but rather do not correlate with features of the world at all. This is obvious enough if we think in terms of the concepts embodied in various subsidiary parts of language (there is nothing in the world with which 'if', 'and' or 'why' correlate), and also, say, the case of imperatives, where the 'shut' in 'Shut the door!' need not link in any way with something in the world. But we have seen already the possibility that this is also true of judgments which do, on the face of it, purport to relate to a feature of the world: there is the argument, for example, that the judgment that an action is *just* is not really a judgment about an independently existing aspect of the action. Cases of this type exemplify, in Hume's phrase, the propensity of the mind to spread itself on nature, or in other words to project on to the world features which in its own independent existence it does not have.

In terms of language this can be expressed as a distinction between those contexts where language is used, so to speak, creatively as a vehicle for an original response to the world, and those contexts where it is used to reflect the nature of the pre-existing world, to map what is already there. Which of these two functions a particular judgment is used to fulfil may not be apparent from its superficial form, but this is precisely what we should expect to deduce from an adequate analysis of the judgment in question. Perhaps no one has done more than Austin to draw attention to various creative uses of language, and we shall consider what he has to say about this in chapters III and IV.[2]

A possible outcome of analysis, then, is the discovery that some concept expresses an original response rather than reflecting some pre-existing feature of the world. Where this is so, the shape of analysis will itself be affected. Rather than singling out some recurrent features which license the application of the concept in question, it will entail much more giving the purpose, point and interest in responding in the way implied by using that concept. But this represents a change in emphasis rather than a completely new type of analysis. Even where a concept does correlate in some way or other with features already 'there' in the world, an analysis giving the principles for applying it must still, at least implicitly, bring out the point in applying it. It is, after all, possible to group together any recurrent features of our experience and invent some term for applying to them: analysis should reveal the reasons which explain and justify doing so in one way rather than another.

At this stage it may be easier to see why analysis may lead us to change the way we describe the world. Where 'description' is a misnomer and it is really a response which is analysed, we may decide that an adequate rationale for the response in question cannot be given, i.e. that there are not good enough reasons for responding in that way. But even when the concept being analysed does relate in some way to something already 'there', what begins as a purely academic, analytical enquiry may end with our being assailed by doubts, of varying degrees of sweepingness, about how we are to interpret and categorise the world. At this point, what was mentioned earlier as a possibility may now be sketched a little more fully, though still in a wholly abstract way. Suppose that we apply the concept C in a number of different situations, or types of situation, $S1, S2, \ldots Sn$, and that with this in mind we attempt to arrive at an analysis of C, an account of the principles governing its application. Suppose, too, that we achieve an analysis which is successful in explaining the application of C in all situations except $S2$: the analysis gives a good and enlightening account of the meaning of C, and explains what it is about the various situations which entitles us to apply C to them, with this one exception of $S2$. If this happens, then we may justifiably feel that we ought *not* to link C with $S2$ any more. Thus, although we may begin by measuring proposed analyses of a concept against the cases which we take the concept to cover (and this is itself only one test of an analysis), when an analysis is seen to have a high degree of acceptability it itself may come to be used as a means of testing the cases and determining whether or not they do fall under the analysed concept.

There probably could be no general rule to tell us when such a reversal may occur, certainly not in terms of the *number* of situations $S_1 \ldots S_n$ which such an analysis must cover. So many other factors will enter in — how happy we are in applying the concept to just those situations prior to any analytical thoughts about it, how informative and systematic the proposed analysis is, and so on. But a point can be reached in this way at which, as a result of an analytical investigation, we modify our views on how to describe the world.

This possibility, to repeat, has been sketched so far only at an abstract level. Nevertheless, it already implies two points of methodological importance. One is that the way we speak cannot be taken as an absolute, unalterable datum; the other is that an analytical enquiry will be intimately connected with normative questions, questions about how we *ought* to speak. Both of these points will assume greater importance in the course of my argument.

So far I have stressed the interconnexion between the judgments we make and analysis of the concepts they contain. There is one respect, however, in which these are distinct. It is true that a successful analysis of a concept will tend to support the retention and use of that concept (because it will reveal reasons which explain and justify operating with it); it is equally true that matters may come to light in the course of seeking an analysis which give reason for abandoning a concept (the conditions for applying it may turn out to be irremediably confused, the concept may turn out to apply vacuously to all situations, it may express something inconsistent, and so on). But the mere absence of an analysis of some concept is not in itself a reason for abandoning the concept. We may employ a concept in our judgments which is perfectly acceptable but yet be unable to *state* what the rationale is for our use of it. (The point of analytical philosophy is to remedy that inability.) In the absence of an analysis which gives compelling grounds for using or not using a given concept, we shall have to base our decision on many other considerations: whether the concept allows a sufficiently sophisticated view of, or response to, the world, whether it allows adequate explanation of the data to which it applies, whether it fits in well with other concepts we employ and see good reason to employ, and so on.

7. Austin's method

Austin's way of dealing with philosophical problems finds its place within the analytical, conceptual and linguistic tradition outlined so far. It is now time to consider the specific principles guiding his work, which differentiate him from other philosophers in this tradition. The most explicit statements of the method he follows are to be found in his papers 'A Plea For Excuses' (PP, pp. 175–204) and 'Three Ways of Spilling Ink' (PP, pp. 272–287).

According to Austin, one philosophical method — and it is the one he goes on to elaborate – is 'to proceed from "ordinary language", that is, by examining *what we should say when*, and so why and what we should mean by it' (PP, p. 181; Austin's italics). In concrete terms, such a procedure has three phases. In the first, we are to make as complete a collection as possible of all the linguistic items, expressions, idioms, etc., which are relevant to the particular area of thought we are concerned with. For this Austin recommends working through a dictionary and any other appropriate literature. Thus, supposing our interest is in problems of responsibility and blame, we should begin by listing terms such as 'accident', 'on purpose', 'inadvertent', etc., and then follow up cross-references in the dictionary until we are simply coming upon repetitions. We should then turn to other useful sources, such as law books, which will contain details of various types of pleas in mitigation, and pyschology books, which will contain various interesting classifications of different types of behaviour.

When we have added to our list of expressions in this way, the second phase consists in breathing life into them. This we do by imagining, in as precise and detailed a way as possible, different situations and attempting to reach agreement on what we should say when they obtained. In this way we attempt to differentiate between idioms and expressions by reference to the different situations to which they are allocated. As well as discussions about *what we should say when*, this second phase also sometimes involves decisions about when we should say what. That is, sometimes we begin by specifying a situation and then determine which of a number of possible expressions is appropriate to it, but at other times we begin by selecting the expression and then working back to a specification of the kind of situation in which the expression would be appropriate.

Austin suggests that if we can reach agreement in this second phase then we have acquired some 'data' which we may go on to explain in the third phase. Such an explanation will consist in 'an account of the meaning of these expressions, which we shall hope to reach by using such methods as of "Agreement" and "Difference": what is in fact present in the cases where we do use, say, "deliberately", and what is absent when we don't' (PP, p. 274).

This is the barest outline of Austin's stated method. It will have to be amplified, and it will be necessary to determine how far his practice is in step with his theory. But in any case there are many distinctive features of his practice which are not conveyed in the outline. Perhaps the most immediately striking feature of his method in practice is the concern with *minutiae*, with minimally small differences in idiom. For example, in the course of particular arguments he attempts to distinguish between knowing that some bird is a goldfinch *from* its red head and knowing it is a goldfinch *because* it has a red head (PP, p. 84); between acting *deliberately*, acting *intentionally* and acting *on purpose* (PP, p. 274); between what I do *in* saying something and what I do *by* saying something (W, pp. 121–31); between *looks*, *seems* and *appears* (SS, pp. 33–43); and even between *precisely* and *exactly* (SS, p. 129). This may prompt the suspicion that in his work Austin is worrying away at a microscopic level which cannot possibly hold any philosophical significance, since the minute differences he draws attention to are merely accidental variations in idiom, confined to a particular language.

At least to some extent, one simply has to be pragmatic about this and just decide in particular cases whether distinctions of this order of magnitude hold any philosophical importance. Certainly the argument given here for supposing they do not is less than compelling. A philosophically significant distinction or assimilation might very well fail to be reproduced in different languages. It may be, for example, that the difference between knowing a person and knowing a fact is sufficiently important to merit distinction by the use of two different verbs, as occurs in French with *connaître* and *savoir*, and that English is philosophically indadequate in the way it is structured at this point. Conversely, it might be that English marks a philosophically important *similarity* between the two kinds of knowledge, which French fails to notice. The problem for Austin is not that he deals in language-relative distinctions but, as we shall see, that his reasons for proceeding as he does leave him helpless when it comes to *adjudicating* between languages, as we must when they conflict.

If the two verbs, *savoir* and *connaître*, do mark an important difference then it will be possible to argue for this in other ways. However, Austin would probably regard it as unnecessary to do so, since he would reject the idea that such differences might be merely accidental. He implicitly holds something like a principle of sufficient reason with regard to language: if there is a difference in idiom there will be some reason for it, even if that reason is not immediately apparent to us. This is comparable to the Freudian assumption that slips of the tongue and the forgetting of familiar names are not just things which we happen by chance to do, but things for which there will be an explanation. In both contexts the assumption, considered as heuristic, is a sound and sensible one for the purpose of acquiring full and systematic knowledge. Assuming that there is a reason means that we shall not miss it if there is. But there are limits — that is the point of heuristic principles. When, in a discussion of the nature of reality, Austin is led to speculate on why we speak of *false* teeth but *artificial* limbs we may well feel that the limit has been passed. (cf. SS, p. 72. He in any case ignores the mock-genteel expression 'artificial dentures'.) Moreover, it is not just that he sticks to his assumption through thick and thin fare. There is a difference between believing there is a reason for something and believing there is a *good* reason for it. To draw a Freudian parallel again. Every time I see a policeman I experience feelings of guilt and uneasiness: I am sure there is a reason why this is so, but it is evident that there is not a good reason for reacting in this way (at least not always). We shall see that Austin's beliefs lead him to hold the second, stronger and less defensible, position with regard to distinctions in the language.[3]

This meticulous, almost obsessive, attention to matters of very fine detail has been transmitted by Austin to the tradition he inspired, so much so that it was once suggested to me that this branch of analytical philosophy could be known as anal philosophy for short. Yet this has not been the most influential aspect of his method, nor is it the most important in his own work. Austin's central concern is with *ordinary* language, the language spoken prior to specialist (including philosophical) theorising, the language of 'the plain man' who makes many appearances in his work. Now we have considered earlier some reasons for paying attention to language in general, and Austin endorses some of these: the power of language to mislead is something he is alive to, as is the fact that language mediates our interpretation of the world (cf. PP, pp. 181–2). The concern with one particular kind of language, however, requires some further justification.

When he is giving such a justification, Austin sometimes presents it as though his concern with ordinary language were simply a matter of tactics and emphasis. He argues that ordinary language already contains finer and subtler distinctions than is often realised, and that if these are explored in preference to rushing into some hastily-defined new technical terms then it may be possible to reach agreement and make some progress in philosophical discussion (cf. SS, pp. 3, 63, PP, pp. 175ff.). As a cautionary reminder, that we should appreciate just what is involved in a certain way of looking at or speaking about the world before we decide to reject it, this is no doubt acceptable. But it would not be sufficient on its own either to explain or to justify Austin's single-minded devotion to ordinary language, and at other times he commits himself to a stronger view regarding the concepts embodied in ordinary language:

> '[O]ur common stock of words embodies all the distinctions men have found worth drawing, and the connexions they have found worth marking, in the lifetimes of many generations: these surely are likely to be more numerous, more sound, since they have stood up to the long test of the survival of the fittest, and more subtle, at least in all ordinary and reasonably practical matters, than any that you or I are likely to think up in our arm-chairs of an afternoon — the most favoured alternative method.'
>
> (PP, p. 182)

In this passage, which is central to an understanding of Austin's approach to philosophy, the argument is not merely that we need to examine ordinary language so that we are clear on what we are rejecting if we reject it; it is rather that, on neo-Darwinian grounds, there is reason for *not* rejecting it. In short, the concepts we already operate with have a claim to superiority, for otherwise they would not have survived but would have been replaced by more adequate ones.

This commitment to the adequacy of ordinary language appears, at least, to be qualified. Whilst contending that ordinary language embodies 'the inherited experience and acumen of many generations of men' Austin concedes that 'it has not been fed the resources of the microscope and its successors' and hence that it may be necessary 'to be brutal with, to tortue, to fake and to override, ordinary language' (PP, pp. 185–6). However, even at the theoretical level such a concession is itself well qualified elsewhere:

'Certainly, when we have discovered how a word is in fact used, that may not be the end of the matter; there is certainly no reason why, in general, things should be left *exactly* as we find them; we may wish to tidy the situation up *a bit*, revise the map *here and there*, draw the boundaries and distinctions rather differently.'

(SS, p. 63; italics added)

At the practical level, in his actual discussion of traditional philosophical problems, we shall see that Austin does resist attempts to supersede pre-philosophical, ordinary language. He almost always defends what the plain man says (or rather what Austin says the plain man says) against any way of speaking meant to replace or improve upon it.

What emerges, therefore, from this aspect of Austin's method is his ingrained *conservatism*. The tendency is always to preserve from change those descriptions of the world which happen to be the current ones, in the belief that they would not be current if they were not worth preserving. As far as I can discover, the only general argument Austin ever puts forward in favour of such conservatism is this neo-Darwinian one. It is therefore crucial to his case, and

we shall see that unfortunately it is a very bad
argument, amongst other reasons because it is self-
defeating. In the absence of any valid general
argument in favour of such conceptual conservatism, it
will be necessary to give some justification for any
piece of current usage on its own account —
something which Austin rarely does. The other side of
this conservatism is, inevitably, a hostility to new
terminology and new ways of looking at the world —
again in practice, if not officially. Austin may appear to
concede the importance of scientific findings for our
view of the world, yet in his discussion of sense
perception he does not consider even the commonest
argument which has scientific findings as its starting-
point, namely the causal dependence of what is
perceived upon the condition of the perceiver.
Indifference to new, and possibly disturbing, findings is
hardly surprising where longevity is taken as the main
sign of worthiness.[4]

The conservative concern with what we should
ordinarily say is thus one dominant aspect of Austin's
philosophy, as well as his concern with minutiae. A
third aspect, which has also been influential in
inspiring others, is that the concern with what we
should ordinarily say really is with what we should
ordinarily *say*. That is, the method is founded pre-
eminently on an examination of *spoken* language,
concrete verbal communication in a specified context,
what people say out loud rather than what they think
or what they would agree to be true (cf. SS, p. 41, W, p.
144, PP, pp. 63–5). It is possible that such an emphasis
may lead to a systematically distorted picture of things
(and I shall argue later that it does), for there are
particular constraints in operation in speech situations,
to do with what it would be relevant to say, what there
would be any point in saying, etc., which do not
operate where we are concerned, in some more
general way, simply with what is true.

In Austin's concern with spoken language, we see an
example of the connexion between philosophy of

language as a method and philosophy of language as a subject. Taking language as his subject, Austin was able to formulate some important theories of concrete speech acts, actual utterances in a social context rather than some abstraction from them. When someone senses and even begins to realise the possibility of a systematic study of concrete linguistic acts, it is natural that he should entertain greater hopes, such as that systematic studies of this kind will enable us to solve or see through many philosophical problems. It is natural, but not necessarily defensible.

This completes the preliminary examination of Austin's method. The final test of its value must be to see it in action in dealing with the kind of question outlined at the beginning of this chapter. In the meantime, however, I believe it is possible to formulate some difficulties in the way of practising the method which suggest that it can be productive of only a very limited success.

8. The method's limitations

To begin with, there is something which may seem a merely procedural difficulty but which will in fact serve to bring to the surface some of the radical flaws in the method. Suppose that we begin to practise it, as outlined at the beginning of the previous section. Having chosen an area we wish to investigate and collected all the relevant linguistic items, we go on to compose stories about apposite situations and ask what we should say when they obtained. An example: I intend to shoot my donkey but in fact shoot yours, who looks very similar, thinking it is mine. Should we say that I shot your donkey *by mistake* or *by accident* (PP, p. 185n.)? It should be noted that the scope of 'we' in this talk of *what we should say when* must be something like all, or most, competent native English-speakers. It could hardly be thought to hold any philosophical interest that I and a few other people in a room gave a particular reply to the question 'What should we say when....?' unless this did hold some such wider implication.

The existence of this implication gives rise to the apparently procedural difficulty. Although Austin deprecated the idea of constructing new idioms from the armchair, it seems that he had no objection to the adoption of that posture for the practice of his own method. Certainly he never advocated any alternative. But if we, i.e. a small group of socially and culturally homogeneous philosophers meeting in an Oxford college, do pronounce from this position on what we, i.e, all or most competent native English-speakers, should say in different situations, how can we be sure that our pronouncements are correct? Does the method not cry out for some form of empirical verification? If we hold that most people would say so-and-so, should we not test this claim by observing their linguistic behaviour or at least by asking them whether they agree? Otherwise, it may be felt, the professional philosopher who pronounces upon *what we should say when* has no greater claim on our credulity than the professional politician who pontificates about what the ordinary people of this country are sick and tired of.

This is a difficulty which has been taken seriously by some of the philosophers influenced by Austin's method. While it has led some to attempt to supplement the method by the use of questionnaires, others have argued that this is unnecessary since we, the philosophers, are ourselves part of the source of the evidence which would validate any claim about what we should say. One weakness in the latter reply is that under any normal circumstances we shall be only a minimally small part of the appropriate evidence. But there is another weakness which affects both replies, and that is the shared assumption that native language-speakers will be reliable *reporters* of their own linguistic habits. In other words, it may be suggested that what we now have is a problem which faces any sociological approach to the gathering of information. Just as a man may *say* that his attitude to something is such-and-such when in fact it is not, so we or the people we question may *say* that we should have such-and-such a linguistic response to a given situation when in fact we should not (cf. Fodor and Katz, 1963). If this new difficulty is a genuine one, its effect will be to move Austin's practice even further away from the armchair, for what it implies is that it may not be adequate to question either ourselves *or others* about what we should say, and that as a check on our information we need actually to observe the response elicited in the appropriate situation. And the information gathered in this way will be very incomplete, since many of the situations we set up will be hypothetical rather than actual ones — we can hardly go around arranging for people's donkeys to be shot in confusing circumstances in order to see what other people then say.

Again an attempt might be made to rebut the objection. It could be argued, for example, that part of what is necessarily involved in being a competent speaker of a language is that one should be able to say with accuracy what one's own verbal behaviour would be, so that it is logically impossible for the alleged difficulty to arise (cf. Searle, 1969, pp. 12–13). But this may be, in a way, too defensive a rejoinder. The point is that the apparently unambiguous question 'What should we say when …?' is capable of being construed in more than one way, and whether there is a difficulty here depends partly on how it is understood. In the first place, when a situation is described and we are asked what we should say when it obtained, we could take it that we are being asked for a *decision* about how to describe it, from the outside, as it were. The question is not, 'What would you say in that situation?' but rather 'What do you say, here and now, about it?' These are the facts, and the question is what we are prepared to say about them. But secondly, and distinct from this, we might suppose that the request is precisely for us imaginatively to project ourselves into the hypothetical situation and *predict* what our verbal behaviour would be in it. It is clear that we may well return different answers to the original question, depending on which interpretation of it we adopt. In particular, a constraint upon what we believe we should say *in* a situation, though not what we should be prepared to say *about* it, would be considerations of what there was any point in speaking about at the time. This may lead us to predict that we should say nothing at all, or something quite irrelevant to what the setting up of the situation is designed to clarify.

The following (true) story illustrates the danger of confusing the two interpretations of the question.When I was a student a number of us became absorbed in the question whether the mind could just be identified with the brain, or whether on the contrary it was conceivable that someone might have a mind but no brain at all. In the jargon, is the concept of a mind logically tied to the concept of having a brain, and would it be self-contradictory to say something like 'Mr X has a mind, though his head is filled with porridge'? Unconsciously influenced as we were by Austin's method, we thought it proper to canvass the opinion of a philosophically uncontaminated friend, the nearest thing we knew to Austin's 'plain man'. Since the friend failed to understand our jargon, we asked him to imagine a situation where someone he had taken to be in all respects a normal human being falls down, breaks his head and porridge pours out. What would the friend say? He paused before replying, 'I should say, "I'm not surprised he fell over".'

This may suggest that the original difficulty, about verifying any answer to the question 'What should we say when …?', is in fact spurious. Any reply which rests on the predictive interpretation is potentially irrelevant in the manner of our example, and this is not something which can be avoided merely by tightening up the way in which we ask for the predicted response. It will not be sufficient, for example, to say 'What should we say if asked, "Does this man have a mind?"?', for the prediction might still be that we should, perhaps, say nothing at all, since we should be too nonplussed. Now it is precisely the predictive reply which is beset by a problem of verification — it might turn out that when the situation did obtain we did not in fact say what we predicted we should. But the reply which involves offering a decision or judgment, here and now, on the hypothetical situation is not open to the same difficulties, since it does not allow the same possibility of a mis-match between predicted and actual response. If, therefore, it is the reply involving a decision which is the appropriate type to give, then the original difficulty can be ignored.

Now it seems clear to me that it is indeed the reply involving a decision which is relevant in philosophical enquiry, so that there is no danger, at least on this score, of philosophy's needing to transform itself into the sociology of language. For all that, it may be that the original difficulty is a genuine one specifically for Austin's method. This is not so straightforward. Certainly his concern with the context in which words are literally uttered, with interpersonal, spoken communication, suggests an emphasis on the predictive interpretation, and there are many examples of particular answers which Austin gives to the question that appear to be predictive. But the sharp contrast between decision and prediction is one which Austin would probably wish to reject. He argues, for example, that truth itself stands 'only for a general dimension of being a right or proper thing to say, as opposed to a wrong thing, in these circumstances, to this audience, for these purposes and with these intentions' (W, p. 144). I shall return to this.

Meanwhile, there is another reason for thinking that it is the reply involving a decision which is philosophically significant. There is a second ambiguity hidden in the question 'What should we say when ...?', an ambiguity which cuts across the first. We may understand it as a request either for a *descriptive* or for a *normative* reply. This ambiguity is hidden since, by an accident of English grammar, 'we should say' can mean either 'we would as a matter of fact say' (to put it into bad grammar), or 'we ought to say'. So we may reply *either* by stating what, as a matter of fact, we do say of a situation or would say in it, *or* by stating what we feel would be the correct thing to say in or about the situation. Now it is important to notice that for Austin this choice does not in practice arise. Since, as we have already seen, he pledges his faith in the appropriateness and adequacy of ordinary language on account of its survival, his answers to either of the two questions would be equivalent. For Austin, what we do or would say is, because of its proven fitness, what we ought to say. For anyone who does not share Austin's commitment to the adequacy of ordinary language there is no guarantee that answers to the two questions will coincide. In some particular case we might well believe that what we do or would say is not, for some reason, what we ought to say. Where this does occur, it seems clear that it is the normative reply which holds philosophical interest.[5] Many of the questions raised at the beginning of this chapter were about the proper or best way of looking at the world, and these are already normative rather than merely descriptive questions. This explains why, as I suggested, paying attention to this second ambiguity in 'What should we say when …?' gives support to the claim that it is decision or judgment, rather than prediction, which is involved in philosophical investigations — for to give a normative answer, to say what you believe ought to be the case, is a matter of making a judgment rather than a prediction. It also explains why it is important that Austin should have good reasons for thinking that descriptive and normative claims will coincide, for he approaches his question under its descriptive interpretation and considers what anyone would or does say.[6] Further weight is therefore placed on his argument that ordinary language has shown its adequacy by its survival.

There is a further connexion between the normativeness of philosophical questions and Austin's neo-Darwinian argument in favour of ordinary language. He was not so parochial as to believe that it was only mid-twentieth century English which had shown its philosophical worth by survival, and he believed that it was important that the type of research he advocated should go on in other languages which had shown fitness by survival (CR, p. 351). This is a commendably consistent attitude, but it does raise the question what we are to do in a case where two languages, both well-proven by longevity, happen to disagree with each other. In his explicit discussion of methodology, Austin's response to this possibility of conflict is sanguine, not to say complacent:

'If our usages disagree, then you use "X" where I use "Y", or more probably (and more intriguingly) your conceptual system is different from mine, though very likely it is at least equally consistent and serviceable: in short, we can find *why* we disagree — you choose to classify in one way, I in another ... if there are "alternative" descriptions, then the situation can be described or can be "structured" in two ways, or perhaps it is one where, for current purposes, the two alternatives come down to the same. A disagreement as to what we should say is not to be shied off, but to be pounced upon: for the explanation of it can hardly fail to be illuminating.'

(PP, p. 184)

Yet there is no further indication *how* such differences are to be explained, or how such disagreements may be resolved. On the contrary, the implication is that there is no need to resolve them, and that we can simply record that we talk in different ways. But this is unsatisfactory precisely because of the normativeness of philosophical questions. Very often the situation is that there are advocates of different and incompatible ways of interpreting experience, and we wish to know which is to be preferred. For example, are we free agents, choosing between genuinely open alternatives when we act, or is everything we do already predetermined by processes byond our control? Again, do we live in a world of three-dimensional, coloured, noisy objects, or is each of us merely locked in an awareness of his own conscious experiences? It is an evasion of questions like this to say merely that these are alternatives which are equally serviceable and consistent. As Austin himself seems to realise elsewhere, something of more than academic significance may hang on how we 'structure' a situation (cf. PP, p. 285). We should, for instance, structure the description of someone's behaviour in different ways depending on the importance we attached to the agent's own way of seeing his behaviour; and in a context where questions of responsibility and blame are at stake we are likely to *act* differently towards the agent, depending on whether we see his actions in one light or another.

There is this permanent possibility of conflict both between different languages or conceptual systems and within one conceptual scheme. When such conflicts cry out for resolution, the conservatism which the neo-Darwinian argument is used to justify will be worse than useless, for there is nothing at all to be said for the preservation of incompatible theories. Moreover, there is a tension between Austin's conservatism and the evolutionism he uses to underpin it which can be brought out more directly. The fact that different, and rival, ways of looking at the world abound is one reason against a philosophical method which is essentially a 'legitimating' descriptive account of the present conceptual state of affairs. Yet even if this were not so, we might still feel that various improvements could and should be made to some existing way of looking at the world. *This is just what consistent evolutionists would expect.* If the neo-Darwinian argument can be used to demonstrate the conceptual superiority of the present over the past, then it can equally be used to justify the conceptual superiority of the future over the present. There is no reason to believe that conceptual evolution has come to an end at any given moment in time. Moreover, we stand in a quite different relation to the conceptual future, at least if we have begun to reflect philosophically on our ways of looking at the world. Rather than waiting helplessly to see what it will be we can, within certain limitations, *decide* what it will be. Consciousness of one's interpretation of the world, we might say, is the first condition of changing both one's interpretation and the world. Just as, in evolution proper, an awareness of the influence of the environment upon us can contribute to our control over the environment, so an awareness of the nature of the concepts we use may be a prelude to the conscious construction of alternative and more adequate concepts.

However, when it comes to a choice between conservatism and the conscious control of conceptual evolution, Austin opts for conservatism. We shall see that this is so very often in practice, but it is also so in theory. In his paper 'The Meaning of a Word' he appears to make a concession in the direction I have indicated, namely the formulation of new and alternative ways of conceptualising experience. He says that it 'will not do, having discovered the facts about "ordinary usage" *to rest content* with that, as though there were nothing more to be discussed and discovered. There may be plenty that might happen and does happen which would need new and better language to describe it in' (PP, p. 69; Austin's italics). If that is so, then the most natural reaction is to suggest that an attempt be made to formulate such a new and better language. Yet earlier in the same paper Austin had not seemed even theoretically interested in an enterprise of that kind. He had said:

'Ordinary language breaks down in extraordinary cases. (In such cases, the cause of the breakdown is semantical.) Now no doubt an *ideal* language would *not* break down, whatever happened. In doing physics, for example, where our language is

tightened up in order precisely to describe
complicated and unusual cases concisely, we
prepare linguistically for the worst. In ordinary language
we do not: *words fail us*. If we talk as though an
ordinary must be like an ideal language, we shall
misrepresent the facts.'

(PP,p. 68; Austin's italics)

But if we do not prepare for the worst (or at least
foreseeable difficulties) in ordinary language, then that
is something which we could, and ought to, alter. If
there are cases where words fail us then we should do
something about it and develop an alternative
language which can cope — though we may or may
not take the language of physics as a model to aspire to.

9. Conclusion

Bearing in mind these doubts and difficulties in
Austin's method, I now want to return to the
classification of philosophical questions introduced in
section 2. In the light of these general considerations,
how well can we expect the method to cope in
answering analytic, borderline and comprehensive
questions? It will perhaps have become evident that it
will enable us to deal with comprehensive questions
about existing concepts in the most drastic possible
way — by excluding them from consideration.
Generalised doubts, fears that an entire way of
speaking may be founded on sand, these are explicitly
or implicitly rejected by Austin (cf. SS, pp. 11, 63, PP, p.
113n.). He will not countenance any claim that we may
always be wrong in supposing that we know
something, or that we may never know what someone
is feeling, or that we may never be responsible for our
actions, or that there may be no world of public,
physical objects. But insofar as the rejection of these
sceptical possibilities rests on the belief that the plain
man's language is aptest for describing the world, and
insofar as this belief is ill-supported, then so is the
rejection of scepticism. Given the failure of Austin's

general argument in favour of the adequacy and applicability of 'ordinary' concepts, each must be justified on its merits, and similarly each sceptical argument will have to be met on its own ground. A wholesale and unargued rejection of scepticism will be no more defensible than the belief that all is for the best in the best of all possible languages.

In contrast to this, Austin's method may seem on the face of it to be an excellent one for dealing with analytic and borderline questions. By tracking down nuances and determining what we should say in different situations we may hope to gather a good deal of data relating to the application of various concepts; and it may seem that if we distinguish from one another superficially similar situations, and what we should say in each, then we shall get clear on how to handle borderline cases. However, it is implicit in the general criticisms made already of Austin's method that even in these two areas it will be both incomplete and defective.

The incompleteness may be brought out by reference to something which often happens in philosophical discussion and which is likely to puzzle anyone not familiar with it. In the midst of a discussion of some concept or other it is not unusual for highly unlikely and outlandish cases to be put forward for consideration. Consider two examples which relate respectively to the concepts of *knowledge* and *causation*.

Normally, if someone always knows my position as I walk back and forth behind a wall this will be because he is always able to see where I am, or because someone else is keeping him informed about my location, or something similar. But now imagine that someone can always successfully locate my position even when none of the channels along which the appropriate information might pass are open. Should we still say that he *knew* where I was, or only that somehow he always managed to guess correctly?

Secondly, with things as they are we call one event the cause of a second only if the first is earlier in time than the second (or at best simultaneous with it). Suppose, however, that on a large number of occasions when separate individuals were asked to draw any pattern of their choice they all produced the same pattern, which was also subsequently produced totally at random by some machine. The fact that the same pattern was chosen by a number of independent people would stand in need of some explanation. If the correlation between this and the machine-produced pattern were sufficiently impressive, should we say that the later event of the machine's randomly producing the pattern had a causal influence on the earlier event of the individuals' producing the same pattern?

What is the point in putting forward such cases for comment when we may have no reason to believe that they actually occur? One point is this. If we are to give the rationale of a concept, the principles governing its application, this is closely connected with plotting the limits of its application. A consideration of actual cases will provide us with the limits of application where this means the range of cases over which we do apply the concept in question, but not where 'limits' is taken to mean the range over which we might, could or would be prepared to apply the concept. There are reasons for thinking that it will be useful to know the limits in the latter sense, and not just the former, if the rationale of a concept is to be given. As we pare away from the hypothetical situation more and more of the features normally present where the concept applies, then if we are still prepared to apply the concept we shall come nearer to finding out what, in the situation, actually gives the grounds for the concept's application, as opposed to being merely accidentally present features wherever it applies. In this way, a consideration of fantastic cases may serve as an aid to the better understanding of actual cases. Similarly, having to reach decisions on imaginatively constructed hypothetical cases more or less forces us to consider what *reasons* we have for saying what we do of the normal cases, in order to see whether those same reasons carry across to the hypothetical cases (cf. Fodor, 1964). In other words, we are forced to go beyond ordinary language and to theorise — which is just as it should be.

How does Austin's method serve in these circumstances? It is plain enough that research into ordinary language will not of itself tell us what to do about hypothetical cases. Since they do not occur there is nothing which we ordinarily say about them. But instead of drawing the conclusion that in that case we shall have to do something besides researching into ordinary language, Austin apparently prefers to draw the conclusion that we simply do not know what to say of them. It is in connexion with such a hypothetical case that he makes the point that in ordinary language words fail us, though in an ideal language they would not. But this is in any case short-sighted. There are some philosophically important possibilities which would force us to a reconsideration of what we say — for example, the possibility that every action which a person performs is causally predetermined. It is the lamest possible reply to say that if this turned out to be true we should not know what to say. This is to feign a kind of fatalistic conceptual helplessness, and to ignore the *creative* possibilities in philosophical analysis.

The defectiveness of Austin's method is apparent in its third stage, that of giving the meanings of the expressions collected from ordinary language, which we may equate with attempting to give the rationale for the application of a concept. At its most unspecific the proposed way of explaining the meaning of a term consists in giving examples of sentences where the term occurs, and getting one's hearer to imagine situations which would be correctly described by such sentences (PP, p. 57). Alternatively, Austin speaks of arriving at the meaning of expressions by considering what is in fact present in cases where we do use the expression in question and what is absent when we do not (PP, p. 274). This is doubly inadequate. First, we have seen that it is not always possible to get to the heart of a concept merely by considering what is *in fact* present when we apply it, for in that way we may pick out features which are always present but are irrelevant to the concept's application, or features which are only instrumentally important as indicating the presence of something else. Secondly, the search for what is present when we do in fact say something, that is, for the features which accompany the expressing of some concept in a concrete speech situation means that the most we shall end up with is a rationale for the *saying* of something rather than a rationale for *what is said*.

These *prima facie* criticisms of Austin's method must be substantiated by an examination of his discussions of particular philosophical questions. However, there is one area where there is no place for my general criticism that he ends up talking only about language instead of using a consideration of language as a medium for reaching conclusions about the world. That is, obviously, where he takes language as his explicit subject matter. Indeed, there is reason to think that there his procedure will have to be different from — and more promising than — that outlined in the present chapter. Ordinary language does not contain much in the way of theories about itself, not even embryonic ones. We ordinarily say many things about the world, but we ordinarily say very little about what we ordinarily say. As a consequence, when he talks about language as a subject Austin is forced to a large extent to abandon his ordinary language approach and proceed constructively and creatively, forging new theories about language and raising philosophical questions about them. These theories, in their turn, react back on his philosophical method. The next stage, therefore, is to look at Austin's theories about the nature of language.

III

Philosophy of Language as a Subject: Performatives

1. Introduction

There are at least two features of human beings which are absolutely fundamental to their nature. The first is that of *agency*, the fact that human beings are capable of intervention in nature in a way no other creatures are (so far as we know), namely as a result of a deliberate, conscious decision to intervene. This is what gives human beings the possibility of quite literally creating their own environment, and it is not in the least surprising that the god which man created in his own image should have as his chief property that of Creator.

Already involved in the idea of agency is the second feature — the capacity which human beings have to *map* the structure of the world. By this I mean that in some way people can reproduce, in their thought, speech and perception, a representation of some part of reality.[1] When beings possess this capacity it is one further step in sophistication to be able to map not only the actual world but also possible worlds. It can then be argued that in order to act, in the fully human sense, we must be able to form a conception of the world as it is and also as it might be, and be able to bring about the change from the first to the second.

When Austin approaches language as a subject for philosophical reflection, he does so in an empiricist temper. His primary interest is in language understood as a set of actual concrete utterances in actual concrete situations, rather than as something more abstract (W, pp. 52, 100, 147). His greatest contribution to philosophy was to show how far language, understood in this way, is bound up with *both* the features of human nature which I have distinguished. There is a natural tendency to think otherwise, to suppose that language relates only to the mapping aspect, so that broadly speaking the only virtues or deficiencies in a language reside in its success or failure in reflecting reality. In *How To Do Things With Words* and 'Performative Utterances' (PP, pp. 233–52) Austin reminds us that there are many other dimensions to language, and he demonstrates that in various ways the idea of people as agents is deeply embedded in the idea of them as language-speakers. This he does by developing two theories, which I shall refer to as the *theory of performatives* and the *theory of illocution*. Ironically, however, he failed to appreciate just how well the two features of human nature coalesce in the use of language which he christened 'performative'. He is therefore led to develop the theory of illocution as a *replacement* for the first theory. I shall argue that he did not need to do so but that each theory makes its own separate and important point.

2. The introduction of performatives

Clearly, language very often is used with a mapping function. If I say 'I am running' or 'There are three people in the room', then my statement, if true, reflects a fact in the world. Utterances of this kind Austin calles *constatives*: they 'constate' something true or false (W, p. 3). He then tentatively draws a contrast (later to be questioned and abandoned) between constatives and utterances which are superficially similar in structure to them, but which do not, in my terminology, have a mapping function. The initial examples of *performatives* are the following:

'(E.*a*) 'I do (sc. take this woman to be my lawful wedded wife)' — as uttered in the course of the marriage ceremony.

(E.*b*)'I name this ship the *Queen Elizabeth*' — as

uttered when smashing the bottle against the stem.

(E.c)'I give and bequeath my watch to my brother' — as occurring in a will.

(E.d) 'I bet you sixpence it will rain tomorrow.'

(W, p. 5)

These are not in any way nonsensical utterances, but yet

'A. they do not "describe" or "report" or constate anything at all, are not "true or false"; and

B. the uttering of the sentence is, or is part of, the doing of an action, which again would not *normally* be described as saying something.'

(*ibid.*; Austin's italics)

Thus, to say 'I bet....' in the appropriate circumstances is not to describe anything else which I am doing, it is actually to *do* something, namely to bet.

The qualification 'in the appropriate circumstances' is important, and it serves to discourage the excessively simple view that marrying is just saying a few words, or that in saying a few words you can marry someone (W, p.8; PP, p.236). Associated with each of these utterances there is a ritual procedure, a set of conventions. If the act of, say, marrying is to be performed then the utterance must be made in the context of the appropriate conventional procedure and a number of other conditions relating to the procedure must be satisfied (W, pp. 8–9; PP, pp. 236–7). We could put this briefly by saying that there must be an accepted conventional procedure involving the uttering of the words in question, that this must be properly and correctly invoked by the parties to the exchange, and that they must all perform correctly and completely according to the principles of the procedure they are invoking (cf.W, pp. 14–15; PP, pp. 237–8). What is *not* required, however, for the successful issuing of a performative utterance is some inner, 'spiritual' act of promising, bequeathing, etc. To suppose so is precisely to miss the point about performatives — that they are not true-or-false descriptions of some independent act or state of affairs (W, pp. 9–10; PP, p.236).

What emerges from the requirements concerning conventions is that although, according to Austin, performative utterances are not assessable for truth or falsity they do become open to assessment in another dimension. They can be successfully or unsuccessfully uttered, or as he puts it, they can be *happy* or *unhappy*, depending on whether or not I succeed in *x*ing as a result of saying 'I *x*' (W, p. 14; PP, p. 237). Austin then goes to great lengths to classify and describe the various ways in which performatives can be unhappy, the various 'infelicities' they can suffer from (W, pp. 14–44; PP, pp. 237–40). These range from the possibility that the conventional procedure just does not exist in the context where the words are spoken (e.g. I say to someone 'I order you to chop wood' in a community where there is no convention according to which anyone can give or accept orders) to cases where a party to the procedure makes some mistake in executing his part of it (e.g. I write a will saying 'I leave everything to my son' and then forget to sign it).

At this point it is worth making a distinction in the conditions governing the happy issuing of a performative utterance. We have just mentioned ways in which someone can *fail* to perform that action which is identified by the key term in the utterance — betting, naming, etc. But we can separate from this another set of conditions. In the case of this second set, failure to meet the conditions does not constitute failure in issuing the performative utterance, but it does mean that the utterance will be in some *looser* sense 'unhappy'. Some conventional performative procedures are associated with independently existing thoughts, feelings and intentions, and provide for a conventional expression of them — such performatives as 'I advise you to leave', which provides a conventional expression of the belief that someone would do well to leave, or 'I bid you welcome', which provides a conventional expression of a feeling of gladness on someone's arrival. And again, some of these conventional procedures exist in order to provide the expectation of a certain kind of *conduct* subsequently, on the part of the person issuing the performative — for example, 'I promise to visit you tomorrow'. Now on the basis of this we might be tempted to say that it is also a condition of my issuing a performative happily that in the appropriate cases I should actually *have* the thought, intention, etc., connected with the performative, or that I should actually perform the action associated with the performative. The force in such a suggestion would come from cases where I say to you 'I advise you to give back the money' and then say you are a fool when you do, or where I say 'I bid you welcome' and then spend the whole evening grumbling that your arrival has disturbed me. Clearly enough, *something* has gone wrong in such cases. But Austin suggests, quite plausibly, that what we have here are instances of *abuse* of the procedure, rather than instances where the performance is actually abortive or void (W, p. 39). If I say 'I declare you man and wife' when I have not had vested in me the right to conduct the marriage ceremony then I have not succeeded in marrying you. But if I say 'I apologise' when I think I was perfectly justified and do not feel at all sorry, then I have succeeded in apologising, but I have made an *insincere* apology. The difference is one which is worth marking.

The initial characterisation of performatives is partly negative, in that it rests on a contrast between them and constatives and the claim that, unlike constatives, they are not true or false. At one point Austin suggests a way of further developing this characterisation by way of contrast with constatives:

(a) In the case of a *constative* utterance, e.g. "he is running", it is some independently existing fact, separate from the utterance, which makes the utterance true.

(b) In the case of a *performative* utterance, e.g. "I apologise", it is the happiness of my utterance which *makes* it a fact that I apologise.

(cf. W, p. 47)

In other words, it is suggested that performatives and constatives exhibit a difference in 'direction of fit' with the world. It is how the world is which determines how we assess a constative in its appropriate dimension, *viz.* truth and falsity; whereas it is our assessment of a performative in *its* dimension of happiness and unhappiness which determines how the world is. We shall see that this suggestion is in several respects oversimplified, but all the same Austin's point here contains an important insight which he fails to exploit sufficiently in his later discussion.

3. Austin's analysis of performatives

In introducing the notion of the performative use of language Austin is doing what in practice he is highly resistant to in other areas of philosophical enquiry. He is proposing a new concept with which to interpret a part of our experience. Now in one respect a proposed new concept is in a more exposed and vulnerable position than a concept already in use and accepted. It may be that the users of an accepted concept cannot give an explicit analysis, an account of the principles governing its use; but if, nevertheless, they are able to apply it with widespread agreement to an open class of particular cases, this creates a weak presumption in favour of the acceptability of the concept. It creates no more than a weak presumption since it shows only that the concept in question can be applied systematically, not that it is a fruitful concept to apply or that it is free from false assumptions. (After all, no doubt people in mediaeval times were able to apply the concept of witchcraft in agreement with each other.) Nevertheless, weak as this kind of evidence is, it is not available in the case of a proposed new concept. Here we cannot point to the fact that people have always used the concept successfully to make some discrimination or that they will continue to do so in the future. A successful explicit analysis of the concept would obviate this difficulty, and though there is no less reason for demanding an analysis of an accepted concept, it is perhaps more immediately evident that analysis is profitable in the case of a new one. Whether for this or for other reasons, Austin attempts to provide an analysis of the concept of a performative utterance. He considers and then rejects several possibilities. At this stage I summarise his arguments with a minimum of critical comment. My disagreement with many of the things he says will emerge later on.

The first possible analysis is in terms of *truth versus felicity*. It consists in considering the information already used in the preliminary introduction of performatives, to see whether it can be elaborated to provide an adequate characterisation of them and an adequate means of contrasting them with constatives. Despite having originally put the relevant points forward, Austin now rejects them. One of his reasons for doing so is this. Imagine that I issue the performative utterance 'I warn you that the bull is about to charge' in circumstances where the bull is *not* about to charge. Then it may very well be that the utterance is neither void nor insincere, i.e. that it is not defective in any of the ways mentioned earlier, but yet in this situation there is clearly something wrong with it. And the temptation — which we should perhaps succumb to? — is to say simply that the warning is *false* or mistaken (W, p. 55; cf. PP, p. 250). If that is so, then it will cease to be a distinguishing mark of performatives that they are open to criticism in terms of felicity/infelicity and not in terms of truth/falsity.[2]

Consider now an alternative suggestion. The examples of performatives which have been mentioned so far ('I promise', 'I bequeath', etc.) are all strikingly similar in *grammatical form*, and this may give us a clue to the means of characterising them. Perhaps it is a feature of performatives that they are always couched in the first person, present tense, indicative mood and active voice (W, p. 57; PP, p. 241).

Now this may seem a hopeless way of attempting to analyse the concept of a performative, on the grounds that grammatical form could not be more than an accidental feature which has nothing to do with the essence of performativeness. Moreover, it is obvious that at best this feature would be only a necessary, not a sufficient, condition for an utterance's being performative, since many utterances have this grammatical form though they are clearly constative — e.g. 'I clean my teeth three times a day' or 'I want to go to bed'.

Austin has answers to these two objections. First, if a successfully uttered performative constitutes an action then the agent must necessarily be the speaker. The first person form would then appropriately draw attention to this and also make clear *what* action the agent was performing (W, pp. 60–1, 67). Secondly, it might be possible to strengthen the grammatical criterion by adding to it a subsidiary criterion for pre-selecting performative verbs. In this connexion Austin observes that there is crucial systematic asymmetry between this grammatical form and all other forms in the case of performative verbs only. When I say 'I promise' then (other things being happy) I promise; but when a parent says of his child 'Johnny promises to come' this cannot make it the case that the child has promised — he has to do his own promising. Nothing like this asymmetry occurs in the case of non-performative verbs. 'I run' and 'Johnny runs' are exactly alike in respect of their function (W, pp. 63, 68; PP, pp. 241–2).

The second part of this reply is not entirely successful, for we are entitled to ask how we are to judge that the crucial asymmetry is exhibited in the case of any particular verb. It looks as though we shall already have to know how to pick out performatives if we are to be able to answer this and thus be able to draw up the necessary list. Be that as it may, Austin himself decides that conformity to the given grammatical form cannot operate as a criterion for performatives. As a counter-example to the requirement of the first person and active voice, he points to the possibility of a performative utterance such as 'You are hereby warned that ... ', or even 'Passengers are warned that ... ' (W, p. 57; PP, p. 242). We might then try to extend our grammatical criterion, in the belief that these forms are essentially transformations of the originally favoured form (cf. PP, p. 243). But worse counter-examples follow. According to Austin, performatives need not be cast in the present tense — instead of 'I find you guilty' I can simply say 'You did it'. Nor need they be cast in the indicative mood — instead of 'I order you to turn right' I can say 'Turn right' (W, p. 58; cf. PP, p. 243).

These alleged counter-examples are, in fact, significantly different from the original cases of performatives. To utter them may well be to do something, but (unlike the originals) not that very thing, e.g. promising, which is specified in the utterance itself; nor is it doing something by virtue of the special felicity-conditions indicated in connexion with the originals. This represents the first move in the dilution of the idea of a performative in a way which suggests that Austin himself did not fully comprehend the phenomenon he had singled out.

One more attempt might be made to save the grammatical criterion as a means of distinguishing performatives from constatives. It is interesting that in defeating the straightforward claim that all performatives must have the favoured grammatical form Austin refers to cases where there is an *alternative* form. Perhaps, then, it may be said that although all performatives do not have to be couched in that form, they must all be *reducible* or *expandible* or *analysable* into it (W, pp. 61–2; PP, p. 244)?

Austin rejects this amended criterion, too, though his reasons for doing so are of uneven quality. One objection (a perfectly cogent one) is that even if we preselect only those verbs with the required asymmetry noted above and couch them in the favoured grammatical form, we do not necessarily end up with a performative utterance (W, p. 64). Thus, *betting* is a verb with the required asymmetry, and 'I bet you that ... ' gives us the required grammatical form. Yet consider the utterance 'I bet you that my team will win far too often'. This need not be a performative utterance. It could just as easily be a constative, a *description* of an action which I habitually perform. Similarly, I might say 'I find the defendant guilty whenever he has long hair'. Even in the case of performative verbs, then, just this grammatical form can serve more than one purpose. Austin claims that something similar is true of an utterance like 'I call inflation too much money chasing too few goods': it can be used simultaneously as a performative and as a description of a 'naturally consequent performance' (W, pp. 64–5).

Two further objections this criterion elicits from Austin are of particular interest, in view of my claim that he has now begun to dilute the notion of a performative. These are the complementary objections that the criterion would let in too many utterances as performative and also not let in enough. First, consider the utterance 'I state that p'. It is couched in the required grammatical form and there is also the required asymmetry between 'I state ... ' and 'He states ... ', for to say 'I state that p', if the felicity-conditions are fulfilled, *is* to state that p. But, Austin objects, the point of the performative/constative distinction is to separate the kind of uttering which is the performing of an action from the kind of uttering which is merely stating (W, p. 61). He therefore concludes that any criterion which has to count 'I state that ... ' as a performative must be defective (W, p. 68). Secondly, when I say something like 'You are a fool' I may be characteristically *doing* something, viz. insulting someone; but there is no formula 'I insult you' whereby I can make this explicit. The criterion of reducibility to favoured grammatical form would therefore fail to allow as a performative something which is (W, pp. 65, 68, PP, p. 245).

The dilution of the notion of performatives is now more apparent. By this time it is explicitly stated that we are to count as performative *any* case where there is 'something which is at the moment of uttering being done by the person uttering' (W, p. 60), and the consequent diversity of the phenomenon is given official recognition by the division of performatives into two kinds, primary and explicit. For, having originally cited many performatives which take the favoured form, and then pointed out that many others neither take nor are reducible to it, it is natural that Austin should distinguish these two kinds. This he does by means of the two examples:

(1) Primary utterance: "I shall be there".
(2) Explicit performative: "I promise that I shall be there."

(W, p.69)

The additional words in (2) make plain exactly how my utterance is to be understood, because in their absence it could be understood as a promise, *or* as an expression of a firm intention, *or* as a vague aspiration, and so on. Austin compares this to the way my uttering 'Salaam' when I bend before you makes it plain that my action in bending is that of greeting you, not that of stooping to observe the flora or easing my indigestion (W, p. 70; PP, pp. 245–6). He then discusses several of the ways in which one can make explicit the force of an utterance other than by adding a performative prefix, such as mood, tone of voice, gesture, etc. (W, pp. 73–6). All of this is questionable, but I shall not question it for the moment.

One more main attempt to analyse performatives can be extracted from Austin's discussion.[3] He draws attention to a class of utterances whose status is doubtful as between performatives and constatives. There are situations where, given certain facts and conventions governing behaviour in our culture, it is expected that a person will and should experience a certain feeling or have a certain attitude, such as repentance or gratitude. On the one hand there are utterances which are clearly descriptive of such states, and are therefore constatives, e.g. 'I feel repentant' and 'I feel grateful'. On the other hand, there are associated with these states utterances which are clearly explicit performatives, e.g. 'I apologise' and 'I thank you'. But standing between these two sorts of utterances there are others which are not so easily classified, utterances like 'I am sorry', 'I am grateful to you'. Are these performatives or constatives (W, p. 79)?

Austin suggests some tests for deciding the matter, and this is of some interest, since if the tests are adequate here then of course so should they be elsewhere. The questions we should ask ourselves, in order to determine whether or not such utterances are performatives, are:

(a) When someone has issued the utterance, does it make sense to ask 'Does he really?'?

(b) Could one be performing the action in question without actually saying anything?

(c) Can we qualify the putative performative with the idea of 'being willing to' and 'deliberately' (as we ought to be able to, since any action is in principle qualifiable in this way)?

(d) Could what is said be literally true or false, or only insincere?(cf. W, pp. 79-80)

The implication is that if the utterances in question are genuinely performative then the answers to questions (a), (b) and (d) will be negative and the answer to (c) affirmative (cf. W, p. 86).

Austin clearly has misgivings about these tests, however, and rightly so. Even if someone uses an uncontroversially performative formula, such as 'I promise ... ' it will still make sense to ask whether he did really, because it is also necessary for the felicity-conditions to be met (W, p. 84). Again, Austin himself points out that we often *can* perform the same kind of action as done in uttering a performative, but by some other means. I can bet, for example, by putting a coin into a slot-machine (W, p. 8; PP, p. 237). These uncertainties reflect Austin's lack of clarity in his own conception of a performative, as I shall try to show later. This applies equally to question (*d*). Performatives, I shall argue, *can* be true or false, so this will not help to distinguish them either.

4. Borderline and comprehensive doubts

The mere existence of borderline cases does not of itself threaten the viability of a concept or of a distinction between two concepts, such as the performative/constative distinction. The existence of twilight, for example, does not threaten the validity of the distinction between day and night. What matters, for the purpose of calling a concept into question, is both the *number* and the *nature* of borderline cases. If there are very many unresolvable borderline cases, we may begin to wonder how clear and serviceable a concept is, and if there is frequent disagreement about which side of a distinction to place a given case, or if it seems to fit neither, then we should begin to treat the distinction with suspicion.

Austin produces many borderline cases with this stronger purpose in mind. We have already seen examples like 'I am sorry', 'I blame ... ' and 'I approve ... ', which we may regard as formulae that are sometimes performative and sometimes constative (W, p. 78) or else as not purely performative but half descriptive (W, p. 79). These, however, present a less than compelling case against the performative/constative distinction, for it may only be the absence of an adequate analysis of performatives which prevents us from placing them firmly on one side or the other. The instrumental importance of analysis is thereby stressed once again. But further cases present a stronger threat. Thus, there is a class of utterances which appear in a context where one is fairly self-consciously laying out one's views, and their peculiar characteristic is that they consist in their main part of an apparently straightforward constative utterance, with a performative verb at their head which shows 'how the "statement" is to be fitted into the context of conversation' (W, p. 85). Examples are 'I conclude that p', 'I argue that p', 'I predict that p'. Now these seem in one way to be clear examples of performatives — to say 'I predict ... ' *is* to predict, and so on. But two features of them worry Austin. The first is that they are inextricably linked to utterances which are true or false, in that such utterances always form their core; the second is that there are other utterances which seem to share the general characteristics of those mentioned but which are not so easily classifiable as performatives. Austin cites as examples 'I assume that p', 'I suppose that p', 'I agree that p'. His worry here seems to be that in these cases we should be more willing to concede that the speaker's behaviour on other occasions might give us grounds for saying that *notwithstanding his assertion* he does not assume, suppose, agree that p (cf. W, pp. 86–8).

There are other similar cases, such as 'I hold that ... ' which, when said by a judge, may constitute a performative, but not when said by a layman (W, p. 88), 'I class x's as y's', which may be performative on one occasion and descriptive on another (W, p. 89), and the worst case of all, 'I state that p', which is both performative and straightforwardly true or false (W, p. 90). In all these cases it is not merely the existence of borderlines but their nature which leads Austin to his comprehensive doubts about performativeness.

Something similar could be said about the various failed attempts at analysis discussed in the previous section. It is not the mere failure to arrive at an analysis which is crucial, but what is revealed in that process. The initial characterisation of performatives, which it was the purpose of analysis to elaborate, rested on a contrast with 'ordinary' statements in two respects: in the uttering of a performative something is *done* (beyond the mere saying of something), and the utterance is open to criticism not in terms of truth and falsity but in terms of felicity. Austin's comprehensive doubts about the notion of performativeness rest finally on his belief that none of these initial contrasts can be maintained. For a start, the two distinguishing features do not necessarily go together — there is no conflict between an utterance's being the doing of something and *also* being true or false (W, p. 134). But in any case truth and falsity can be brought into the assessment of performatives (W, pp. 139–40; PP, p. 250) and felicity into the assessment of constatives (W, pp. 135ff.; PP, p. 248). Finally, the abandonment of the notion of performativeness, which has turned out to apply to all utterances rather than a special type, is equally an abandonment of the polar opposition between performatives and statements: 'I state ... ' is itself exactly on a level with 'I bet ... ' (W, p. 133, PP, p. 247). Indeed, it would be more accurate to say that it is the original constative/performative *dichotomy* which has been abandoned (cf. W, pp. 145ff.). As an alternative to this Austin develops his second theory of the connexion between saying and doing, the theory of illocution (W, pp. 91–163).

5. An alternative analysis [4]

I shall now argue that Austin's despair was premature. I shall attempt to show that it is possible to characterise performatives in such a way that they can be regarded as a distinct type of utterance. But this will involve fairly radical disagreement with him, in that one half of his initial characterisation of them — as being not capable of truth or falsity — will be rejected. Austin regards his claim here as obvious enough not to need any argument (W, p. 6; PP, p. 235). He does argue specifically against the idea that a performative like 'I promise ... ' is a true or false description *of an inner spiritual act* (W, pp. 9–10; PP, p. 236), and he points out that when someone utters these or similar words but fails to perform the action in question — say, because another concomitant condition is absent — we do not speak of a false bet or promise (W, pp. 10–11). But the first point does not show that the words are not a true or false report of *anything*, and the second point is an exceedingly weak reason for Austin's conclusion, representing one of his few lapses into ordinary language philosophy while discussing language as a subject. We may have many reasons, good or bad, for saying or not saying something, and it is our reasons, rather than our not saying something, which are of paramount importance. I stress the disagreement with Austin over whether performatives can be true, because I think it is precisely through a consideration of the peculiarity of the conditions in which they are true that we may best understand them.

Now since Austin originally contrasts performatives with true-or-false constatives, it may seem that my suggestion will in any case lead to the same conclusion as Austin's, *viz.* that performatives cannot after all be kept distinct from constatives. But this does not follow. Rather, as a consequence of misunderstanding performatives Austin also misunderstands the nature of the distinction between them and constatives. For similar reasons he is also mistaken in what he takes to be the extent of their range. Having erred in his description of the four original paradigms of performative utterances, he then errs in the way he projects the use of the term in connexion with further examples. Roughly speaking, only what he distinguishes as *explicit* performatives are performatives at all (and even they do not all qualify).

I cannot at this stage[5] offer an informative analysis of truth which shows how it is that performatives can be true, though as we proceed I hope to remove some objections which might be raised to the idea. Let us say for the moment that a statement is true if it corresponds to the facts. This will do as a commonplace if not a philosophical analysis, and Austin, at least, would not quarrel with it (cf. PP, p. 121). One of the problems for anyone who wishes to hold this view *as a theory* about the nature of truth is that of keeping the statements and the facts to which they correspond as two distinct entities. But apart from any general difficulties of this kind, there are some troublesome cases where a statement itself seems in some way to guarantee its own truth. Imagine that on three different occasions I speak as follows:

(1) I am alive
(2) I am saying something
(3) I am speaking in English.

In each case, provided only that certain minimal conditions are met — conditions which govern the making of *any* statement, e.g. that the speaker is a rational being who understands the meaning of the words uttered, etc. — then in speaking as I do I make a true statement. All the statements I make here are in that respect self-verifying. However, although each is sufficient for its own truth, they differ with regard to their dispensability. For instance, (1) can be dispensed with altogether, in that *what* I say here may very well be true *even if I do not say it*, or indeed say anything at all (it is true that I am alive at moments when I am making no statement whatsoever). In contrast to this, (2) and (3) are indispensable in the following sense: if we imagine my utterance removed from the situation and nothing put in its place, then what I *would* have said *if* I had spoken is no longer true. This does not mean, however, that (2) and (3) are indispensable in an absolute sense. There are various allowable substitute utterances which would make what I say in (2) and (3) true, and a different range of allowable substitutes in each case. If I make any utterance at all, (2) will be true, whereas (3) will be true if I make an utterance from a more restricted range, *viz.* utterances made in English. A further point of contrast with (1) is that some *utterance* is required for the truth of (2) and (3), and no other substitute will make them true.

Let us now bring performatives into the comparison, and take as obvious the reverse of what Austin takes as obvious. Let us assume that my statement 'I promise ... ' is true if and only if it is a fact that I promise in the situation where I so speak, and so for other performatives. In one respect these resemble (2) and (3) rather than (1): if we subtract the statement from the situation and make no replacement, it will no longer be true that I promise, bet, etc. The situation regarding allowable substitutes is different for different performatives. In some cases something other than an utterance can make what I say true (e.g. my putting a coin in a slot instead of saying 'I bet ... ' can make it true that I bet); in other cases not (e.g. the only way I can make it true that I find the defendant guilty is by *saying*, in the appropriate circumstances, 'I find the defendant guilty'). However, in two other respects performatives differ from all three utterances. First, where the allowable substitution is of another utterance, there is a much stricter limitation than for (1)–(3). To make it true that I promise there is little else that I can *say* besides uttering the words which identify that performative, or a synonymous form of words (or, say, uttering the word 'Yes' in reply to the question 'Do you promise?'). That is to say, the *content* of a performative utterance is far more germane than is the case with (1)–(3). Secondly, we saw that the utterance of (1)–(3) was, in a fairly straightforward way, sufficient for their truth. Not so with performatives. There is the additional, crucial requirement that the performative be uttered *in the appropriate circumstances*, or that the felicity-conditions associated with it be fulfilled. Saying 'I promise ... ' does not make it true that I promise if no one is around to hear; saying 'I bet ... ' does not make it true that I bet if no one takes me up.

These considerations suggest the possibility of some further interesting comparisons. Imagine a teacher carrying a delicate balance across a school laboratory. Just as he passes, a pupil shouts out at the top of his voice

(4) YOU'VE DROPPED IT!

The utterance is delivered so suddenly and at such a volume that its own truth is thereby assured.[6] Next, another malicious pedagogic relationship. A student is on the point of entering an examination room. His tutor, who happens to be invigilating, says to him

(5) You will fail this examination.

Ill-prepared and unconfident though the student was, he would have just scraped through the examination had this remark not been made. Finally, in a newspaper column highly regarded for its accuracy as a barometer of the market, it is stated that

(6) The price of gold will fall tomorrow.

As a consequence, the price of gold does indeed fall the following day.

Each of these statements is, in the circumstances envisaged, self-confirming, and not only that but indispensably so, in the weaker sense that if it is subtracted without replacement from the situation then it would no longer be true. None is indispensable in the stronger sense: someone could bring it about that any of (4)–(6) is true other than by making just that statement, and indeed other than by making a statement at all. I might make it true that the teacher drops the balance by pushing him, make it true that the price of gold will fall by assassinating the prime minister, and so on. There are two partial parallels with performatives. In (5) and (6), though not in (4), when that particular statement is made in a self-confirming situation then the content of the statement is highly germane to the result. If, instead of (5), I say 'You will pass the examination' my statement may have a different (even opposite) result. In addition, and again like performatives, statements (4)–(6) are not self-confirming completely on their own. In these cases, moreover, something more substantial than the mere fulfilment of felicity-conditions is required. The respective statements play a role in bringing about some separate state of affairs which is constitutive of their truth, whether in a relatively brute fashion as in (4), or through the mediation of a hearer's understanding and belief as in (5) and (6).

In one respect we may hesitate to compare performatives with *any* of the statements (1)–(6). There is nothing about (4)–(6) considered in themselves to indicate how they may be productive of their own truth in certain circumstances — that they are is a contingent matter of fact. In contrast, it is something which follows directly from the *meaning* of (1)-(3) that they have this self-confirming property. We may call the first kind of self-confirmation causal and the second kind logical, and then be undecided which of these kinds performatives are. In a way still to be explained, I believe that they lie between the two.

However, before I expand on this and draw together the various analogies so far suggested, I must draw attention to a serious ambiguity in the concept of 'statement' in the preceding remarks. It has been used ambiguously to denote (a) the *making* of an assertion, the issuing of a certain kind of utterance (what I propose to call the *statement-act*), and (b) *What* is asserted in the making of an assertion of this kind (what I propose to call the *statement-content*). In other words, it can be used to denote *either* a concrete event in the world, the production of certain sounds or marks (or the sounds or marks themselves), *or* a certain kind of abstraction from such sounds or marks. The difference between these two can be brought out by reference to the criteria they imply for the identification and counting of statements. If I say 'London is the capital of England' and you say 'London is the capital of England', then in terms of concrete events in the world we have made two statements; but in terms of the abstraction of what is said in those concrete utterances we have made one and the same statement. Two statement-acts take place, but there is only one statement-content (cf. Strawson, 1950a and Lemmon, 1966).

If we are going to ascribe truth to statements at all (and there is no reason why we should not), it will be more appropriate to ascribe it to statement-contents than statement-acts. For one thing it is reasonable to suppose that there are true statements which no one has ever uttered, and it is only statement-contents which can exist *without* being uttered. Of course, it may not be possible to identify any such statement without uttering it, but still it will presumably be true in advance of being uttered. I mean, for example, the statement that there is a piece of paper in front of me was true even before it was made. Neither the paper nor the fact to which the statement corresponds come into being only when they are actually referred to. What is true is not *in general* dependent on what is said.

Someone might agree that truth is to be ascribed to statement-contents, and argue that it is precisely for this reason that performatives cannot be true or false. They are, it may be argued, *essentially* statement-acts: the 'I', the agent, is explicitly present in all of the original examples, and arguably must be implicitly present in all performative utterances. Hence, in the case of performatives there is no detachable content which can be considered in and by itself, apart from its actualisation in a concrete act.

It may be worth pointing out that this is an argument which is not available to Austin. First, it is not clear that he is properly alive to the act/content distinction; secondly, he appears in any case to ascribe truth and falsity to statement-*acts*. Truth, he agrees, is ascribable primarily to statements, but a statement 'is made and its making is an historic event' (PP, p. 119), and the term 'statement' has 'the merit of clearly referring to the historic *use of a sentence by an utterer* (PP, pp. 120–1; italics added). Indeed, this may be one reason why he will not allow truth and falsity to performatives. In their case there is no radically separate state of affairs which can stand in a relation of correspondence to the statement-act, since it is, e.g., the statement-act 'I promise' which is the major constituent in the state of affairs by virtue of which it is true that I promise. But this would not help Austin's case, partly because (as I shall argue in Chapter VII) his correspondence theory of truth is unacceptable, and partly because, as we have already seen, there are perfectly genuine true statements, such as (2) and (3), the making of which is a constituent in the state of affairs which makes them true.

In any case, the original argument which I said was unavailable to Austin is equally defective. It may be that we think of performatives as *primarily* statement-acts, but their containing so-called token-reflexive terms like 'I' does not make them different from constatives such as 'I am tired'. In all these cases we need to settle what the relevant terms are, in the particular context, being used to refer to, but once that is done we can go on to consider merely the content of the statement in question. Both Mr Jones' performative utterance 'I name this ship *Queen Elizabeth*' and my constative utterance 'Mr Jones names that ship *Queen Elizabeth*' have as their content the statement that Mr Jones names the ship in front of him *Queen Elizabeth*, a statement-content which we can consider on its own, detached from its actualisation in someone's utterance-act. Hence, there is no good argument here for withholding truth and falsity from performatives.

The act/content distinction is relevant to my earlier remarks in the following way. When I spoke of cases where 'the statement guarantees its own truth' this can now be more accurately put by saying they are cases where the statement-act guarantees the truth of the statement-content which it expresses. For any ordinary, common or garden statement this is not so. The statement-content 'the books are on the table' can be true regardless of whether it has been actually expressed in a statement-act, since what determines its truth is the presence of certain physical objects in a certain place rather than what anyone says. What is peculiar about (1)–(3) is that the mere occurrence of the statement-act is itself sufficient to guarantee the truth of the statement-content expressed. One thing which is peculiar about a performative utterance is that in certain circumstances it becomes sufficient for the truth of *its* statement-content, and not only that but it *non-redundantly* guarantees it. The statement-content would not be true unless that statement-act were performed.

Effectively, the occurrence of a performative statement-act is sometimes an INUS-condition of the truth of the content it expresses.[7] My uttering the statement 'I bet ... ' is not on its own sufficient for the truth of its content, but given a background of the appropriate conventions and given, in general, the fulfilment of the felicity-conditions, it is the only other condition which has to be met for that content to be true. The utterance is the one change in the circumstances which creates that truth. Roughly speaking, the description of a performative as this kind of INUS-condition will be correct where there is some other, perhaps non-verbal means of creating the truth in question, as with betting. Where there is not, as with finding the defendant guilty, then the whole complex of circumstances in which the performative occurs can no longer be regarded as *unnecessary* for that result. What we can say in general, however, is that in one way or another the performative brings about the truth of its own content.

But it is *how* it brings this about, and the sort of bringing about in question, which makes performatives distinctive and worthy of attention. It is customary in philosophical discussion to distinguish between logical and causal conditions, and, as I indicated earlier, I believe that in the case of performatives we have a phenomenon not adequately described in either of these ways. The performative utterance does not bring about a substantially separate state of affairs which is responsible for its truth, as in (4)–(6), but neither is it logically sufficient for its own truth, as in (1)–(3). It *conventionally* brings about its own truth in the following sense: the content expressed by the utterance becomes true when the statement-act is performed *because people regard it as being so* as a consequence of the act of utterance. To put it this way is to emphasise that the existence of performatives rests not only on utterance but also upon social attitudes. The latter constitute the indispensable background against which the former operates. If people did not adopt the attitude they do towards a person who says 'I promise ... ' (and they are not forced to), then 'I promise ... ' could not be self-verifying in the way in which it is. We may put this in the form of a definition by saying that *a statement-act S is performative if and only if it brings about the truth of the content it expresses as a consequence of people's so regarding it.*

When it is taken in conjunction with my earlier discussion I suggest that this definition provides an adequate analysis, insofar as it shows in a clear and non-obvious way how performatives work. It also indicates what the *range* of possible performatives is. What is first of all needed for a performative is a performer and an audience: a performer, so that we are provided with a statement-act, and an audience so that a particular attitude can be adopted towards it and the content it expresses. But that is not all. The statement-content must be such that it is *possible* for social conventional attitudes and behaviour to determine its truth. To put it crudely and over-simply, it must be the kind of thing which a combination of saying and thinking can make so and subsequent behaviour confirm as so. This explains why, for example, the statement 'I am six feet tall' could not be used performatively, for it refers to a state of affairs totally independent of its utterance and of a kind which social convention *could* not determine. It also explains why statements concerning human social relations are frequently performative, for the truth of a statement concerning social relations very often does depend on social conventional *attitudes*.

This sets a limit to the utterances which *could* be performative, but a list of those which actually are will vary from one culture to another. Austin notes that there is no performative 'I insult you' (W, p. 68), but himself points out that there was a culture in which such a performative did exist (W, p. 30n.2). This is not surprising, since the question whether a given statement constitutes an insult is very obviously one which social convention can determine. Similarly, although the announcement 'We are the masters now' is not performative, one can imagine a culture in which it acquired the necessary ritual aspect, so that a man in a position of ascendancy would become chief by making the statement 'I am the chief now'. In the reverse direction, just as in our culture the statement 'I insult you' is likely to be greeted by 'No, you don't' or 'Well, go on then', it is conceivable that there should be a culture in which the mere statement 'I promise...' elicited the same response — if, say, there were no convention that you can promise by saying so and it was also necessary to sign some special legal document. In short, the question whether a given statement is performative may be culture-relative.

6. Re-examination of Austin's arguments

The conclusions arrived at in the previous section enable us to see more clearly the limitations of Austin's own discussion. Consider, for example, the attempt to analyse performatives by reference to their grammatical form. It is natural but by no means essential that performatives should be cast in the first person, present, active, indicative. Such a grammatical form helps to make it clear that something is being done at the time of utterance by the utterer, which is *one* essential aspect of performatives. But given that the fact which is created in the uttering of a performative is often a fact about interpersonal relations it is to be expected that many performatives are statable in the second person — as well as 'I authorise you' there is 'You are hereby authorised'. Equally, they are sometimes statable in the third person, as in the transference of a piece of property by means of the utterance 'It's yours'. We should note also that the facts stated and created are not necessarily about either the utterer or his audience, and in that case there need not be even implied reference to either — as when the properly appointed person declares in the proper circumstances, 'Mr Jones is the duly elected member for this constituency'.

These acceptable counter-examples to the grammatical criterion for performatives, some of which are Austin's, differ markedly from some other counter-examples which he puts forward. Thus, he suggests that in place of

(a) I order you to turn right

I may issue as a performative utterance simply

(b) Turn right

or even

(c) I should turn right if I were you (cf.W, p. 58).

On the account which I have given these alternatives would not qualify as performatives at all. This may initially seem puzzling, since (b) and (c) clearly are alternatives to (a) in some sense. But they are alternatives in that their utterance can constitute the same *action* as the utterance of (a). They can be used to issue an order, indeed the *same* order as (a). But what they do *not* share with (a) is the additional important and distinguishing feature of becoming true as a result of being uttered, or being used to create their own truth. Truth does not attach at all to an imperative utterance like (b), and attaches under different conditions to (c). In short, (b) and (c) do not share enough of the special features of (a) to warrant calling them alternative *performatives*. This does not mean that the features which they do share with (a) are not worthy of investigation, and indeed for some purposes they can usefully be grouped together. This we shall see when we come to examine Austin's theory of illocution. Nevertheless, we have seen that there are other cases which support Austin's conclusion that performatives do not have to be couched in the favoured grammatical form.

Just as I have criticised some of Austin's alleged examples of performatives, I should be equally critical, and for similar reasons, of his division of performatives into primary/explicit (W, p. 69). A primary utterance like 'I shall be there' just is not dependent for its truth on the act of uttering, in contrast to the explicit 'I promise that I shall be there', although again the two obviously have *some* features in common.

When we come to the borderline problems which Austin raises about performatives, many can be resolved by means of our analysis. Some borderline cases may remain, but they will be neither so numerous nor of such a kind as to license any comprehensive rejection of the concept of a performative or the performative/constative distinction.

Take, first, those cases which Austin claims are ambivalent between performative and constative — utterances like 'I am grateful', which stands between the performative 'I thank' and the constative 'I feel grateful', or 'I am sorry', which stands between 'I apologise' and 'I repent' (cf. W, p. 79). Most of the examples on Austin's list are not performatives according to our analysis. And it is possible to see *both* why they are not and should not be so considered, *and* why there is some temptation to consider that they are. Yet again, there is a parallel with the similarity between 'I order you to go' and 'Go'. To say 'I apologise' in the appropriate circumstances *is* to apologise; and to say 'I am sorry' in those circumstances is equally to apologise. This is the common feature of the two utterances, and this is what might tempt us to say that 'I am sorry' is also a performative. But this would be a mistake, and for the same reason as in our earlier case. The statement-act 'I am sorry' does *not* create the truth of its own content as does 'I apologise'. There is a mental state of being sorry (however the term 'mental state' is to be understood or analysed), to which the utterance 'I am sorry' *may or may not* correspond even though it is *certain* that it constitutes an apology. There is not, in the same way, an anterior state which may have an effect on the truth of the statement 'I apologise'. As long as the felicity-conditions are met, the statement 'I apologise' is true, and Austin does well not to include amongst those conditions any facts about substantive mental states of the utterer, as opposed to the mental state which consists in speaking with an understanding of one's words, etc. (cf. W, pp. 15–16). After all, the whole point in applying the concept of a performative is to single out those situations where a fact is created by speaking (against a certain social background), where our word is our bond whatever may have been going on in our mind (cf. W, p. 10). A similar procedure can be adopted for all the other cases on Austin's list. We need to ask whether some substantive mental state on the part of the utterer is a necessary condition for the truth of the statement in question. If it is, the statement is not a performative.

Next, there are various minor and peripheral borderline cases, such as 'I call an x a y', which Austin claims can be used *simultaneously* as a performative and a constative (W, pp. 64–5), and 'I hold that ...', which is performative when uttered by a judge in the appropriate situation but not when uttered by a layman (W, p. 88). The first of these can be dealt with in the same way as the previous cases. If, as Austin maintains, the utterance can be a 'description of a naturally consequent performance' (W, p. 65) then a substantially separate state of affairs is relevant to its truth, and it cannot in that situation be a performative. Such a state of affairs could not be *simultaneously* *ir*relevant to the truth of the utterance, and hence it is doubtful whether Austin is correct in saying that the utterance can be performative and constative at the same time. On the other hand, that it, like 'I hold that ... ', should be performative on one occasion but not on another is something which should not worry us. When we think of the importance of surrounding circumstances for the successful issuing of a performative, and when we recall that 'felicity-conditions' is shorthand for a long list of different requirements, including, for instance, the requirement that the particular people and circumstances must be appropriate for invoking the procedure in question (cf. W, pp. 14–15), then it is not surprising that this should happen. It is then quite natural that, for example, the uttering of the words by a *different person* should have a different and non-performative function.

Leaving aside the relatively minor cases, however, it may be felt that those borderline questions which sustain comprehensive doubts about performatives have not yet been touched. First, there is the case of 'I state that p', to utter which *is* to state that p. On the one hand it may seem that this case is in a unique position, since 'stating' or 'constating' is originally taken to be the polar opposite of issuing a performative. But in its general features it is only one of a whole group of utterances which present the same problem, such as 'I argue, conclude, testify that p' (W, pp. 85–6, 89–91). Here, too, to say these things is to do them, but it is also to make a statement which is true or false. Austin's only suggestion for dealing with this problem is to distinguish the verb at the head of the statement, which indicates how the utterance is to be taken, from the that-clause, which is true or false (W, p. 91). But apart from the fact that there is no guarantee that this can always be done (cf. 'I liken x to y'), it is not clear that separating the elements of the utterance in this way actually resolves anything. It does not tell us how to classify such examples in terms of the performative/constative distinction. Indeed, it suggests that it will be unsatisfactory to classify them in either way.

These are the comprehensive doubts which Austin expresses about his distinction. I wish to argue that when the nature of performatives is made clear in the way indicated earlier, the doubts evaporate. As far as the term 'statement' is concerned, it has long since become clear that performatives are themselves one kind (a very special kind) of statement, so that the performative/constative contrast is a contrast between two different kinds of statement, rather than between a statement and a kind of utterance which is not a statement. This means that a comprehensive doubt would not be generated if 'I state that p' were a performative. It would simply follow that this was a statement whose truth is acquired in a peculiar way, different from that of most statements.

But in fact it should *not* be conceded that 'I state that *p*' is a performative. Of course, the truth of the statement follows from its being uttered, but the case of the original examples (1)–(3) in section 5 shows that this is not sufficient for an utterance's being a performative. Indeed, if the truth of a statement really does follow *immediately* from its being uttered, this is sufficient for its *not* being performative; for its truth will not then follow from its being uttered *as a consequence of social convention*, in the way outlined. That is to say, its truth will not depend on people's taking a particular attitude towards the statement, *viz.* precisely that of regarding it as true. The difference between 'I state that *p*' and 'I promise' is this. It is an immediate consequence of the *meaning* of 'state' that someone who says 'I state that *p*' states that *p* — it makes no difference what attitude his audience adopts, and arguably it makes no difference whether he has an audience or not. It is *not* an immediate consequence of the meaning of 'promise' that someone who says 'I promise' promises. To promise means to place oneself, voluntarily, under an obligation, etc., etc. And it is a contingent fact that one can do this *by doing nothing more than saying* 'I promise'. Similarly for bequeathing, betting and naming a ship (as opposed to calling a ship by a certain name).[8] Hence the mediation, in these cases, of social convention in the way noted, which is, of course, something different from the way convention might be said to enter into *any* use of language as a collection of symbols with conventional meanings.

So much for 'I state'. Doubts may remain about some of the other examples Austin cites, but this itself cannot be used to support a comprehensive doubt about performativeness. If we are not sure whether, for example, 'I argue that *p*' is performative or instead self-verifying in the same way as 'I state', this will be a reflexion of uncertainty about the precise meaning of 'argue' rather than uncertainty about the conditions for being a performative.

7. Conclusion

The position now reached may seem bizarre. It was Austin who coined the term 'performative', introduced it by way of examples, explained their nature and finally abandoned the notion, or at least the belief that performatives could be contrasted with other utterances in a straightforward way. I have disagreed with his characterisation and denied that many of his examples are really performative at all. How can this be? Am I not denying him the right to use his own term, and have I not, perhaps, focused attention on something other than performativeness in my discussion? An amplification of the progress of the discussion will help to answer this, as well as shedding further light on the nature of conceptual analysis and its connexion with our actual application of concepts.

Austin introduces his term by way of four examples, which he characterises initially only in the most general way. It is therefore reasonable to look for their highest common factor as providing the basis for describing them by means of a specially invented word. The fact that it is Austin who first singles out these examples gives no special prerogative to the account which he then proceeds to give of what is peculiar about them. And in fact I argued that there were various deficiencies in the elucidation of the nature of performatives which he gives by considering his four original examples as paradigms, in particular his suggestion that they cannot be true or false. Hence I was led to suggest that Austin either fails to describe or misdescribes the important feature which the examples share, the role which the uttering of the statement plays in establishing the truth of its own content.

Now my characterisation of performatives sets a limit to the kind of utterance which can be so described; it sets a limit to how the scope of the term can be extended to further examples. The property which I ascribed to the four original examples is a very special one, and there is no possibility or danger that all statements will turn out to possess it. The fact that Austin believes that there is this danger suggests either that he has misunderstood this property possessed by his four examples, or else that he is focusing attention on some other property which they possess. One can construe in either of these ways the idea he works with that performatives are 'cases of the issuing of an utterance being the doing of *something*' (W, pp. 68–9; italics added). Perhaps he takes *this* property, which is indeed common to all his original examples but not their highest common factor, as definitive of performatives. If so, then all statements may well turn out to be performative *in this weaker sense*. It may very well turn out that whenever I make a statement I am doing something, over and above saying something. I am unsure whether the claim that all statements are performative in this weaker sense can be proved *a priori* or only by amassing empirical evidence. But what I am sure of is that it is true *a priori* that not all statements could be performative in my stronger sense. It could not be the case that all utterances constituted the doing or bringing about of *that thing specified in the utterance*. To say 'I climb Mount Everest' is not and could not be to climb Mount Everest.

It should be stressed that this is not a dispute merely about how to use the term 'performative' — or at least, so far as it is, then either my or Austin's use is possible. My point is rather that once the term is introduced to apply to very special examples it is better to confine its application to other cases which share in this specialness, and find some other term for the similarity between these original examples and many other, more 'normal' statements (and we shall see that Austin provides one in his theory of illocution). Otherwise, we run the risk of obscuring or overlooking what is very special in the nature of utterances like 'I bet you it will rain' and 'I leave my watch to my brother'.

I suggested at the outset that when we issue performatives we are involved both in a *creative* and in a *mapping* operation. When I say 'I bet you it will rain' I both do something and describe truly what it is that I do; the operation is perfectly integrated, because there is only one thing which constitutes both the doing and the describing. But interesting and curious though this is, it involves no illegitimacy. It may be felt that there must already be something there in the world if any successful mapping operation is to be effected, but this is not so. It is sufficient if the state of affairs to be mapped comes into being simultaneously with the act of mapping. To demand anything more would be to fall into the trap of interpreting the mapping metaphor too literally (cf. Chapter VII, below).

By now we have seen that yet a third facet of human nature enters into the workings of performatives. Their operation can only be effective against the appropriate *social* background. The act of speech is one necessary component, but the attitude of those surrounding that act is another. From this an interesting consequence emerges. It is obvious enough that human beings can alter the world by brute, physical intervention in it, and obvious, too, if we think about it, that they can alter the world by using language. If we focus on the audience rather than the speaker in a performative context, then something slightly less obvious emerges, namely that people can change the world, create new states of affairs, by *conceiving* it differently. A world in which people regard a man who says to his wife 'I divorce you' as having done so in uttering those words is materially different from a world in which people do not adopt that attitude. Thus, although everyone already knows that you can place a bet by saying 'I bet', make a promise by saying 'I promise' and so on, an analysis of the concept of a performative can be useful in drawing attention to something we might not have been so clearly aware of: that a sharp distinction between acting in the world and merely conceiving of it in a particular way is untenable.

IV

Philosophy of Language as a Subject: Illocution

1. Introduction

Having, as he thought, shown that it is impossible to isolate the performative, Austin begins all over again in the second half of *How To Do Things With Words* to investigate how saying something can also be doing something. In fact, this is a far more general phenomenon than the performative utterance, but clearly one which it is essential to understand if we are to have a full understanding of language itself.

Austin's procedure is similar to that adopted in the first half of the book. We are introduced to a distinction — this time a triple one — and an attempt is made to clarify the distinction in terms of examples. To some extent, therefore, it is possible to adopt the same procedure in assessing his suggestions. But a study of the more general phenomenon of speech acts inevitably brings in larger issues, to do with communication and meaning in general. To begin with I shall again lay out Austin's views more or less without criticism.

2. Locution, illocution and perlocution

Austin initially distinguishes three ways in which the saying of something is or may be the doing of something.

(a) Locution. First, there are all those things which must be done if someone is to say something in the central and basic sense of 'say', the sense in which a human being can, but a parrot or tape recorder cannot, say something. Saying something in this basic

and central sense involves doing something, because it consists in uttering certain sounds which one knows to be words bearing a definite sense and making definite reference to something (W, pp. 92–3). In short, to say something you have to utter noises which you know have meaning. To do this is to perform what Austin christens a *locutionary act*.

(b) *Illocution.* Even when it is clear that someone has said something in the sense of performing a locutionary act, indeed even when it is clear *what* he has said, it may still not be clear what the force of the utterance is, or how it is to be taken. He said 'It's going to charge', but was this a warning or a prediction? He said 'That's a dandelion', but was he identifying it or describing it? (cf. W, p. 98). From this kind of doubt about how an utterance is to be taken Austin draws a second way in which the saying of something may be the doing of something. I may be doing something *in* saying something, or performing what he calls an *illocutionary act*. This idea is introduced via a series of examples of illocutionary acts:

asking or answering a question,
giving some information or an assurance or a warning,
announcing a verdict or an intention,
pronouncing sentence,
making an appointment or an appeal or a criticism,
making an identification or giving a description (*ibid.*).

Before he gives any further characterisation of illocution, Austin mentions a third way in which saying can involve doing.

(c) *Perlocution.* Sometimes, when a person says something, he may, by design, bring about certain effects on his hearer as a result of what he says. He may, for example, convince someone that something is the case, or persuade someone to do something. One may, in other words, do something *by* saying something. Such doing Austin calls the performing of a *perlocutionary act* (W, p. 101).

Finally, all three ways of doing something may coalesce in one operation. On a particular occasion the locutionary act of saying that I am tired may constitute the illocutionary act of warning you and also the perlocutionary act of persuading you to leave.

Austin's declared concern throughout the book is 'essentially to fasten on the second, illocutionary act and contrast it with the other two' (W, p. 103). The theory of illocution plays a central part in his own philosophy, and it is almost impossible to exaggerate its influence in contemporary philosophy. It has been a major preoccupation of those discussing language as a subject, and it has also had a profound influence on the way philosophy of language has been employed as a method for dealing with philosophical problems in general. In this respect it provides a support for the Austinian method discussed in Chapter II, *what we should say when*, and is a locus for a fusion, or confusion, of his views on the nature of language and his examination of language as a means to dealing with other phenomena. This is a point which will crop up again and again as we examine Austin's attempts to deal with philosophical problems. For the moment, however, the question is whether the concept of illocution is a viable and fruitful one for understanding the nature of language itself. Starting from the examples first given, is it possible to work out what conditions must be met for a description to count as a description of an illocutionary act, and how do we decide *what* illocutionary act has been performed on a particular occasion?

As a first step towards testing the adequacy of the idea of illocution, we may ask whether it is something which can be kept firmly separate from locution and perlocution. It is important that it should be, and various of Austin's critics have argued that it cannot. His theory has, so to speak, been squeezed at both ends.

Let us begin with the relation between illocution and perlocution. Austin points out that more or less *any* perlocutionary act can be performed by issuing more or less any utterance (W, p. 109). You may convince me that someone is an adulteress by asking whether it was not her handkerchief in X's bedroom (W, p. 110), and it will in general be a matter for detailed empirical investigation what utterances constitute what perlocutionary acts. This is precisely what needs to be avoided in the case of illocution. Austin clearly envisages the study of illocutionary force as an *a priori* philosophical one, and hence the importance for him of keeping a sharp distinction between perlocution and illocution. It might be objected against him that this is not possible and that illocutionary force is itself an empirical notion. That is, it might be said that the question to what uses an utterance can be put is an empirical one, about the 'pragmatics' rather than the 'semantics' of language (cf. Mates, 1958), so that perlocution and illocution cannot be kept radically distinct.

Both the premise and the conclusion of this argument are suspect. First, even if illocution and perlocution both relate to 'the way we use utterances' we ought not to suppose that this itself is an unambiguous phrase indicating something which can be pinned down only by empirical investigation (cf. W, p. 99). There are in any case other ways of separating illocution from perlocution. Admittedly, not all Austin's attempts to do so are of equal worth. Lecture X of *How To Do Things With Words* is unprofitably spent considering whether the distinction can be defended on the grounds that an illocutionary act is performed whenever one does something *in* saying something, and a perlocutionary act whenever one does something *by* saying something (W, pp. 120–31). Not surprisingly, Austin answers in the negative. Such a suggestion seems doomed from the start when, apart from anything else, we do not use 'in' and 'by' with sufficient precision in ordinary language to enable us to keep a clear distinction between them (whatever Austin's unsupported intuitions may tell him). But more promising for the distinction is the fact that perlocution is an essentially *consequential* concept, in a way that illocution is not (cf. W, pp. 101, 110ff.). So for example, if I am to perform the illocutionary act of *telling* you to leave then all that needs to happen is that you understand what I say; but for me to perform the perlocutionary act of *persuading* you to leave it must also be the case that you do something, *viz*, leave. This means that the formal conditions for the successful performance of each kind of act will differ crucially. For the successful performance of any perlocutionary act it will be necessary that some consequential *change* occur in the attitudes, beliefs or actions of one's audience; whereas for the successful performance of an illocutionary act all that need occur beyond the utterance itself is that the audience understand it. As Austin puts it, 'the performance of an illocutionary act involves the securing of *uptake*' (W, p. 116; Austin's italics).

This way of keeping a distinction between the two kinds of act provides us with a minimal and negative characterisation of illocution: it can be said that it is not a necessary condition for an act's being an illocutionary act that it be productive of any consequences (at least of substantial consequences. Cf. W, pp. 115–16). It is also important because it serves to throw some doubt on the premise of the previous objection. It seems that, in order to identify illocutionary acts, we do not have to go beyond the utterances which are constitutive of them, together, perhaps, with the circumstances in which the utterances are issued. If these things, in themselves, allow us to identify illocutionary acts then perhaps we may hope for something approaching a general, *a priori* study of them after all. Certainly we shall not need to look, in each case, to see what happened as a result of the utterance before we can decide questions of illocutionary force.

Before we consider whether such a minimal characterisation can be improved upon, there is the second difficulty which has been urged upon Austin's theory that I mentioned earlier, namely that he cannot keep illocution separate from locution. Again, as in the case we have just considered, it is important that he should succeed in maintaining the separation. Keeping a distinction between the illocutionary and perlocutionary force of utterances is the first step towards the possibility of a systematic, *a priori* study of illocutionary acts; what must now be avoided is a slide to the other extreme, which would leave the study of illocutionary forces in no way distinct from a study of the *meaning* of utterances. Austin's claim in his theory of illocution is to have drawn attention to a dimension of utterances which is something other than their meaning but which is of equal if not greater importance for understanding them (cf. W, pp. 73, 148). It is in this light that his claim, construed as a contribution to the philosophy of language as a subject, is to be judged. We might express the dilemma by saying that Austin has to draw illocution near enough to meaning to enable him to make it the object of philosophical rather than detailed empirical enquiry, but not so near that it ceases to be distinguishable from meaning. It has been argued by Cohen (1964) that such an absorption does take place and Austin is unable to avoid the dilemma. This is the argument we must now consider.

First, it is claimed by Austin that, with certain unimportant exceptions, the issuing of *any* utterance will constitute the performance both of a locutionary and of an illocutionary act (though not necessarily a perlocutionary act, since no substantial consequences may follow from the utterance). He says, 'To perform a locutionary act is in general, we may say, also and *eo ipso* to perform an *illocutionary* act' (W, p. 98; Austin's italics). Austin is not claiming that two acts go on in the way that two quite separate processes are involved if, say, I simultaneously tie my shoe lace and issue an order. Rather, the two acts are abstractions from one and the same physical phenomenon. I utter the words

'Go west, young man!', and this is at once to say something which has a determinate meaning (locution) and to issue a piece of advice (illocution).

This is the starting point of Cohen's objection. He suggests that there is a significant class of cases where even this degree of separation and abstraction is not possible. The class is that of so-called explicit performatives. If, instead of 'Go west, young man!', I utter the words 'I advise you to go west, young man', then the locutionary act which I perform already determines the illocutionary act I am performing. Or rather, in this case it is not even possible in the abstract to separate the one from the other. The *meaning* of the utterance 'I advise you ...' already makes clear what the content of the utterance is *and* how it is to be construed, and so here there is nothing left for the job which, supposedly, only a theory of illocutionary forces can perform.

The next stage in the objection is to argue that what is manifestly true for explicit performatives is also true (though less obviously) for all other utterances. When I expand the utterance 'He caught a big one' into 'John caught a big trout' then I am simply rendering explicit something which is already part of the meaning of that original utterance; and the same is true, Cohen suggests, when I expand my utterance 'Go west' into 'I advise you to go west'. Austin himself, after all, says that illocutionary force is '*conventional*, in the sense that at least it could be made explicit by the performative formula' (W, p. 103; Austin's italics). But in general, so it is argued, his basic mistake is that of tacitly assuming that to one verbal form, such as 'He caught a big one' or 'Go west', there corresponds one statement with one meaning. In reality such a verbal form cloaks a multiplicity of meanings, since it can be used to make many different statements, depending on the circumstances in which it is uttered, what its constituents are used to refer to, the intonation of the utterer, and so on. Hence, when the meaning of an utterance, as determined by all these factors, is made clear and explicit, there is nothing left on which to pin the name 'illocutionary force'. Austin's alleged discovery of a philosophically important dimension of statements, hitherto neglected, is bogus. He has simply given a new name to an old problem, that of meaning.

Whatever our final assessment of this argument, its great merit is to focus our attention on the fact that Austin's theory has to be placed in the context of a theory of language, meaning and communication in general. It is necessary, indeed, to place it in this broader perspective in order to decide how useful the objection is. We must therefore now broach these wider, and exceedingly complex, issues. What I have to say will be unsatisfactorily brief, but I hope it will prove valuable in later discussion of particular philosophical problems.

3. Meaning

Austin, I said, approaches language as a subject for study in an empiricist temper, preferring to examine it as a concrete phenomenon rather than in any more abstract way. This is reflected in his view that the 'total speech act in the total speech situation is the *only actual* phenomenon which, in the last resort, we are engaged in elucidating' (W, p. 147; Austin's italics). His whole theory of illocution rests on his belief that something besides the *meaning* of linguistic utterances is important for a full appreciation of their significance. And, far from disputing this point, Cohen's objection involves being more Austinian than Austin, for it rests not on denying the importance of the total context in which linguistic utterances occur but on arguing that that context is itself a determinant of the meaning of any utterance. This may give rise to the suspicion that the dispute between Austin and Cohen is empty, that they are simply giving different names to something whose substance and significance they agree upon. I wish to argue that the issue here is not an empty one. Even if we are agreed on attaching importance to the 'total significance' of linguistic utterances, a great deal still hangs on how we go about characterising this and how we structure our theories about it.

Language as a phenomenon is obviously the concern of several different disciplines (which is why linguistics is itself a multi-disciplinary discipline). It has many aspects — biological, psychological, sociological, philosophical, and so on — and the practitioners in these different fields will differ in what they regard as the basic units of language. For the *users* of language, however, the basic units are words and sentences. We form sentences out of words and use sentences not only to make statements but, as Austin would be anxious to remind us, to issue orders, ask questions, swear, etc. As long as we do not forget the diversity of uses to which sentences can be put, we may take statements as our example for discussing meaning in general.

We are able to make statements because the sentences we use have meaning. How is the meaning of those sentences determined? Partly by the meaning of the words of which they are composed. The meaning of the sentence

(1) The boy loves the girl

obviously depends partly on the meaning of 'boy' and 'girl'. But a second point, the obviousness of which should not blind us to its importance, is that the meaning of sentences is not merely a function of the meaning of the words they contain. In the sentence

(2) The girl loves the boy

the constituent words are the same as those in (1) and there is no reason to suppose that they change their meaning from one sentence to the other; but for all that, it is obvious that (1) and (2) themselves differ in meaning. As a minimum, therefore, the meaning of sentences is a function both of the meaning of their constituent words and of the structure which the words form. Now I want to say that, on one level, this completely determines the meaning of what a speaker says. Clearly Cohen disagrees and wishes to include several other factors as determinants. Without embarking on a full discussion of theories of meaning I want to discuss the nature and importance of this disagreement.

We have an option here between what I shall call a *wide* and a *narrow* theory of meaning. Cohen's theory is a wide one in that he holds the meaning of a given verbal form to depend on a large number of factors, and therefore to vary considerably from one use to another. A version of a narrow theory is implicit in a series of articles on meaning by H.P. Grice (cf. bibliography). Insofar as Austin's theory involves a separation of illocution from meaning it, too, is a narrow theory. The strategy of a narrow theory is to distinguish rather than assimilate. It involves an insistence that we keep separate the idea of the core meaning of an utterance, something which remains fairly constant across different contexts and in different uses, though recognising that in a concrete case the issuing of an utterance and the context in which it occurs will combine to produce further 'dimensions of significance' besides that core meaning. Among such further dimensions we may distinguish the following: the meaning of the speaker — what *he* means may be different from, even the opposite of, what his utterance means (I may say, 'What an extremely funny remark!' when what *I* mean is, 'What an extremely *un*funny remark!'); *how* the speaker means his utterance (as a threat, a promise, etc.); the implications of what is said, i.e. of the utterance-content; the implications of the utterance-act in the actual situation in which it is issued; and probably several more besides. There may be disagreement over which of these dimensions is most basic and what relations they stand in to each other, but it is only in the context of a narrow theory, where the distinctions have been drawn, that such questions can even arise. For the purposes of the present discussion I shall assume without argument (and in opposition to Grice) that it is utterance-meaning which is basic, and that this is determined by the two factors I suggested, the meaning of its constituents together with the structure they form. I shall call the meaning of an utterance as determined in this way its *sense*, without wishing to imply that my view is necessarily the same as Frege's (cf. Geach and Black, 1952; and Wiggins, 1971).

It is a natural corollary to a narrow theory to aim to give just *one* meaning for any verbal form, rather than postulating several different senses. The aim will be to assign one meaning to an utterance like 'John knows the train has arrived', rather than arguing (as I have heard philosophers argue) that sometimes this means 'John sees the train has arrived', sometimes 'John infers that ...', and so on. In that way a narrow theory of meaning follows the spirit of the principles which I suggested should govern analysis (cf. Chapter II section 6, above). It aims for unity, and in the context of language this means *univocity*, or singleness of sense.

This is where we are likely to find an echo of the complaint that the dispute between Austin and Cohen is an empty one. For it may be said that it just does not matter whether we choose a wide or narrow theory of meaning. In either case we agree that a number of different messages can be conveyed in issuing a linguistic utterance, so it is not as though adopting one theory rather than the other made any difference to what we believe is true of the world.

There are several things to say in reply to this. First, such confidence that a theory of meaning can have no 'pay-off' in the way we describe the world may be misplaced. I argued in Chapter II that analysis could lead to a change in the judgments we make about particular cases, and to the extent that a search for meaning is itself a form of analysis the same will apply. In particular, if we isolate an element in an utterance which remains constant, and take the view that certain other possible messages associated with it vary, then this may well affect our view of the situations in which we think the utterance itself has application. When we come to consider particular philosophical problems and analyses of the concepts relating to them, we shall see several instances where one's theory of meaning (both one's adherence in general to one type rather than the other, and the particular theory about the meaning of some particular term which such a general commitment leads one to have) has an effect on what one believes to be true of the world.

However, even if such consequences did not follow, the choice between a wide and narrow theory would be significant. A narrow theory is preferable *for theoretical reasons*. One such reason is that it meets the demands of theoretical economy. Occam's razor bids us not to multiply theoretical entities beyond necessity, and the narrow theory obeys this injunction by not multiplying the senses of a word or sentence beyond necessity. In aiming to associate just one sense with some verbal form it aims for theoretical simplicity, in contrast to a wide theory which will postulate a change in the meaning of a given verbal form whenever there is a change in any of a large number of factors governing its total import.[1]

It might be objected that this is false economy, because what we save in sense of expressions we lose by an accretion of different dimensions of speaker's meaning, implications of various kinds, etc. But this is not quite fair. What the speaker means when he says something, how he means his utterance to be taken, etc., these are all aspects which are organically connected, so to speak, with the concrete action of issuing an utterance. They are thus a greater distance from being the abstract theoretical entity which the postulated sense of an expression is, and it is to such theoretical entities that Occam's razor relates. A theory cannot reduce the number of actual utterances in the world, but it can and should reduce, where possible, its commitment to abstract senses.

But though the number of senses assigned to any particular expression should be kept low, the notion of sense cannot be dispensed with altogether. This gives a second theoretical reason in favour of a narrow theory. One task for any theory of meaning is to explain how we manage at all to use the sounds and marks of language to talk about a world quite separate from them. And one aspect in particular of this process calls for explanation — what I should call the essential generality or re-applicability of language. I made the point in Chapter II that most uses of language are very different from the activity of naming, and there are many respects in which this is so. A name is a sound or mark associated with a particular object, but even those constituents of language most like names, *viz.* nouns, are associated rather with a whole class of objects *of some general kind*. The name 'Pete' relates to a feline object in my kitchen, but the noun 'cat' relates to an indefinitely large number of objects. When we come to complete sentences, the analogy with naming is even more strained. Sentences like 'He cannot perform that task' or 'He knows what time the train leaves' can be applied in countless situations which are in no immediately visible way similar to each other. To postulate a sense associated with a given verbal form is to suggest a route from language to the world. And to postulate *one* such sense leads us to abstract from all the particular circumstances in which that verbal form is used, to move away from superficial features up to a higher level of generality in extracting what is common to all those circumstances, and thus to show how we can use the verbal form in innumerable different situations and be understood.[2] In contrast, if the meaning of sentences like these is constantly changing according to circumstances, then it becomes more of a mystery how we can use them and be understood at all. We do not, after all, have to learn a new meaning each time such a sentence is uttered, as a wide theory seems to imply. Thus, a narrow theory is also preferable on the grounds of its greater explanatory power.

The principles of a narrow theory give a grounding to the conviction that, at one level, for me to understand the meaning of what is said when someone utters a sentence like one of those mentioned above, all that is required is that I should understand the English language. I may not know what reasons there are for issuing the utterance, what particular features make it true or false, but still I have a clear and unambiguous understanding of it. I am not in the position of someone who hears the utterance 'My wife is at the port', and is at a loss whether to conclude that the person referred to is a lover of boats or of alcohol. Two qualifications are necessary, however. First, it is not always possible to realise the narrow theory's aim of postulating one sense for each verbal form, and not only in cases of straightforward homonymy, like the last example. It would be more accurate to say that the aim is to postulate one sense, provided that doing so is consistent with thereby expressing the specific content of the verbal form in its different contexts. For example, we could preserve the univocity of 'My wife is at the port' by saying that its one and only sense is 'My wife is somewhere'. This is clearly unacceptable as an account of the meaning of the utterance because it is too unspecific. Hence we see that the price to pay for univocity is sometimes too high, and that sometimes we do have to multiply senses to give a satisfactory account of a verbal form at all. (We shall see an example of this in Chapter VI, when we consider the language of perception.) The point is that this should be seen as a last resort rather than the first option in explaining meaning.

Secondly, I should explain further why knowing the sense of an utterance like 'He cannot perform that task' enables me to understand what is said *at one level*. Someone might object that knowing only the sense does not enable me to understand what is said at all, because if that is all I know then I do not know what *thing or situation in the world* is being spoken about. *Who* cannot perform the task? Cannot perform *what* task? In short, I do not know what statement is made, as 'statement' was being used in Chapter III, if all I know is the sense. The proper response to this objection is not to take in further factors as determinants of the meaning of an utterance, but rather to stress what is already implied by the narrow theory, *viz.* that there is more than one level of meaning (cf. Strawson, 1973, pp. 47ff.). Certainly we should not simply regard reference, the thing in the world spoken about, as itself part of the meaning of an utterance. Austin does so in isolating locution from illocution (cf. W, p. 148), and to that extent his own theory is an imperfectly narrow one. To take reference into meaning in this way is to give up the attempt to explain the move from language to the world. It is the meaning of an utterance (together with the identity of the speaker, the situation in which it is issued, etc.) which leads us to its reference, not vice versa. What does follow from the objection, however, is that we need to distinguish firmly between sentence-meaning and statement-meaning (a point which may have been obscured by my wilfully ambiguous use of the expression 'utterance' in the preceding discussion). If I say to you 'You are drunk' and you say to me 'You are drunk' then sentence-meaning is the same in both cases, though statement-meaning is not. And sentence-meaning is a level of meaning, complete in itself, which ought not to be ignored.

The aim of a narrow theory, then, is to isolate the core meaning of an utterance, and then trace the moves from this to further levels of meaning. If the aim is justified by the arguments I have given, Cohen's criticism of Austin will not stand, since it will rest on a conflation of things which need to be distinguished, a lumping-together of all possible factors into one undifferentiated concept of meaning. In contrast, Austin's theory of illocution represents an attempt to differentiate. We cannot yet say, however, that the concept of illocution is safe. Whether it can stand as one such level of meaning depends on whether the idea of an illocutionary act can be made clear on its own account.

4. Determinants of illocution

Suppose that I perform some locutionary act. I say, for

example, 'There is a man in the next room', or 'Will you open the door?' What factors determine the illocutionary act which I perform in saying what I do? That is, what determines that I am giving information, or making an appeal, or asking a question, or any of the other examples which Austin gives of illocutionary acts (W, pp. 98, 152–62)? An answer to this question should also help us to see what determines that a given act finds its way on to the list of illocutionary acts in the first place: it should help us to see what it is to be an illocutionary act. Several candidates suggest themselves as determinants of illocution. I shall argue, however, that we cannot say that a particular candidate just is, in general, the determinant of the illocutionary act which a speaker performs in saying something. The reason is that 'illocution' is a blanket term which covers too many different types of act.

To begin with, we should return to the starting point of Cohen's objection, that in the case of explicit performatives such as 'I promise ...' the sense of the utterance itself determines what illocutionary act is being performed. Now this is not strictly true, since I may say 'I promise ...' in infelicitous circumstances, and then (although my utterance has the same meaning as it carries in more felicitous circumstances) it will not be true that I have performed the illocutionary act of promising. All the same, we might try to make something of Cohen's point here, and be encouraged to do so by the fact that there are other cases where the nature of the locutionary act itself has a crucial effect on illocution. When Austin is discussing the reporting of a *locutionary* act from different points of view, he gives as examples:

' "He said 'Get out' ", "He *told* me to get out";
"He said 'Is it in Oxford or Cambridge?' ";
"He *asked* whether it was in Oxford or Cambridge".'
(W, p. 95; italics added. Cf. W, p. 97, where he appears to give 'advise to' as a possible description of a locutionary act.) Now 'tell' and 'ask' are both names of *illocutionary* acts (W, p. 161), and since nothing else is said

about these examples — nothing, for instance, about the context of their utterance — it looks as though some feature of the locutionary act itself is a determinant of illocution. The most obvious conclusion is that it is *grammatical structure* which is responsible for this: the imperative form is the standard form for the illocutionary act of telling to, the interrogative for asking, and so on. This might be one way of interpreting Austin's repeated insistence that illocutionary acts are conventional (e.g. W, pp. 103, 105, 118). The idea would be that there are conventional grammatical forms for illocutionary acts. On this view, then, locution is itself a determinant at least of the broader and less specific illocutionary acts (cf. Strawson 1973, p. 55; Searle, 1968, p. 148).

Is the view acceptable? One obvious drawback is that it is an incomplete account. It is easy to postulate a conventional grammatical form for asking and telling, but not for, say, warning, making an appeal or toasting. Something else, then, would have to determine when these other acts were performed. But a more serious criticism might also be raised. Suppose that a sergeant-major says to a soldier under his command, 'Would it inconvenience you too much to pay a visit to the barber when you have a few minutes to spare?' According to the grammatical criterion, this would have the illocutionary force of asking; but surely, it will be said, it is most likely that the sergeant-major was doing no such thing but rather *ordering?* This suggests the alternative view that the determinant of illocution is *how the speaker means his utterance*, a view which can also claim support from Austin. He implies that illocutionary force can be captured by means of the formula 'he meant it as ...' (W, p. 100) and makes reference to the commonness of 'deliberate or unintentional failure to make plain "how our words are to be taken" (in the illocutionary sense)' (W, pp. 114–15n.; Austin's parenthesis). If it is this failure which obscures the illocutionary force of a given utterance then it must be the speaker's failure, and this suggests that the means of making the illocutionary force plain does indeed lie with him.

The idea that it is a speaker's meaning or intention which determines illocution has found favour with some of Austin's commentators (e.g. Strawson, 1964; Skinner, 1972). It is not without its own difficulties, however. First, a tension naturally appears between this claim and the claim that illocutionary acts are conventional. Admittedly, it may be conventional relations holding between speaker and audience in my example which determine that an order has been given, but in other cases this will not be so. I may say 'If you move a muscle you will not leave the room alive', and mean this as a threat, but it is not clear what kind of convention is involved in my meaning it in this way.[3] Austin himself says that the illocutionary act 'is constituted *not by intention* or by fact, essentially but by *convention*' (W, p. 127; first italics added). So if illocutionary acts are essentially conventional, it looks as though my meaning my utterance as a threat will not determine that I have performed the illocutionary act of threatening. Of course, this is open to the reply that since I plainly do threaten by meaning to threaten, Austin's insistence on the importance of convention must be mistaken. But that does not leave a free run for the claim that it is speaker's meaning which necessarily determines illocution. Overlooking and neglecting are both illocutionary acts (cf. W, pp. 159, 162), but I may perform them *whether I mean to or not*. (Strawson, *op. cit.*, p. 397, argues that in the case of some illocutionary acts, unintended performance is 'essentially deviant', but I see no reason to accept this in the case of the examples I give here.)

If we allow speaker's meaning and intention to recede and concentrate again on convention, we do not necessarily end up at our starting point, equating convention with standard grammatical form. Rather, we might take our cue from my sergeant-major example, together with Austin's warning, when he first introduces the idea of illocution, that 'the occasion of an utterance matters seriously, and that the words used are to some extent to be "explained" by the "context" in which they are designed to be or have actually been spoken in a linguistic interchange' (W, p. 100). What is suggested by a joint stress on convention and context (especially when we recall that the theory of illocution is intended to be a more adequate replacement for the performative/constative distinction) is perhaps something like this: that some conventional, socially sanctioned procedure has to be gone through for an illocutionary act to have been performed, and that if we scrutinise the background conditions of the utterance and the conventional relations obtaining between the speaker and his audience, we shall be able to discover which illocutionary act has been performed.

Once again, however, the suggestion cannot be generalised to account for all the different illocutionary acts. It will be appropriate for some cases — for example, a scrutiny of the conventional background will be material in determining whether a particular utterance of the words 'You will go to prison for three years' constitutes the pronouncing of a sentence. But it will not fit the common run of illocutionary acts. If I say 'These measures will lead to unemployment' then I may be merely stating a fact, or I may also be warning or protesting, but no accretion of facts about the conventional relations and background obtaining when I make the utterance will tell us which, if either, of these other acts I am performing. I can warn whatever my conventional role and my conventional relations with my audience (unless we are talking of those explicitly conventional contexts where I might issue, as we significantly say, a formal warning or protest, e.g. in a game or at a meeting. But most acts of warning or protesting are not of this type, and will not therefore be determined by the conventional situation.)

Let us make one final attempt to interpret the idea that illocutionary acts are conventional. At one point

Austin remarks that the use of language to perform illocutionary acts is '*conventional*, in the sense that at least it could be made explicit by the performative formula' (W, p. 103; Austin's italics). Strawson (*op. cit.*) points out that there is in fact no such sense of 'conventional', but that nevertheless this may indicate how illocutionary acts are determined. Certainly Austin remarks elsewhere that 'the whole apparatus of "explicit performatives"..... serves to obviate disagreements as to the description of illocutionary acts' (W, p. 115n.). This will not of itself give us a means of determining the illocutionary act performed where a speaker does not use the 'explicit performative' device, but we could say that it is determined by the performative the speaker *would* have used *if* he had done so. (This may be one of the thoughts behind the subtle theory developed by Strawson, *op. cit.*) But the suggestion fares no better than our previous ones. Austin makes the point perfectly, in contradiction of his earlier statement. Although on his view 'I favour' is an explicit performative, 'To say "I favour X" may, according to context, be to *vote* for X, to *espouse X*, or to *applaud X*' (W, p. 157; Austin's italics). That is to say, in issuing an 'explict performative' I may perform illocutionary acts *other* than the one specified in the performative formula itself. The distinction I insisted on in Chapter III, between (a) saying being the doing of *something* and (b) saying being the doing of *the thing said*, returns to haunt us. Austin's comments here suggest, once again, that he did not take the distinction seriously enough.

Our discussion so far has been unsatisfactorily inconclusive. We have a number of rival candidates as possible determinants of illocution — speaker's intention, context, grammatical form — and we seem to be hovering in a no-man's-land of indecision. No candidate looks impressive enough to warrant its being used to rule out counter-examples which would be urged against it by the proponents of a rival candidate. I want to suggest that this is not because Austin himself put forward inconsistent views on our question (though that may be true), nor because there is some more promising line of approach which we have ignored. Rather, it is because the concept of illocution is so broad that it *cannot* be dealt with in the ways we have been considering.

When the idea of illocution is introduced with the original examples (W, p. 98), its characterisation is even more minimal than the initial characterisation of performatives. It is simply the idea of an action which is performed in saying something rather than as a consequence of saying something. By the end of an avowedly inconclusive discussion Austin has increased his list of illocutionary acts to several dozen (cf. W, pp. 151–61) and he believes that the full number is 'of the order of the third power of 10' (W, p. 149n.). The final lists contain acts as diverse as stating, planning, toasting, siding with, convicting, calculating, praying, declaring open, grumbling about and conjecturing. The diversity is so great, and the discussion of the concept of illocution so inconclusive, that we have been given no good reason to suppose that any one set of general conditions will govern *all* our examples of illocution. We have no reason to suppose that they have anything in common beyond the initial minimal characterisation, i.e. that they are all acts which we can perform in saying something. But what general conditions must obtain for me to perform such an act will depend on *which* act is in question. Certainly convention of a fairly obvious kind will govern some illocutionary acts, such as pronouncing sentence, but not others, such as asking or reporting. Certainly speaker's intention will be crucial to some, such as pledging oneself, but not others, such as informing or warning. But we shall not be able to generalise any such factor across the whole range of illocutionary acts, any more than we should expect to be able to do so over the whole range of acts performed non-verbally. Nor should we expect, given the diversity, that any interesting disjunctive analysis of the determinants of illocution can be given.

Of course, it does not follow from this that the whole concept of illocution should be abandoned (even though Austin introduces it tentatively and expresses misgivings about it). That an adequate and informative analysis is not available does not support that conclusion. Once we have recognised that 'illocution' is an umbrella term covering many different speech acts, it may be more profitable to attempt a sub-categorisation and develop analyses in relation to sub-categories of speech act. It is a curious fact that Austin and his commentators tend both to give verbal recognition to the diversity of illocution and still to seek for a *general* account of it.[4]

5. Conclusion

Austin is chiefly concerned with the *analysis* of the concept of illocution. We knew before we began that you can, literally, perform actions with words. But the detailed discussion of the various actions which can be so performed, the different conditions governing different actions, and so on, all this has the beneficial effect of leading us to view this perfectly familiar fact with greater insight. The implications of the discussion, moreover, have far more than merely analytical interest. When we are reminded of the sheer extent and diversity of the acts which can be performed in speaking, this ought to put us on our guard against any facile distinction between speech and action in, say, a political context. It should warn us against underestimating the importance of political propaganda as itself a form of political *activity*, and it should warn us against supposing that freedom of speech is an issue entirely separate from freedom of action (cf. Edgley, 1975).

Austin's work here also carries implications for other disciplines, such as history and the social sciences. Often these involve the attempt to understand an alien culture, and this will naturally include an attempt to understand the language and thought of its members.

The discussion in *How To Do Things With Words* gives an indication of the different dimensions which such enquiries will have to deal with. It also gives emphasis to one particular and central difficulty. In many cases, as we have seen, the illocutionary force of an utterance is dependent upon facts about conventions or the context in which it occurs, and certainly not dependent solely upon the locutionary content of the utterance. This means that even where we have an adequate system of translation we cannot just assume that an utterance with a given core message will carry the same illocutionary force in a different cultural setting as the one we might standardly associate with it in our own. Understanding the full import of utterances, as opposed to their core meaning, is difficult enough in our own, familiar, social environment. When interpretation has to be carried out across large distances of time and space, the problems are multiplied (cf. Skinner, 1970). In these and related ways, Austin's theory of illocution is an extremely important contribution to our understanding of language as a concrete and many-sided phenomenon.

It is probably inevitable that this stress on the concreteness of language should lead Austin at times to look askance at attempts to abstract from it. The picture of linguistic communication which his theory rightly condemns is that of a speaker and audience respectively transmitting and receiving a 'pure' message which is unaffected by and does not affect their actual situation, social relations, etc. But I have argued (section 3, above) that it is important to be able to isolate such a 'pure' message *as one component* in linguistic communication. I argued for the importance of isolating a relatively stable and re-applicable statement-content as the core of an actual linguistic utterance. It is not clear how much sympathy, in the end, Austin would have for this. He inveighs, for example, against 'the traditional "statement" ', to which my statement-content could be likened, as being 'an abstraction, an ideal, and so is its traditional truth or falsity' (W, p. 147). Indeed, in the matter of truth he has decided preferences in favour of concrete statement-acts (though he does not use that term):

> 'It is essential to realize that "true" and "false", like "free" and "unfree", do not stand for anything simple at all; but only for a general dimension of being a right or proper *thing to say* as opposed to a wrong thing, in these circumstances, to this audience, for these purposes, and with these intentions ...
>
> ... The truth or falsity of a statement depends not merely on the meanings of words but on *what act you were performing in what circumstances.'*
>
> (W, p. 144; italics added)

Now we must take care in the inferences we draw from these remarks. Austin's commitment to the distinction between locutionary and illocutionary acts is less than absolute (cf. W, p. 148) and he recognises in any case that *both* types of act are abstractions (W, p. 146). Similarly he is prepared to allow that the traditional conception of truth is 'an artificial abstraction which is always *possible and legitimate* for certain purposes' (W, p. 148; italics added). As Strawson (1973, p. 56) remarks, we are uncertain whether the conception is an abstraction and none the worse for that, or an abstraction and a good deal the worse for that. But we should resist the drift of some of Austin's remarks as they affect the idea of truth, and not only because they conflict with the conception of truth which he advocates elsewhere (cf. Chapter VII, below). This applies in particular to the identification of what is true with what to say. Something may be true but not the thing to say in these circumstances because it is irrelevant to anyone's concerns in the situation, or because to utter it would mislead everyone in the situation, or because no one in the situation has grounds for a rational conviction of its truth. Again, truth cannot always depend either on the statement-act or on the illocutionary act anyone was performing. We can debate the truth of statements which no one ever has issued, and more importantly there are many general statements whose truth or falsity hangs in no way at all on who uttered them in what circumstances. If I want to know whether it is true that all events have a cause or that all knowledge rests on good evidence, I need have no interest at all in what surrounds the *saying* of these things.

There is an important connexion here with Austin's philosophical method. I have already mentioned several times how his work on language as a subject coalesces with his approach to philosophical problems in general, and this is a connexion to which he explicitly draws attention himself. Of the theory of illocution he says, 'The real fun comes when we begin to apply it to philosophy' (W, p. 163, cf. p. 100), and he suggests moral philosophy as a place to start. An uncountable number of philosophers have followed this exhortation, both in the recommended area and in general, and many continue to do so. The question is whether they have been led to the promised land or up the garden path.

On a brief recollection of the principles behind analytical philosophy which I outlined in Chapter II, it may seem appropriate to follow Austin in this way. After all, a consideration of the actual circumstances of utterance will certainly provide us with information about what is present when we say such-and-such, and it could well be argued that an account of the illocutionary force of an utterance will serve to bring out its *point* (cf. Skinner, 1972, p. 146). Can we not, in this way, arrive at solid conclusions about what is involved in speaking in certain ways about the world, and the reasons for doing so?

I believe that this question should be answered in the negative, and that the theory of illocution is damaging rather than beneficial as an instrument for dealing with philosophical problems about anything other than language. I noted in Chapter II, section 8 the ambiguities in the idea of examining 'what we should say when' as a means to analysis. The theory of illocution provides us with information about what we should say in *precisely the wrong sense* of that ambiguous phrase. It relates, obviously, to the actual *saying* of various things, and if it furnishes a rationale at all, it is a rationale for utterance-acts rather than utterance-contents. It gives the grounds for the *saying* of something *in* a given situation, not the rationale for *what* should be said *about* it. Much of what Austin has to say about philosophical problems connected with knowledge, perception, and so on, is indeed, 'applied theory of illocution'. The result is that what he has to say is still about language (the language of knowledge, perception, and so on) rather than about those phenomena which the language is itself *about*. An examination of his arguments will, I hope, bear this out.

V

Philosophical Problems: Knowledge

1. Introduction

The two central questions of theory of knowledge, or epistemology, are (a) what is knowledge? and (b) what (kinds of) things do we know? We have, in other words, one question about the *nature* of knowledge and one question about its *scope*. This is a division which will crop up again in subsequent chapters of this book, in relation to other areas of enquiry. It is fairly obvious that questions of this kind will be interrelated, and the initial view one has about the answer to one of them is likely to have some influence on the way one answers the other. If you hold the view that knowledge is a kind of mystical union with an eternal, unchanging, intangible entity, then you are not likely to allow that one of the things of which we have knowledge is the price of eggs. Conversely, if you hold the view that I *can* know something like this then you are not likely to accept the former characterisation of what knowledge is.

At first sight this may seem to suggest that it is impossible to get started on a theory of knowledge. How can we decide what we know until we have decided what kind of thing knowledge is, and how can we decide what knowledge is except by considering cases where we do know something and seeing what is involved in them? But we are not really trapped in any such impasse. The point is that in advance of any self-conscious theorising we already apply a concept such as knowledge to particular cases. We also have at least some idea why we do so. And this means that there is some raw material for a self-conscious theory to work

on. We already hold views on what we know and what
knowledge is, although our views may be only implicit
and inchoate and they may be more or less articulate,
consistent and coherent, and more or less widely
agreed upon. The problem for a philosophical theory is
then to expound these views and relate them to each
other in an informative and structured way, and to
decide whether they are acceptable. What is essential to
remember is that our initial views provide us with a
starting point and no more. They may become
transformed or even abandoned in the course of
examining them. Theory of knowledge is therefore a
good testing ground for the provisional criticisms
which I made of Austin's method in Chapter II and for
the alternative approach which I advocated. We need
to look at cases which we should initially be prepared
to say are cases of knowledge, and then we must try to
say why we regard them as such, what features they
share in common and what distinguishes them from
similar cases which we say do not amount to
knowledge. And we must decide how much
enlightenment results from pursuing these enquiries in
Austin's preferred way.

The attempt to say what knowledge is is as old as
philosophy itself, and it will be as well to give a brief
description of some of the analyses which have been
advanced before we turn to Austin's own discussion.
Any claim to knowledge, if it is to be allowed, must
satisfy certain requirements. If it fails to do so it is likely
to be reclassified as a *belief*, and the ideas of knowledge
and belief stand so close to each other that any theory
of knowledge will have to make clear what relation
holds between them. The tone was set by Plato in his
Theaetetus, where he asked what the difference was
between knowledge and true belief, and the
commonest attempts to analyse knowledge still consist
in defining it as 'true belief plus'. On the face of it, the
distinction between knowledge and true belief is an
essential one. I may at this moment believe, for no
reason at all, that a man has been injured in a road

accident two blocks away, and it may turn out that my belief is correct. But if there is no discernible reason why I should hold this belief there is an initial resistance to accepting that I *know* that such an incident has occurred. This is the starting point of what might fairly be called the *classical* analysis of knowledge. It is suggested that those of my beliefs amount to knowledge which are true and for which I do have reasons, that knowledge is true belief which is well-grounded or for which I have adequate evidence or which I have a right to be sure about (cf. Ayer, 1956; Chisholm, 1966).[1]

However, there are difficulties facing this theory which are almost as well known as the theory itself, in particular the suspicion that it suffers from a certain kind of circularity, which I consider later. It may be partly in response to these difficulties that an alternative theory has arisen. The *causal* analysis is like the previous one in regarding knowledge as 'true belief plus', but it locates the differentiating factor in the origin of a belief rather than in its accompaniments. The suggestion here is that sometimes a true belief is induced in a subject by that very state of affairs which the subject believes to obtain, and that it is in just such cases that belief amounts to knowledge, whereas when the belief is induced by some other means it is *mere* belief. For example, when it is the very presence of a vase before my eyes which causes me to believe that there is a vase before my eyes, then I *know* that this is so. But if, say, hypnosis causes me to believe this, then even if my belief is true I do not know (cf. Goldman, 1967).

A further alternative is the analysis of knowledge as a *capacity* (cf. Watling, 1955; Ryle, 1949). In contrast to the previous theories there is no emphasis here on the origin or accompaniments of belief (or indeed on the existence of belief at all). The idea is rather that a person knows something in virtue of possessing a competence in getting it right. To know, even to know facts, is to know *how* to do something. What this analysis shares with the others is the attempt to show why it is *no accident* that a person who knows can get something right.

2. Conditions for knowing

There is room for disagreement over whether Austin provides any account of the conditions for knowing comparable to the foregoing attempts. His main discussion of knowledge appears in 'Other Minds' (PP, pp. 76–116), part of a symposium with John Wisdom (1946) which has as its subject a question about the scope rather than the nature of knowledge, a question to which I return in section 4, below. At the very least, however, Austin has much to say which carries implications for any such account, and for the relation between knowledge and belief.

Wisdom's concern had been with how, if at all, I can know what another person is feeling, and whether it is like the way I know other things — that a kettle is boiling, or that there is a party next door, for example. Austin focusses on the question 'What we should say if asked "How do you know?" these things' (PP, p. 77), and he sets about answering it in the way his method dictates. He considers 'what sort of thing does actually happen when ordinary people are asked "How do you know" ' (*ibid.*).

The example discussed is one where I claim that there is a certain bird in the garden, am asked 'How do you know?' and make various responses. Such responses exhibit a bewildering variety, which perhaps suggests that the person who raises the question may himself have different things in mind in asking it. Now some of the answers which I may give to this question are very obviously substantively different from each other: there is a very obvious difference between saying 'Because I heard it' and 'someone told me'. But as well as these, Austin purports to discern distinctions which are not so immediately evident. He says, for example:

' "*From* its red head", given as an answer to "How do you know?" requires careful consideration: in particular it differs very materially from "*Because* it has a red head" ... Any answer beginning "From" or "By" has, intentionally, this saving "vagueness". But on the contrary, an answer beginning "Because" is dangerously definite. When I say I know it's a goldfinch "Because it has a red head", that implies that all I have noted, or needed to note, about it is that its head is red (nothing special or peculiar about the shade, shape, &c. of the patch): so that I imply that there is no other small British bird that has any sort of red head except the goldfinch.'

(PP, pp. 84–5; Austin's italics)

When claims of this degree of specificity are made, it becomes apparent why doubts have been expressed over whether it is satisfactory simply to rely on one's linguistic intuitions in the matter of distinguishing idioms and saying why they are distinct. For the claim which Austin makes here seems to me, at least, to be mistaken. Whether my reply to the question 'How do you know?' is vague or definite hangs not on whether I begin with 'Because' or 'From', but rather on what follows these. Suppose I say that I know what the bird is 'from its red head, black top, white ears and pointed beak'. There is nothing at all vague about such a reply: it is precisely as definite as the reply '*Because* it has a red head, black top, white ears and pointed beak'.

However, rather than disputing the validity of Austin's claim it is probably more important to ask what its point is. Otherwise, one is seduced into a discussion which may turn out to be entirely without significance. Why, then, does he go into so much detail over the ways in which we may reply to the question 'How do you know?'? Consider one possible answer (though it is not entirely clear to me whether this is an answer which Austin would himself wish to use). If we can collect the mass of different possible answers to the question, and introduce some sort of systematic order into them, it may be possible to correlate these with a set of different challenges which lie behind the question. And then it may be possible to correlate these challenges with the various conditions for knowing an empirical fact. I am asked how I know, and I reply by citing an authority, or something about my past experience, my present position, and so on. Perhaps, then, one or more of these conditions is necessary for me to know, and perhaps some of them are sufficient to ensure that I do? This would certainly give some point to the broader distinctions which Austin makes, if not the more minute ones, and it is consistent with some of his further remarks. He implies that for me to know, in the type of case he deals with (knowledge of 'particular, current, empirical fact'; PP, p. 77), I must (a) in general have had the opportunity to learn about objects of the kind in question and acquired a certain acumen in recognising them, and (b) in the particular case have had an opportunity for getting the answer right and actually succeed in getting it right (PP, pp. 79–80).

If this is the correct way of construing the import of Austin's remarks, should we agree that the particular conditions he lists really are necessary for knowledge? There is at least room for doubt. In Chapter II, section 9 I mentioned the possible case of a man who is always able to give my position as I walk along behind a wall, although he has not, in any proper sense, had an *opportunity* to find out where I am (cf. Watling, *op. cit.*). Or again, focusing on the first part of Austin's conditions, what if someone has *not* in general had an opportunity to learn about the objects in question but yet successfully identifies them on all occasions? What if someone is born able to recognise goldfinches? Do the people in such cases *know*? My own inclination is to say that they may, and that the conditions Austin lists do not stand in such an intimate relation to knowledge that we should say without any hestitation that their absence *guarantees* lack of knowledge. The nature of the role they play in connexion with the concept of knowledge explains why we are and ought to be hesitant when we find them absent. In normal cases we pay attention to the features in question not because they are themselves indispensable conditions for knowing, but rather because they are generally reliable guides to something else, and it is that something else which is indispensable to knowing. Hence, when those original conditions are removed from the situation we are unsure whether to describe it as one of knowledge or not. It may be and it may not be: we are uncertain because the guide normally used to decide the matter is absent.

These remarks may appear rather gnomic. What is this 'something else' the presence of which really is necessary for knowledge, according to me? We may begin to answer this by re-phrasing Plato's question in a way suggested by our discussion of analysis in Chapter II. What is the *point* of the concept of knowledge? We can ascribe beliefs to someone, and we can add that the belief is true, so why do we need as well as this the possibility of ascribing knowledge? The difference lies in the fact that the man who has knowledge can safely be relied upon, whereas to rely upon a man who happens to have a correct belief is a more risky business. The knower does not just happen to get something right, it is no accident that he gets it right. It is this consideration which provides the impetus for a causal analysis of knowledge, of the kind mentioned earlier. But the idea of knowledge as a capacity is an alternative way of construing the fact that it is no accident that the knower gets something right. The man whose belief just happens to be correct can be seen as getting something right by fluke, and the contrast with fluke successes is successes which arise as a result of possessing the *capacity* to perform tasks of the required kind. It is this idea of possessing a capacity which I should suggest is fundamentally involved in the concept of knowledge. The man who has knowledge of facts has the capacity to discriminate amongst a certain set of true and false statements. The man who knows a person or a place has the capacity to recognise them, to distinguish them from other people and places. This interpretation emphasises the unity of the concept of knowledge. In all the different cases what is at bottom involved is the possession of some skill, either in the performing of some action (as when someone knows how to swim) or in making some discrimination. It is also made clear that knowledge is not just a passive attribute of human beings, something simply fed in through a reliable route. To know something is to be able to do something, and in that sense there is substance in the dictum that knowledge is power.

The idea of knowledge as a capacity, as I said, explains why Austin attaches importance to the conditions he mentions, in the case of knowing a particular empirical fact. Those conditions are normally fulfilled, and would normally be insisted upon, because people do not normally have the *capacity* to recognise, distinguish and identify particular objects unless they have learnt about them in general and had the opportunity to identify them in the particular case. But if this is true it is a contingent and not a logical truth, stating what is causally necessary for the acquisition of a certain capacity. The *possession* of the capacity is something in principle distinct from its manner of acquisition, and from the point of view of knowledge it is the possession of the capacity which matters.

What further follows from this is something which may seem at first sight rather startling — that the connexion between knowing something and having evidence or good grounds for it is not a logically necessary connexion. It is traditionally taken to be such, and the traditional view is reflected in Austin's discussion by the demand that I be able to answer the question 'How do you know?' with replies like 'I learnt about them at school' or 'It has the right shape head'. But I am not sure that we ought to be startled by this. The traditional view is notoriously beset by a problem of circularity which I mentioned earlier, a problem of which there is already a hint in the closing stages of

Plato's *Theaetetus*. If in order to know that something is the case I have to have evidence for it, what relation must I stand in to that evidence? Do I have to know that it is true or may I simply believe it? If I merely believe it then my 'knowledge' is after all being anchored in something accidental, and since the introduction of the requirement of having evidence is intended to avoid this, it looks as though it will be insufficient for me only to believe the evidence. On the other hand, if I have to *know* the evidence then the danger of an infinite regress immediately suggests itself. For, in conformity with the original requirement, my knowing the evidence will require my having evidence for that evidence, which will require me to know the evidence for the evidence, and so on *ad infinitum*. This difficulty suggests that sooner or later it will have to be admitted that there is something which I can know without necessarily having evidence for it. But if we are forced by perfectly general considerations to the conclusion that this must be possible in some cases of knowledge, then why not in all? Why not simply discard the view that having evidence is a conceptual requirement of knowledge?

One reply would be that there are two kinds of knowledge: *immediate* knowledge, which does not have to be anchored in having evidence, and *mediate* knowledge, which does; and hence, that the requirement of having evidence cannot be allowed to slip out of the picture altogether. This is a plausible reply, and one which can be plausibly elaborated, as it is, for example, by Armstrong (1973, part III). We have so far simply given an argument to the effect that there must be *some* cases of immediate knowledge, and it might be possible to make a reasoned division of cases into mediate and immediate, in terms of the kind of empirical fact which is known. For example, it might be said that my knowledge that the train leaves in ten minutes must be mediate, whereas my knowledge that I have a headache may (or must) be immediate, perhaps because one has a peculiarly intimate acquaintance with one's own mental states such that evidence for them is superfluous.

Probably the shortest way with this reply is to point out that it introduces needless complications. On the general grounds outlined in Chapter IV, section 3, if we can give an explanatory account of some concept which is also unitary and simple, then so much the better. I believe that the account of knowledge in terms of capacities has such advantages. Unlike the elaborated traditional account, it does not force upon us the belief that some kind of pun is involved when I say that I know two things, that I have a headache and that you have a headache. My knowing either of these things requires fulfilment of exactly the same kind of general conditions. To say this and no more, however, is to do less than justice to the subtlety of an account like Armstrong's. Once the unity of a concept has been exhibited there may well be a point in making further distinctions and sub-divisions within it, distinguishing different types of knowledge. This will act as a further qualification of the injunction to aim for a univocal analysis of any concept. We may still say, however, that such sub-divisions should be made only *after* a more general analysis has been constructed which displays the unity of a concept (in cases where such unity does exist). The analysis of knowledge as a capacity would conform to this.

It may or may not be possible to elaborate the account I have suggested into a plausible theory of knowledge.[2] But the debate on that question is one which Austin's method does not even allow him to join in. A review of the arguments of the last few pages will explain why.

We began with a putative analysis of knowledge drawn from Austin's remarks. One general criticism which could be levelled at the analysis concerns the way it is arrived at. We need to go beyond 'what actually happens' in an ordinary, pre-theoretical conversation about knowing something, in order to sift the essential from the inessential, and this is something which Austin does not do. Our preferred method of attack, however, was by means of counter-examples. This is a favourite move in analytical philosophy, but one which has its own dangers. If we present something as a counter-example merely because we normally describe it as a case of knowledge whereas the proposed analysis would disallow it, then our argument is of the same kind as Austin's and just as deficient. It is therefore necessary to justify our description of the counter-example itself, and say *why* we regard it as a case of knowledge. In this way we avoid having to allow a proposed analysis to take precedence over a counter-example and we also avoid having to allow an intuitive counter-example to take precedence over a proposed analysis. The pitting of the one against the other tests them both, and in the process often generates a new or amended analysis. This was how the idea of knowledge as a capacity emerged. But Austin cannot follow us along this spiral path. For him, if we talk of knowledge in a given case then we do, and so much the worse for a theory which says we should not. Moreover, he confines himself to actual cases, whereas our examples were by design hypothetical. I noted in Chapter II section 8 his tendency to ignore the creative possibilities of analysis, and this is a case in point. If unexpected things happen, '*we don't know what to say.* Words literally fail us: "What would you have said?" "What are we to say now?" "What would *you* say?" ' (PP, p. 88; Austin's italics. Cf. PP, p. 68.) But we are given no answer. Paradoxically, his method leaves him with nothing to say about just those cases which afford us a greater insight into our reasons for saying what we do about actual cases.

3. Knowledge and performatives
I now turn to another part of Austin's discussion, one which may be thought to allay any doubts about whether he actually offers an analysis of knowledge.

I said that any analysis would need to establish the relation between the ideas of knowledge and belief.

The tendency of Austin's remarks is to emphasise the distance between them. He points out that saying 'I know ... ' 'is *not* saying "I have performed a specially striking feat of cognition, superior, in the same scale as believing and being sure, even to being merely quite sure": for there *is* nothing in that scale superior to being quite sure' (PP, p. 99; Austin's italics). This seems correct enough, and it is an important point to make. The history of philosophy is littered with attempts to show that knowledge is a state of mind like, but also different from, the state of mind called belief, and Austin implicitly brings out the futility of such attempts. If there is a difference between the man who knows something about the world and the man who believes, this is not to be found in their subjective state of conviction, for this may be total and identical in both cases. I may be in a state of total conviction about some matter and yet have belief rather than knowledge about it, and there is nothing more which can be demanded of me in this respect than being in a state of total conviction, no further change which will transform my state into one of knowledge. If, therefore, there is a difference it will have to be traced to something other than the subject's mental state — perhaps some other difference in the subject or a difference in the subject's relation to the world, in knowledge and belief respectively.

Now Austin clearly does think there is a large difference between knowledge and belief, for he goes on to say: 'We all *feel* the very great difference between saying even "I'm *absolutely* sure" and saying "I know": it is like the difference between saying even "I firmly and irrevocably intend" and "I promise" ' (PP, p. 100; Austin's italics). In consistency with his earlier remark, the suggestion here seems to be that the difference involved is one of kind rather than degree. How, then, are we to understand it? What exactly is it in the parallel case of intending and promising which should interest us? According to Austin,

'[W]hen I say "I promise", a new plunge is taken: I have not merely announced my intention, but, by using this formula (performing this ritual), I have bound myself to others, and staked my reputation, in a new way. Similarly, saying "I know" is taking a new plunge ... When I say "I know", I *give others my word*: I *give others my authority for saying* that "S is P".

When I have said only that I am sure, and prove to have been mistaken, I am not liable to be rounded on by others in the same way as when I have said "I know".'

(PP, pp. 99–100; Austin's italics)

Finally, Austin points to the error which is responsible for our failing to see that this is the difference in function between 'I know' and 'I am sure':

'To suppose that "I know" is a descriptive phrase, is only one example of the *descriptive fallacy*, so common in philosophy. Even if some language is now purely descriptive, language was not in origin so, and much of it is still not so. Utterance of obvious ritual phrases, in the appropriate circumstances, is not *describing* the action we are doing, but *doing* it ("I do").'

(PP, p. 103; Austin's italics)

We have here a series of claims about the speech acts 'I know' and 'I believe *or* am sure'. Postponing for a time the question what broader conclusions could be drawn from such facts, let us ask simply whether Austin is correct in the claims he makes, construed as claims about these utterance-acts. First, there is the idea that I generate the right for people to round on me when I say 'I know' and am in error, but not when I say 'I am sure' and am in error. This, I suggest, cannot be sustained as a claim merely about the two different utterances. Much depends on surrounding circumstances. If I say 'I am sure' in a situation where you have reason to trust me and where I enter no proviso or qualification, then you may well have a right to round on me if, for example, I turn out to be mistaken through carelessness.

Austin might reply that it is precisely the matter of whether one can enter provisos which is crucial. You can cover yourself against possible reproach in the case of 'I am sure' by adding 'but I may be mistaken', but you cannot do this in the case of knowledge. You cannot say 'I know, but I may be mistaken' (cf. PP, p. 98). Hence, in the case of claims to knowledge you carry a burden from which you cannot so to speak release yourself in advance. The point is well taken, but it is not quite enough to establish the conclusion he wants. The question at issue is whether any right is created verbally in saying 'I know' and whether that right may verbally be withheld. In view of this and the comparison between saying 'I know' and giving others my word, it would therefore be more help to Austin's case if it were equally illegitimate to say 'I know that this is so, but you can take it or leave it'. Things are not so clear here, however. Although it is true, as Austin notes, that when I say 'I know' I do not *mean* 'You can take it or leave it' (PP, p. 100), nevertheless it seems to me that this message can fairly be added to the original in a way which is not possible with 'I may be mistaken'. There is not, in the same way, anything in the statement-content 'I know' which prevents me from adding to it 'But you can take it or leave it'.

So far, of course, this is to conduct the argument merely at the level of linguistic intuition. If Austin's main claim, that 'I promise' and 'I know' are both creative of the relevant kind of obligation, is correct then so much the worse for any intuitions to the contrary. Specifically in this connexion he argues that for the proper use of either speech act I must *be in a position* to know or to promise respectively. If I say 'I promise' I must be prepared to show that something is *within my power*; if I say 'I know' I must be prepared to show that something is *within my cognizance* (PP, p. 100).

It is crucial that neither this specific parallel nor the parallel in general between promising and knowing can be sustained.

On the specific point, Austin considers, and tries to answer, an objection:

'We feel, however, an objection to saying that "I know" performs the same sort of function as "I promise". It is this. Supposing that things turn out badly, then we say, on the one hand "You're proved wrong, so you *didn't* know", but on the other hand "You've failed to perform, although you *did* promise". I believe that this contrast is more apparent than real. The sense in which you "did promise" is that you did *say* you promised (did say "I promise"): and you did *say* you knew. That is the gravamen of the charge against you when you let us down, after we have taken your word. But it may well transpire that you never fully intended to do it, or that you had concrete reason to suppose that you wouldn't be able to do it (it might even be manifestly impossible), and in another "sense" of promise you *can't* then have promised to do it, so that you *didn't* promise.'

(PP, p. 101; Austin's italics)

Now this looks suspiciously like a piece of special pleading, designed to keep the specific parallel between knowing and promising intact. In the first place, there is no sense of promise in which *merely* to say 'I promise' is to promise. As Austin himself stresses elsewhere, the ritual phrase must be uttered *in the appropriate circumstances*, and that is a crucial consideration in connexion with the role which such phrases play (cf. W, p. 8; PP, p. 102). Elsewhere, too, he recognises that I may very well promise, whether I intend to perform the promised action or not (W, p. 40). But there is a more important point. Although I may very well fail to perform a promised action for the kind of reason Austin gives, there are many more possible reasons besides. In particular, it may be that an action *is* within my power at the time of my saying 'I promise', that I know that it is within my power and that I fully intend to perform it, but things still 'turn out badly', i.e. I fail to perform it, because I subsequently change my mind.[3] In such a case there is not the least tendency to say that after all I did not promise. But this is precisely where the parallel breaks down. If we imagine analogous conditions fulfilled in the case of knowing, i.e. that something is within my cognizance, that I have an abundance of evidence for it and that I believe it, and then imagine that things turn out badly, i.e. that I am wrong, then it does follow that after all I did not know. There is thus still a crucial asymmetry between the two cases even if I am 'in a position' with regard to both.

This should be enough to make us deeply suspicious of the general parallel, and in fact it is indefensible. In its negative aspect it is equivalent to the claim that some mistake is involved — indeed, a fallacy — in regarding 'I know' as a descriptive phrase (PP, p. 103), and reference is made to that use of language in which we are 'not *describing* the action we are doing, but *doing* it' (*ibid.*; Austin's italics). Now the conclusion that 'I know' is not a descriptive phrase does not follow from anything which has gone before. In particular, it does not follow from the correct claim, already discussed, that 'I know' is not a description of my state of mind, for this leaves open the possibility that it is descriptive of something else (cf. my suggestion that it is descriptive of a capacity). It is interesting that there is the same lacuna here in Austin's argument about knowledge as there was in his argument about promising, for we saw in Chapter III, section 5 that there too he moves too hastily from the premise that 'I promise' is not descriptive of some inner, mental performance to the conclusion that it is not descriptive of anything at all (cf. W, pp. 9–10).

Consider a possible rejoinder. In my own discussion of performatives in Chapter III, I was at pains to stress that 'descriptive' and 'performative' are not mutually exclusive labels. An utterance like 'I leave my watch to my brother' can be both productive of and simultaneously descriptive of a state of affairs. If I now say that 'I know' is a descriptive expression then I must equally concede that this does not preclude its also being performative. This is correct, of course: 'I know' is not precluded on those grounds alone. Nevertheless, it does follow plainly from my discussion that it is not a performative utterance. When I say 'I promise' against the appropriate social background, i.e. one where my audience adopts the attitude of regarding my utterance as true in consequence of its being uttered, then I perform that action specified in my utterance. But speaker's utterance and audience's attitude could not combine in the same way to create knowledge. To say 'I know' is not and could not be to know. We should all be much wiser if it were. I stressed in Chapter III, section 7 that the nature of performativeness itself places a limit on the potential material for performative utterances, and knowledge is a matter which clearly falls outside that limit. Saying 'I know' is neither sufficient for knowing (since what I claim to know may not be so) nor necessary (since I may know something but keep my mouth firmly shut).

This provides further justification, if it were needed, for insisting on a separation of the theory of performatives from the theory of illocution. The suggestion that 'I know' is a performative utterance has no plausibility at all when it is subjected to scrutiny; the suggestion that it has a certain characteristic illocutionary force at least has some.[4]

'I know that p' may sometimes have something in common with 'I give you my word that p' or 'I give you my authority for saying that p'. That is, it may be true that in saying 'I know' I give someone my word. But it is another matter how useful this is in giving an analysis of the concept of knowledge. Apart from the looseness of the notion of illocution itself, we know that the illocutionary force of an utterance with a given content may vary according to circumstances, speaker's intentions and other factors. We should therefore need to ask when, and why, 'I know' carried this force. (It is not, after all, like the utterance 'I give you my word' in carrying it *ex officio*.) But even then the information at our disposal might not be acceptable as an analysis of knowledge. I explain why in section 5, below.

4. Other minds

What is the scope of our knowledge? To put the matter at its broadest, we normally take ourselves to know a good deal about at least three different things: ourselves, people other than ourselves, and the brute physical world. It is the security of our knowledge of other people which will concern us in the present section, in the form of the *problem of other minds*. Our knowledge of the physical world will be discussed in Chapter VI, and the status of our knowledge of ourselves both in Chapter VI and in Chapter VIII. Doubts have been expressed by philosophers about the security of our knowledge in all three areas, but perhaps most frequently in relation to our knowledge of other people and the physical world. A basic similarity of approach can be discerned in the way these two problems have often been raised. It consists in setting up a dualism between two entities: immediate entities with which we have some kind of direct contact, and mediate entities whose existence is less assured. (Curiously, such a move often has the effect of reinforcing or preserving the certainty felt about our knowledge of ourselves.) Austin's response in both areas is to reject the dualism which the doubts are founded upon.

In the problem of other minds the dualism is set up between, on the one hand, the thoughts, feelings and mental experiences in general which a person may have and, on the other hand, the phsyical and behavioural manifestations of those mental experiences. Thus, there is the actual feeling of anger on the one hand, and the white face, the red neck and the quavering voice on the other. The argument then is that whereas each individual has direct awareness of his own mental experiences, other people do not; all they have to go on is the existence of the physical symptoms of that experience. But since the experience can occur without the symptoms (where we hide our true feelings) and the symptoms can occur without the experience (where we pretend to have feelings we do not really have), it is concluded that any claim to know that another person is having a certain mental experience is subject to doubt.

Do I know when people other than myself are having some mental experience? Do I know the character of such experiences? Do I, indeed, know that there are other people? The answer depends partly on one's conception of knowledge. If my own earlier suggestions were correct, the question whether we can know about other people's mental states is equivalent to the question whether we can acquire the capacity to discriminate truths and falsehoods about those states. A complete answer would therefore involve considering what is necessary to acquire a capacity of that kind, and whether there is anything to prevent us from acquiring one in this particular area.

What does Austin say here? Characteristically, he insists that there is a distinction between '*How* do we know someone is angry?' and '*Do* we know?', and asserts that he will stick to the first (PP, p. 76). In fact, he makes several comments relevant to the second question (e.g. PP, pp. 110–12). But in view of his arguments about the performative nature of the speech act 'I know' we should notice that for him either question will have to be construed in a peculiar way. If a claim to know really is a claim that something or other is so, then it makes sense to ask under what conditions such a claim would be correct, what has to be the case for what is claimed to be true. But we saw that Austin rejected such a view, and said that 'I know' is not a descriptive claim but a performative. And that means, according to his own lights, that we cannot ask the question 'Under what conditions is it true?' but only the question 'Under what conditions is the utterance happy, i.e. under what conditions does someone succeed in performing the act in question?' He is not saved by the fact that, contrary to his own view, performatives *are* true or false, or by the fact that his claim is better construed as one about the illocutionary force of 'I know'. For the conditions for the truth of a performative utterance and the conditions for the performance of the action it specifies are identical; and it is absurd to suppose that the conditions under which I know something are the same as those under which I succeed in giving my word that that thing is so.

I have presented these consequences of Austin's view as unacceptable ones which provide a persuasive argument against it. Yet in his discussion of the problem of other minds Austin seems implicitly to exploit these paradoxical consequences. The conditions under which we may *say* 'I know' and the conditions under which we do actually know are constantly treated as interchangeable (as indeed they would be, if the parallel with promising were a valid one). For example, at one point he considers the possibility that previous familiarity with a particular kind of person may be important for knowing what a person of that kind is feeling, and he concludes that if we have had such familiarity 'then we can, in favourable current circumstances, *say* we know: we certainly can *recognize* when some near relative of ours is angrier than we have ever seen him' (PP, p. 104; italics added). The implication seems to be that the conditions for saying one knows and the conditions for actually knowing are identical (cf. PP, pp. 105, 107–8 for the same assumption).

It looks as though Austin's performative view of knowledge leads him into these errors, which result in some evasion of sceptical questions about the scope of our knowledge. But his non-sceptical stance may receive reinforcement from another direction. I noted in Chapter II the general assumption behind his philosophy that there are strong reasons for endorsing what we do already normally say as adequate and appropriate, and certainly the normative commitment to ordinary language is present in the direct attack which Austin makes on the duality of mental feeling and physical symptom. He objects that such a dualism involves 'a dangerous oversimplification' on the grounds that in this context ' "symptoms" (and also "physical") is being used in a way different from ordinary usage, and one which proves to be misleading' (PP, p. 105). 'What is important' he suggests, 'is the fact that we never talk of "symptoms" or "signs" except *by way of implied contrast with inspection of the item itself* ... And hence the words "symptom" and "sign" have no use except in cases where the item, as in the case of disease, is liable to be *hidden* ... ' (PP, pp. 105–6; Austin's italics). Thus, 'to say that we only get at the "signs" or "symptoms" of anything is to imply that we never get at *it*' (PP, p. 107; Austin's italics).

When I criticised Austin's method in general terms in Chapter II, I pointed out that his defence of existing usage by virtue of its evolutionary superiority would not do. Given the failure of this general argument, it becomes necessary to give a particular justification for any particular way of speaking which we happen to have. Austin is presented with just such an opportunity in the present case. All he has shown so far is that if the sceptic about the problem of other minds has his way then we shall be adopting a usage different from ordinary usage. What needs to be explained in addition is why this proposed usage should be rejected and why we should instead favour actual usage. But in the event Austin foregoes this opportunity. Having pointed out that setting up the dualism of symptom and feeling and then saying that we only get at the symptoms of other people's anger carries a certain implication, *viz.* that we never get at the anger itself, he objects:

'But *is* this the way we do talk? Surely we do not consider that we are never aware of more than *symptoms* of anger in another man?.

"Symptoms" or "signs" of anger tend to mean signs of *rising* or of *suppressed* anger. Once the man has exploded, we talk of something different — of an expression or manifestation or display of anger, of an exhibition of temper, and so forth ... "Symptoms" of anger are not, at least normally, contrasted with the man's own inner personal feeling of anger, but rather with the actual display of anger. Normally at least, where we have only symptoms to go upon, we should say only that we *believe* that the man is angry or getting angry: whereas when he has given himself away we say that we *know*.'

(PP, pp. 107–8; Austin's italics)

These remarks can be interpreted in one of two ways. Either Austin assumes that the sceptic is himself trying to give an account of the way we normally speak, or at least not to say anything which conflicts with it — which is an absurd assumption. The sceptic would doubtless concede that what we ordinarily say reflects what we ordinarily believe, and it is precisely what we ordinarily believe that he thinks is unwarranted. Or alternatively, Austin assumes that the sceptic's proposed usage can be shown to be misleading merely by pointing out that it does diverge from the ordinary. In other words, it is not that the proposed usage has two separate features, *viz.* differing from ordinary usage and being misleading, but rather that its misleadingness just consists in its being different from ordinary usage. The argument, under either construction, rests on the assumption that there is nothing wrong with our current way of speaking. When that is just what the sceptic wishes to question, it will not be sufficient merely to reiterate the claim.

But is this a fair account of Austin's argument? Is his point not, rather, that there is something faulty with the sceptic's picture of two quite different and easily separable kinds of entity, *viz.* the private, mental feeling and the public, physical symptom? And does

Austin not object against this that 'being angry' is descriptive of a whole pattern of events, so that it is simply futile to ask 'What, really, is the anger itself?' (PP, p. 109)? The trouble with this suggestion is that Austin does concede that the pattern is arranged in a way which allows the sceptic to express his doubts, for he agrees that it is possible for someone to 'exhibit all the symptoms (and display and everything else) of anger, even *ad infinitum*, and yet still *not (really) be* angry' (PP, p. 111; Austin's italics). Indeed, at this point his position seems to be not that the sceptic's expressed doubts rest upon a misleading picture of the phenomena, but rather that they can be straightforwardly dealt with when they have been expressed. In this connexion he makes two comments.

First, he agrees that problems of the kind the sceptic raises 'arise in special cases, and occasion genuine worry' (PP, p. 112), but he argues that they are 'contrasted with the normal cases which hold the field' (PP, p. 113). 'Extraordinary cases of deceit, misunderstanding, &c. (which are themselves not the normal) do not, *ex vi termini*, ordinarily occur' (*ibid.*). The comprehensive doubt, that we may *never* know what someone's feelings are, is rejected. But the reason for rejecting it is inadequate. The fear, after all, is that the cases which we *think* are exceptional and extraordinary may not be exceptional, and that our confidence in our general ability to discern whether someone is having a mental experience (and if so, of what kind) may be misplaced. Austin all but concedes that this is possible when he agrees that there may be varieties of mistake which are common without our yet having become aware of the fact (*ibid.*). Perhaps, in that case, they may yet prove to be the commonest? If there is something wrong with such a speculation, then at least some further indication of *what* is wrong with it would have to be given.

The only thing which might be taken as such is the second general remark which Austin makes in this connexion. This is that in the present case, unlike some other focuses of scepticism, we have a unique piece of evidence for our belief, in the form of the man's testimony that he is having a certain experience. But this is a successful differentiation only if sceptical doubts cannot be raised about that testimony itself. Isn't talk of 'testimony' here already to presuppose that there is another mind in communication with one's own, and isn't the security of that assumption precisely one of the things at issue? Here Austin's reply is disappointing. He states that 'believing in other persons, in authority and testimony, is an essential part of the act of communicating, an act which we all constantly perform' (PP, p. 115), but he agrees that 'there is no "justification" for our doing them as such' (*ibid.*).

One concession should be made here, however. The tenor of some of these later remarks suggests that Austin may intend not so much to meet the arguments of the sceptic as to show what price he has to pay for his scepticism: if he is serious about his doubts then they must extend to wondering whether he ever communicates them to anyone. If there is no intelligence at the receiving-end when he expresses them, he may only be speaking to himself. If this is Austin's aim then I have some sympathy with it, though none at all for the points he makes in support of it. It is perhaps significant that the problem of other minds is one internal to philosophy. It arises not from any commonly-expressed worry existing outside philosophical discussion — as is the case with the problem of free will, for example — but rather from the consequences of a particular philosophical picture of the nature of human beings, *viz.* that deriving from Descartes. But the way to settle the problem is to show what is wrong with that philosophical picture, not to refer to existing linguistic idiom.

5. Conclusion
A number of times in this chapter, I have raised the possibility that Austin does not, properly speaking, give an analysis of knowledge (rather than simply that he

gives a defective one which leads him into error). It is now time to say explicitly why I think this is so.

Reversing, as he sometimes does, the procedure of asking *what we should say when*, Austin approaches knowledge by taking the idiom first and building back to a situation which it fits. He asks when we should say 'I know'. And his interpretation of the question is the one I suggested he would adopt in Chapter II, section 8. He gives a descriptive account of the circumstances where an actual uttering of those words would be likely. Throughout his argument he is preoccupied with concrete, spoken exchanges, as, for example, when he suggests that 'I know' is not (or is not merely) descriptive of a state of mind because 'it functions differently in *talking*' (PP, p. 79; italics added). 'It' here can only refer to the statement-act.

As I have said already, this approach fits in very well with a concentration on the illocutionary aspect of language. An examination of the common features of the contexts where these words are spoken, and an account of the point in speaking them, may produce a rationale for the utterance which is in practice indistinguishable from its illocutionary force. In saying that we know something we give others our word for it. The drawback is that this concentration on the illocutionary force occurs at the expense of any attention to the locutionary force and the sense of the utterance. The general theory of illocution is a theory about one of the many, disparate ways in which language can be used 'creatively', as a response to the world rather than as a reflexion of it. In his theory about the illocutionary force of 'I know' Austin systematically neglects the fact that the utterance is *both* a response *and* a reflexion. In saying 'I know' I may give others my word and also describe something, a capacity which I possess. And there is a strong case for saying that the first is at least in part a consequence of the second, that the illocutionary force is dependent on the locutionary content, that the role which this statement-act performs rests on the specific nature of the statement-content. All the more reason, then, for not neglecting the statement-content, as Austin does.

There is a further limitation on Austin's discussion. Not only does he conduct it in terms of situations where knowledge is actually spoken of, he confines his attention to situations where someone says *of himself* that he knows. But there is reason to think that situations where someone says '*I* know' are special, and specially complicated. A person would not, in general, say sincerely 'I know' unless he was aware, or at least believed, that he knew. This follows from the perfectly general truth that a person would not, in general, sincerely make *any* claim unless he was aware, or at least believed, that things were as he claimed. Once again, some of Austin's contentions are affected. He says, for example, 'Whenever I say I know, I am always liable to be taken to claim that, in a certain sense appropriate to the kind of statement (and to present intents and purposes), I am able to *prove* it' (PP, p. 85; Austin's italics). There is nothing wrong with this, as long as we remember that this ability is liable to be inferred from *my saying* what I do, from my making a claim (any claim at all). It is not something which may be inferred from *what* I say, and cannot therefore be taken as a condition of my knowing something, as opposed to my justifiably *saying* I know something.

The upshot of all this is that Austin has no chance of arriving at an analysis of knowledge by examining language along the principles I advocated in the early sections of Chapter II. He does not use facts about language as a means to getting at the truth about something else; his theses are essentially *about* language. But knowledge is not itself essentially linguistic in the way that something like promising is. It does not depend for its existence on communication between human beings, for people know things whether they talk about it or not. To put it shortly, Austin does not give us a theory about what it is to know something. He gives us a theory about what it is to *say* that you know somthing.

VI

Philosophical Problems: Perception

1. Introduction

I said in Chapter I that the widest tradition in which Austin could be placed is that of empiricism, though by virtue of temperament and orientation rather than the sharing of specific doctrines. It is commonly observed that it is a central and misguided part of that tradition to treat our passive perception of the physical world as our prime source of information about it — misguided, because we in fact learn as much about the world by acting in it, pushing it around, and so on, as we do by suffering its effects. Such a tendency is probably reinforced by an almost exclusive concentration in philosophical discussions on visual and to a lesser extent aural perception, for seeing and hearing, as well as being the most remote modes of perceiving the world, are themselves far less directly connected with action on our part. Nevertheless, there can be little doubt that our perception of the world, and especially our visual perception, is *one* prime source of knowledge. An examination of perception is to that extent also a continuation of the discussion of knowledge begun in the previous chapter.

We may start by asking the two questions about the nature and the scope of visual perception which parallel those asked about knowledge: (*a*) what is seeing? (*b*) what (kinds of) things do we see? We may again expect that an answer to either question should be conditioned by one's views on the other. This is especially pertinent here, since until recently, and certainly at the time when Austin was discussing these

139

matters, it was comparatively rare to find a complete and direct analytical answer to (a) — that is, an answer which constituted an attempt to explain the notion of seeing (or perception in general) without in any way making use of that notion in the course of the explanation. This was probably a direct result of an almost obsessive preoccupation with question (b).

Now we can doubtless classify the things we see into many different kinds, and the number of kinds we end up with will depend on how specific we make our classifications. But it has commonly been claimed that the most general objects of perception are, on the one hand, material objects, which may be characterised as entities which occupy, continuously or discontinuously, a position in space and time and are not dependent for their existence on being perceived by some sentient creature; and on the other hand, a different kind of entity, called by some technical name such as a 'sensum', 'sense-impression' or 'sense-datum', which may be characterised as being precisely not material but mental, and existing only insofar as it is the object of some creature's perception.[1] Answers to question (b) along these lines are extremely widespread, and are by no means confined to the empiricist tradition. (The rationalist Descartes, for example, puts forward a similar view.) They are likely to be found in the context of some more general theory of perception, which may also involve, if only by implication, a partial answer to question (a). There are some fairly well staked-out alternative theories, as was the case with knowledge, and we may distinguish in the present context the *causal* theory, *phenomenalism* and *direct realism*.

According to the causal theory, seeing a material object is a matter of that object's causing us to perceive a sense-datum. This theory can be held in one of two forms. Either it can be said that it is a matter of scientific fact that this is what goes on when we perceive a material object; or it can be said that the only way in which we can make sense of the process of perception is by positing some such causal process, whatever the particular scientific facts about the world turn out to be.

Phenomenalism also involves an acceptance of the dualism laid out in the suggested answer to question (*b*), in terms of material objects and sense-data, but in a rather different way. According to this theory we may regard talk of perceiving material objects as a 'logical construction' out of talk of perceiving sense-data, perhaps in something like the way that talk of the average tax-payer is a logical construction out of talk of particular tax-payers. In other words, the dualism set up in the phenomenalist theory is not one involving two completely separate, independent entities. The sense-data which we do or could perceive are taken to 'add up' to material objects. If they did not, then since it is our perception of sense-data which is the more secure it would be so much the worse for all ordinary talk of perceiving material things.

In contrast to these two theories, direct realism involves a rejection of the claim that there are really two kinds of things which we perceive. It is a view which may be held implicitly, in advance of philosophical theorising, or explicitly as a result of being acquainted with but unimpressed by philosophical discussions of perception. It is most succinctly described as the view that we do directly perceive material objects and that it is either not necessary or not possible to postulate in addition that we perceive some mental entities such as sense-data.

2. The problems
It is impossible to adjudicate amongst these theories about the scope of perception without considering the arguments which surround their formulation. At this stage I give the arguments in outline. They, and Austin's response to them, receive further attention in succeeding sections. They are best approached by a brief consideration of the *nature* of perception. Even if, with the direct realist, we endorse the commonsense

belief that we see, without qualification, such things as tables and chairs (paradigm examples of material objects), what exactly does this involve? Is it possible to analyse the idea of seeing, in an enlightening way, in terms of other ideas?

There is no reason why we should not take our first cue from the language we normally use to talk about perception, though we may end up believing there is plenty of reason to change it. If we consider some ordinary perceptual statement such as 'John is looking at the table', then its surface form suggests that perception is a relation obtaining between a person and a material object, and the analysis of perception would consist in specifying the nature of that relation. For the perceptual relation to obtain, we might say, an object of this kind must be 'presented' to me — in the case of seeing, it must be before my eyes — and I must have some experience of it. Moreover, not just any experience of the object will be adequate for meeting the requirements of perception. A vague, intuitive awareness of it, for example, which is not connected with any of my senses will not suffice. Difficulties may then arise in specifying the kind of awareness required in an informative way: it will hardly do to say that it has to be sensory or visual awareness. Similarly, it may be difficult to specify what *level* of awareness is required for a case of perception, since there are good grounds for supposing that I may certainly perceive an object without holding anything as strong as a belief about it (cf. Dretske, 1969).

These points, and many others, would need elaboration in an adequate analysis of perception. But those who espouse a causal or phenomenalist theory would argue that elaboration is pointless when the original plan is so flawed. They would argue, as we have anticipated, that many cases of perception simply will not fit the model of a person's standing in some relation to a material object. At this point, then, the connexion begins to emerge between one's view of the analysis of perception and what one takes to be the range of cases of perception. The following would be cases which these theorists might cite in order to halt the progress of the proposed analysis. When someone looks directly at a bright light and then at a blank wall, he sees an 'after-image' superimposed on the wall. In a famous hallucinatory scene, Macbeth saw a dagger. Delirious travellers in the desert sometimes see oases which are in fact mirages. In these instances, so it is argued, there is no material object before the people concerned, but yet they are all cases of someone's having a visual experience, i.e. seeing. Hence, it is concluded that it is not a necessary condition of seeing that one should stand in some relation to a material object, for there may be no such object in an appropriate position.

Mention might also be made of a different but related type of case, where there is an object in the appropriate position but it does not have the appropriate character. Thus a man may have an experience like Macbeth's of seeing a dagger, not where there is nothing at all before him but where there is, say, a projection on the wall which he mistakenly takes as a dagger. Or again, in the Müller-Lyer diagram someone may see one line shorter than another when in fact the two lines before him are of equal length. What follows from these cases, it is argued, is that it is not a necessary condition of my seeing an object of a certain character that there should be an object *of that character* before me.

I said that an examination of perception would hold implications for theory of knowledge. In fact, if Austin is to be believed, the philosophers whose views he discusses in *Sense and Sensibilia* are interested in knowledge and not in perception at all (SS, p. 104). It is perhaps not difficult to see how the points raised in the last few paragraphs might be utilised for this purpose. In particular, we might envisage a sceptical line of argument about our knowledge of the physical world running as follows. If we compare the case of a man who sees a dagger which exists as a material object with the case of Macbeth who sees a hallucinatory dagger, then so far as their respective experiences themselves go there is nothing to distinguish one from the other. From the inside, from the subject's point of view, the two cases are identical. But this puts an obstacle in the way of moving too swiftly from the fact that I have some perceptual experience to a conclusion about the nature of the real physical world. When I have a perceptual experience which I should describe as that of seeing an object of a certain description, it may be that there is no such object in the world, that I am seeing something only in the sense in which Macbeth sees something. Consequently, there is a gap, and therefore room for things to go wrong, between my perceptual experience itself and what I may claim to know about the world on the basis of that experience.

This argument has a similar form to the sceptical argument about our knowledge of other minds, considered in Chapter V, section 4. A dualism is set up between immediate entities, the sense-data of which we have direct experience, and the only indirectly perceived material objects of the physical world. Once again, scepticism about our knowledge of something separate from ourselves can easily go hand-in-hand with greater certitude about the knowledge we have of ourselves — this time, in the form of the knowledge we have of our own perceptual states. Once again, too, Austin's reaction is to reject the dichotomy on which the argument is founded. His main aim in *Sense and Sensibilia* is to discredit the fundamental assumption of causal and phenomenalist theories, that what we directly perceive are not material objects but sense-data. But he equally disowns the realist theory, if this amounts to the view that we do perceive material objects. 'One of the most important points to grasp' he says, 'is that these two terms, "sense-data" and "material things", live by taking in each other's washing — what is spurious is not one term of the pair, but the antithesis itself' (SS, p. 4). To make good such a claim, Austin has to produce a reasoned rejection of the arguments I have described.[2]

3. The nature of the problems
A number of problems have been introduced so far, together with a number of theories related to them. What is the nature of those problems and theories? They concern what we should say about a certain area of our experience — 'what we should say' understood as a normative decision about what to say (cf. Chapter II, section 8). We are often engaged in activities or undergoing experiences which we describe in such terms as 'looking at the trees', 'hearing a train go by', and so on. One question is the analytical question what such talk means — on what grounds we take these statements to be sometimes true and sometimes false, in what conditions and for what purpose. Another is the comprehensive question whether, taking a broad view of the conditions surrounding such talk, it is appropriate and adequate for the phenomena to which it relates, or whether some other, possibly more sophisticated, vocabulary should be employed.

This way of looking at the problems is superficially similar to Ayer's (1940). He says that we should regard the point of view of direct realism 'not as an assertion of fact, but as a proposal to use words in a certain fashion; and the same is true ... of the thesis that we experience sense-data' (op. cit., p. 48). However, when he suggests that the only grounds on which a rival theorist might be criticised are that his alternative language is 'cumbersome and inconvenient' (op. cit., p. 18), and when he says of his own preferred alternative, 'At best it enables us only to refer to familiar facts in a clearer and more convenient way' (op. cit., p. 26), then I believe he is both underselling the great distance between the alternative theories of perception and taking too narrow a view of the reasons we might have for choosing one alternative rather than another for conceptualising and articulating our perceptual experience. It is a further inaccuracy to suggest that 'these so-called theories of perception are not theories at all in the ordinary sense, and therefore that the notions of truth and falsehood, which we apply to scientific theories are not applicable to them' (op. cit., p. 48). This is inaccurate principally because of the implied contrast between philosophical and scientific theories. It is highly implausible to suppose that a scientific theory of any complexity can be accepted as true or rejected as false by a simple confrontation between the theory and some restricted range of facts. Rather, the theory is better viewed as a kind of framework for interpreting and explaining certain data, and it will be accepted as adequate or rejected as inadequate for that purpose, depending on how well it does so. In this respect, and indeed in general, there will be a difference of degree rather than of kind between the relation in which a scientific theory stands to 'the facts' and the relation in which a philosophical theory stands to them (cf. Quine, 1953, Chapter II). Whether we should call either kind of theory true or false is a question I return to in a moment.

It is interesting that on some occasions Austin takes a view rather like Ayer's. We saw in Chapter II that in 'A Plea For Excuses' he suggests that if two people disagree about the words to be used in a certain situation they may be using alternative conceptual schemes, though each may be equally serviceable (PP, p. 184), and I criticised this on the same grounds as my present criticism of Ayer's view, that it underestimates the importance of the difference between different conceptual schemes. In the present context of the problems of perception Austin also appears to accept the contrast which Ayer draws between philosophy and science. He says:

'There is no *one* kind of thing that we "perceive" but many *different* kinds, the number being reducible if at all by scientific investigation and not by philosophy: pens are in many ways though not in all ways unlike rainbows, which are in many ways though not in all ways unlike after-images, which in turn are in many ways but not in all ways unlike pictures on the cinema screen — and so on, without assignable limit. So we are *not* to look for an answer to the question, what kind of thing we perceive.'

(SS, p. 4; Austin's italics)

So much for my question (*b*), about the kinds of things we perceive, if Austin is right. But it is not clear that he is right, or even that what he says here is consistent. Perhaps he is just saying that a general classification of the objects of perception is possible as long as someone else does it. But then we have to place some interpretation on the contrast between philosophy and science which is again implied. If the suggestion is that science brings us the facts whereas philosophy is concerned only with pure theory I should urge its rejection. Not that the findings of science are irrelevant to the philosophy of perception: on the contrary, it is an unfortunate fact that they have been ignored by nearly all philosophers who have written on the subject, including Austin. What is misleading, however, is the idea of any sharp contrast between digging out the facts and theorising about them. The question how to categorise the objects of perception has to be answered at a fairly general and abstract level in the light of the known empirical data, and I see no reason why both philosophers and scientists should not contribute to it. We should note, too, that Austin fails by his own criteria. He manages to reduce the number of kinds of thing we perceive by concluding that we do not perceive sense-data — and he does so without the aid of science.

However, although Austin is at one with Ayer on the separateness of science and philosophy, in general he is in conflict with him on the way the problems of perception are to be characterised, and he seems implicitly to be in conflict with his own view as expressed in 'A Plea For Excuses'. For example, an alternative conceptual scheme considered by Ayer would accommodate certain facts of illusion and hallucination by postulating that the real shape of an object is something which is constantly changing (*op. cit.*, p. 18). Austin regards as 'astonishing' the idea 'that the words "real", "really", "real shape", "real colour", &c., can perfectly well be used to mean *whatever you like* ... ' (SS, p. 59; Austin's italics). And he goes on:

> 'For if, when one person says whatever it may be, another person may simply "prefer to say" something else, they will *always* be arguing only about words, about what terminology is to be preferred. How could *anything* be a question of truth or falsehood, if anyone can always say whatever he likes?
>
> (SS, p. 60; Austin's italics)

Here we see clearly a far less tolerant attitude towards alternative concepts and languages than the view in 'A Plea For Excuses'. But if that other view underestimates the importance and the consequences of making a choice between such alternatives, the present view errs in its estimation of the room we have for manoeuvre. First of all, it is true that anyone can say whatever he likes in relation to the experiences which he has, and this is not a trivial truth. He may say something which is just unintelligible or self-contradictory, he may say something so outlandish that he fails to communicate with anyone, or what he says may be part of a way of looking at his experiences which is impoverished, perverse or perverted. But for all that, it is a central fact about human beings that they are not just programmed to respond to things in a stereotyped way. This is what makes philosophy, and perhaps any thinking at all, a possibility. There is a choice, people may indeed prefer to say different things, *and the point of philosophical debate is to adjudicate.*

It by no means follows from this that all disputes become merely verbal. In this context a preference for a particular way of speaking is equivalent to a preference for a particular way of talking and thinking about something *in general* — in the jargon, a preference for a particular conceptual framework. The choice is, for example, whether to talk of perceiving sense-data or not. Consider, then, what has to be done by an advocate of this way of talking, or any other way of talking of the same order. He will need to explain the meaning and the point of the terms he uses, show how they connect with other terms, and show how they embody a mode of organisation and interpretation which is plausible, coherent, adequate, fruitful, etc., in relation to the data they apply to. We should recall, too, that no less than this should be demanded by way of justification of an existing and accepted way of talking: only a faulty evolutionary argument, like the one considered in Chapter II, could excuse it from such an examination. Now if a way of talking proves acceptable according to these criteria, it has a fixed and determinate interpretation and mode of employment. In a certain situation it will be either true or false to say that one is perceiving a certain sense-datum, and at this point there is no longer any freedom to 'say what one likes'. Or, more strictly, you can still say what you like, but the price you may pay for this is just being *wrong* according to the criteria of your own conceptual framework.

But Austin might object, and with some justice, that this does not meet his point. Truth and falsity, he might say, have a role *within* a conceptual framework, according to my argument; but if they are not applicable to those frameworks themselves, the problem remains. Two advocates of different conceptual schemes will by that very fact prefer to say different things, and no dispute between them can be settled. My reply to this is that I see no good reason for refusing to extend the ideas of truth and falsity to conceptual frameworks themselves. Given the criteria used in evaluating them, a choice between different frameworks is anything but arbitrary. But more than that, it is governed by just the same sort of considerations as enter into deciding the truth or falsity of many statements made *within* a framework.

I can see a *bad* reason for refusing to regard conceptual frameworks as true or false, and it is a reason to which Austin could easily be attracted. If we hold a picture of truth as something which can be satisfactorily explained by the idea of 'correspondence with the facts' then we may be misled into supposing a far greater difference than there really is between conceptual frameworks on the one hand, and the statements made within them on the other. If a statement's susceptibility to truth and falsity rests on its corresponding or failing to correspond with some particular fact, state of affairs or part of the world, then we are likely to see a large and qualitative difference between 'There is a glass on my table' and 'We perceive sense-data'. The former, we shall say, can be true or false just because we can compare it with the relevant fact; but the latter cannot. We shall see in the next chapter that Austin holds just such a theory of truth. I shall try to say there why it is to be rejected, and for present purposes I shall just say this. The theory gains plausibility from concentrating on a particular, and simple, type of statement, and from the fact that doubtless the truth of most statements does rest in *some* way on the nature of the world. But if we think of other statements which are certainly, on any reasonable view, made within a conceptual framework, such as 'Wage rises do not cause inflation' or 'If Hitler had been assassinated there would have been no Second World War', there is far less plausibility in the idea that their truth rests on correspondence with some easily isolated fact. On the contrary, we should accept or reject such statements by reference to tests and criteria much closer to those we employ for judging conceptual frameworks. The difference here is one of degree, and if we are loath to say that a statement like 'We perceive sense-data' is just simply true or false that is because of the greater complexity of the issues involved in judging it, not because there is something misguided in principle in the idea of its being true or false.

There remains a further objection to my argument. Someone might say that the way I talk of judging the adequacy of different frameworks implies that it is possible to adopt a neutral standpoint, outside all particular ways of looking at or talking about experience, in order to assess their validity. Surely there can be no such position? Must we not ourselves adopt some particular viewpoint, and take our experiences to be of such-and-such a kind, before we ask whether some particular way of interpreting them is acceptable? And does this not already commit us to interpreting them in a particular way? Thus, Austin believes that Ayer himself avoids the consequence that all disputes would become merely verbal on his view of the matter, but only because he illicitly assumes that the real facts which a theory of perception must interpret are facts about sense-data (SS, p. 60).

One response to this would be to counter-attack and point out that after all Austin himself only makes a different assumption of the same kind, namely that the real facts are as common sense describes them, an assumption which is equally unjustified if taken as an unquestionable datum. This is a valid claim to make against Austin, and it is significant that one of his familiar warnings against tampering with ordinary language follows close on the heels of his criticism of Ayer (cf. SS, p. 63). But it is no more than a polemical point, and one which, if anything, appears to reinforce the objection that we cannot judge any frameworks because we must always be using one in the process of judging. The real weakness in that objection is that it points not to an insuperable difficulty but only to a technical one. One must, of course, adopt *some* way of talking in order to discuss the acceptability of other ways of talking, one which may itself be assessed on some other occasion. The problem in any particular context is simply to find a vocabulary for conducting the assessment which all parties to the discussion will accept as uncontroversial. In the context of perception, where the question is whether to talk of perceiving tables and chairs or to talk of perceiving sense-data, this can be achieved by referring in a studiedly neutral way to our perceptions, leaving it open what they may most appropriately be thought to be perceptions *of*. Naturally, we should have to ensure that neutrality really is observed. Austin objects that Ayer's talk of 'perceptions' involves the smuggling in of dubious entities (SS, pp. 11, 47), and against Ayer the objection may be well taken (cf. Locke 1967, pp. 40ff.). But we do not have to follow Ayer. We may use the term 'perception' to refer to the *act* or *experience* of perceiving, which is not to bring in any entity but to refer to something which happens, as all parties to the debate would agree.

In short, arguments of the kind mentioned earlier prompt questions about the language we ought to choose for talking about perception. They may turn out to hide a welter of confusion and obscurity, and it may be that there is after all nothing wrong with the way in which we already do talk about perception. But we cannot fairly come to that conclusion in advance of examining the arguments.

4. Austin's view

As may perhaps be inferred from earlier remarks, when it comes to a consideration of these arguments Austin refuses to a large extent to accept the terms of debate which they involve. It is natural that he should do so, given his philosophical conservatism. In fact, his criticism of the terms of debate depends implicitly on two of the methodological assumptions discussed in Chapter II. He assumes in practice that the way in which people do now, as a matter of fact, describe their perceptual experiences is an adequate way; and he concentrates on the employment of that existing vocabulary in concrete speech situations. This becomes apparent as soon as Austin begins to discuss the arguments, and it also becomes apparent that he is himself imposing contentious, if not question-begging, restrictions on the debate. The scene is set by representing Ayer's as involving a confrontation between the 'plain man' and the philosophers (SS, pp. 6–19), although in fact this implicit contrast appears only on the first couple of pages of Ayer's book. Austin undertakes to acquit the plain man of the confusions and naiveties of which Ayer accuses him, and to convict the philosophers of such faults, thereby vindicating the commonsense view of things.

Consider two examples which illustrate my description of Austin's procedure. He mentions a remark of Locke's, quoted by Ayer, to the effect that the testimony of our senses gives us a certainty of the existence of material objects 'not only as great as our frame can attain to, but as our condition needs' (*Essay Concerning Human Understanding*, Book IV, Chapter XI, section viii). Austin comments:

> 'It suggests that when, for instance, I look at a chair a few yards away in front of me in broad daylight, my view is that I have (*only*) as much certainty as I need and can get that there is a chair and that I see it. But in fact the plain man would regard doubt in such a case, not as far-fetched, or over-refined or somehow unpractical, but as plain *nonsense*; he would say, quite correctly, "Well, if that's not seeing a real chair then *I don't know what is*." '
>
> (SS, p. 10; Austin's italics)

Austin's prediction may be correct, but it is not to the point. What matters, for the purpose of laying a philosophical doubt, is not what people would say in a certain situation but what their reasons would be for saying it, and whether they are good reasons. It may be that in the present case there are good reasons; but there are the arguments, based on the possibility of illusion and deception in perceptual experience, which question this and suggest that there are good reasons for saying something else. These arguments must be disposed of in some way, and it will not do to rig things against them by talking about 'seeing a chair in broad daylight' as though that were an uncontentious and unquestionable description, when the whole point of those arguments is to claim that it is not.

However, Austin would object here that the use of terms like 'illusion' and 'deception' is itself restricted by their ordinary use, and this gives the second illustration of his method:

> 'Next it is important to remember that talk of deception only *makes-sense* against a background of general non-deception. (You can't fool all of the people all of the time.) It must be possible to *recognize* a case of deception by checking the odd case against more normal ones ...
>
> ... The cases, again, in which a plain man might say he was "deceived by his senses" are not at all common. In particular, he would *not* say this when confronted with ordinary mirror-images, or with dreams; in fact, when he dreams, looks down the long straight road, or at his face in the mirror, he is not, or at least is hardly ever, *deceived* at all.'
>
> (SS, pp. 11–12; Austin's italics)

This is a particularly clear example of Austin's refusing to countenance a comprehensive fear, of a kind which has certainly been entertained by some philosophers, namely that we might be permanently deceived in our perceptual experiences. It may be that the fear is ill-conceived, that it is one which could never be laid to rest, or that it is so all-embracing that it could never make any difference to our lives. It is quite another thing, however, to argue that the very expression of this fear presupposes its own falsity, as Austin does in the passage quoted. But Austin's own claim here is crucially ambiguous. There is some plausibility, I suppose, in the view that talk, i.e. *talking*, of deception requires that there be cases where we do not talk of being deceived. After all, someone might say, the point in characterising an experience as deceptive is to mark off some feature of it, to distinguish it from other experiences; and if this is to be possible then we must also distinguish other experiences from *it*, i.e. characterise some experiences as non-deceptive. But there is no plausibility at all in the view that the very fact of our being deceived, whether or not we talk about it as being deceived, requires that there be cases where we are not deceived. Why should it? Those cases where we do not now talk of being deceived may in fact involve some kind of deception which we have not yet become aware of. Why on earth *must* it be possible to recognize this? It is this stronger, less plausible, claim which Austin must aim for if he is to defeat the claim that, whatever we may say, it is possible that we may always be deceived. But his way of doing so is to reduce to nothing the distance between what we may say and what may be the case — as in the later part of the passage quoted, where there is a transition from the plain man's not *saying* he is deceived to the plain man's not *being* deceived. When it is the adequacy of a whole way of talking which is in question, the matter can hardly be settled by pointing out that this *is* the way we talk. It will at least be necessary to look at the cases of perceptual experience which are brought forward in order to throw doubt on that way of speaking.

The possibility of raising this comprehensive question rests in some way on the idea that the content of our perceptual experiences is only an indirect reflexion of the external, physical world. Austin objects equally, and in very similar terms, to the suggestion that we only *indirectly* perceive the physical world:

'We have here, in fact, a typical case of a word, which already has a very special use, being gradually stretched, without caution or definition or any limit, until it becomes, first perhaps

obscurely metaphorical, but ultimately meaning-
less. One can't abuse ordinary language without
paying for it.'

(SS, p. 15)

With regard to the proper (i.e. for him, current) use
of the expression 'indirect perception', Austin makes
six points (SS, pp. 15–18); that it has a use, or rather
various uses, only in special cases; that these usually
have to do with a kink in direction, so that seeing
someone through a periscope would normally be
described as seeing indirectly, whereas seeing someone
through binoculars would not; that this idea probably
has no application with senses other than sight; that
the idea cannot be used without limit; that if we are
seriously to speak of something's being perceived
indirectly then it must at least be possible for it just to
be perceived, *not* indirectly; and that we normally
prefer what Austin calls the 'cash-value' of the
expression 'perceive indirectly' — so that if I say that I
see the ships indirectly, meaning by this that I see blips
on a radar screen, why not just say the latter? On this
basis he rejects the comprehensive claim that we only
indirectly perceive the world: it involves a use of the
expression 'indirectly perceive' which offends against
the canons implied by the points listed.

It is evident that Austin's inadequately-supported
normative assumptions about ordinary usage are at
work again here, but there are further errors of some
importance. Why should we agree that it must be
possible to perceive, without qualification, anything
which can be indirectly perceived? Austin dismisses the
possible complications occasioned by the electron-
microscope, 'about which I know little or nothing' (SS,
p. 18), and it is foolhardy of him to do so.
Considerations from this area, as well as others, might
well lead to a conclusion at odds with his own. Now
any decision on this will depend on how we fix the
criteria for applying the concept of indirect perception,
and this will itself depend partly on our attitude to the

various cases of faulty and deceptive perception, to be examined in a moment. But one general point can be made about fixing the criteria. When Austin says that we prefer the cash value to the metaphorical 'indirect' idiom, then what he says is probably true in relation to actual linguistic exchanges in a concrete speech situation. There our communication is governed by some principle such as that we should give the maximum detailed information consistent with the interests of our audience. Hence, if my claim to have seen the Queen indirectly is likely to draw the further enquiry 'Indirectly *in what way?*' then I ought indeed to say in the first place that I saw her through a periscope. But different principles apply when we are *talking about* the application of a concept rather than using it. Here it becomes important to abstract to some extent from the particular, concrete features of particular cases, to move to a higher level of generality and attempt to isolate the essential features common to different cases which we regard as, in their various ways, indirect perceptions, rather than to focus on what is peculiar to each case.

There is some reason to suppose that Austin is reluctant to look for such general principles. For example, in resisting the application of the label 'deceptive' to many multifarious perceptual experiences, he says:

'That is to say, once again there is no neat and simple dichotomy between things going right and things going wrong; things may go wrong, as we really all know quite well, in lots of *different* ways — which don't have to be, and must not be assumed to be, classifiable in any general fashion.'

(SS, p. 13; Austin's italics)

It is true that he immediately qualifies this in a footnote, but the qualification is itself well qualified:

'I am not denying that cases in which things go

wrong *could* be lumped together under some single name. A single name might in itself be innocent enough, provided its use was not taken to imply either (a) that the cases were all alike, or (b) that they were all in certain ways alike. What matters is that the facts should not be pre-judged and (therefore) neglected.'

(SS, p. 14n.; Austin's italics)

Now it may seem that nothing is at stake here except a question of emphasis. You begin an enquiry into the grounds for applying a concept, and you are either disposed to think that the cases where it applies may be united, in more than name, by some underlying similarity, or you are disposed to think that they may not. But then it must be recognized that such a disposition on one side or the other is likely to have a strong influence on the shape of the enquiry. Certainly this is so in Austin's case, and it affects the approach he adopts to particular cases.

Cases of abnormal or faulty perception may be used in a variety of ways to support the claim that the ordinary language of perception needs to be tampered with. Given Austin's general position, it is to be expected that he deals with the attempt to use the cases for that purpose in a brusque and peremptory manner. Take the most hackneyed case in the whole philosophy of perception, the case of a straight stick partly immersed in water which, through the effects of refraction, looks bent. The stick does not have the property of being bent, but it does present a bent appearance. Someone might then want to argue that since there is nothing bent in the appropriate part of the material world, the bent appearance which I certainly do perceive must exist non-materially. Ayer had considered, though perhaps not entirely endorsed, a similar suggestion. Austin's impatience with it is evident:

'Well, we are told, in this case you are seeing

something; and what is this something "if it is not part of any material thing"? But this question is, really, completely mad. The straight part of the stick, the bit not under water, is presumably part of a material thing; don't we see that? And what about the bit *under* water? — we can see that too. We can see, come to that, the water itself. In fact what we see is *a stick partly immersed in water*; and it is particularly extraordinary that this should appear to be called in question — that a question should be raised about *what* we are seeing — since this, after all, is simply the description of the situation with which we started.'

(SS, p. 30; Austin's italics)

But the raising of this question is not at all extraordinary for anyone who is not wedded to a belief in the adequacy of ordinary language. We might well *begin* with a description of a situation which we come to regard as inadequate and in need of repair or replacement. But is this such an occasion? If so, for what reasons? Austin argues that the misleadingness of appearance does not give a reason for altering the description of the case and that properly speaking it is not a case of illusion at all, since it involves an excessively familiar phenomenon and no one is likely to be taken in by it (SS, p. 26). This may be true, but it is important that something *outside* the experience of seeing the stick is responsible for our not being misled — we know something about the effects of refraction, we move the stick around, etc. If we confine our attention to the context of the perceptual experience itself then we cannot share Austin's confidence about the case and its description, for it is an example of a whole range of cases where the content of the perceptual experience is in itself misleading (and this is what entitles us to call them cases of illusion). Admittedly, this is not yet to show any reason for calling into existence some non-material object of perception. It is to use the example for an epistemological rather than an ontological purpose, *viz.* to show that the move from a description of perceptual experience to a description of the world assumed to stand behind it is one which may involve error.

Other cases dismissed by Austin can be used in a similar way. Compare, for instance, that of seeing an apparently headless woman, of which Austin says

> 'And when the plain man sees on the stage the Headless Woman, what he sees (and this *is* what he sees, whether he knows it or not) is not something "unreal" or "immaterial", but a woman against a dark background with her head in a black bag.'
>
> (SS, p. 14; Austin's italics)

It can fairly be pointed out against this that the question whether a man knows what it is that he sees is crucially important in determining how to describe his perceptions. These cases do, therefore, lead to a reassessment and possibly a restructuring of perceptual language.

The distinction between *illusion* and *delusion*, which Austin usefully calls attention to (SS, p. 23), is relevant here. The term 'illusion' does not suggest that something totally unreal is conjured up, whereas the term 'delusion' does. This distinction can be made to match a distinction amongst the various cases of abnormal perception, and the two different purposes for which they may be brought forward. Cases such as that of the apparently bent stick and the Müller-Lyer diagram are, *pace* Austin, cases of illusion because the relevant part of the physical world presents an appearance which is misleading in itself. As I suggested, they are best used for doubting the security of our description of the physical world, rather than as an argument for the postulation of a *non*-physical world. But cases where something totally unreal is conjured up, such as hallucinations, stand in contrast to these, and may be used for a different purpose. For if we are impressed by the suggestion that anyone who sees must see *something*, and if it is agreed that nothing physical is present in cases of hallucination, then we may seem to have no alternative but to conclude that something non-physical is present in these cases, perhaps a sense-datum in the sense defined in section 1 above. Austin himself is slightly more indulgent than one might expect to such a suggestion. He says, 'The mirage case ... is significantly more amenable to the treatment it is given. For here we are supposing the man to be genuinely deluded, he is *not* "seeing a material thing" ' (SS, p. 32; Austin's italics). But he then goes on:

> 'We don't actually have to say, however, even here that he is "experiencing sense-data"; for though, as Ayer says above, "it is convenient to give a name" to what he is experiencing, the fact is that it already has a name — a *mirage*.'
>
> (*ibid.*; Austin's italics)

This, it seems to me, is simply an evasion. If it is admitted that a man can see a mirage although a mirage is not a material thing, then the question can be raised what *kind* of thing a mirage is, and whether it is the same kind of thing as, say, a ghost, or Macbeth's dagger. Anyone who wishes to avoid these questions may try denying that these are properly regarded as instances of perception at all, but that is not Austin's way out of the difficulty at this point. His way is to resist the raising of such general questions and to reiterate the description normally given of such cases, as though no further question could be raised about its import or validity.

The existence of delusive experience gives some grounds for saying that there are non-material things which we perceive, and better grounds than the existence of illusory experiences. Is it possible to give any further reason why this should be so? I want to suggest a reason which has nothing at all to do with the nature of the language we use to describe perceptual experiences (an all too fallible guide), but rather to do with the introspectible nature of those experiences, however they are described. Consider the difference between perceiving something on the one hand, and talking or thinking about something on the other. Just as cases of seeing something which does not exist present us with a problem, so too do cases of talking or thinking about something which does not exist. Indeed, Parmenides came to the conclusion that there cannot be such cases, that it is not possible to speak or think of what does not exist, and that the belief that we can is itself misguided. Later philosophers have rejected Parmenides' conclusion, and rightly so. It is obvious that I can think of things which do not exist, as, for example, when I wonder whether there are Martians or unicorns. The problem is to explain *how it is* that I can do this, and to meet the challenge that thinking of something non-existent is the same as thinking of nothing, which is the same as not thinking at all. Attempts to provide an answer begin with Plato's *Sophist*, and still continue. What is of interest in the present context is that some of them involve a move analogous to the postulation of sense-data. These are the theories which concede most to Parmenides' view, and argue that if I am to think of something which does not exist in the material world, then it must exist in a non-material world — perhaps as an idea in the mind, perhaps 'subsisting' in some other shadowy realm. Theories of this kind have been widely rejected (cf. Quine, *op. cit.*, Chapter I), and without going into the reasons why at any great length, we can at least say why they compare unfavourably with their analogous sense-datum theory. Perceptual experience is such that it appears to require the presence of a perceived object *immediately*, there on the scene with the perceiver; and it also appears to involve something *separate* from the perceiver, something other than him and his states, in contrast, say, to the experience of imagining, which can more easily be regarded as merely a state of the imaginer. Neither of these things is so obviously true of the experience of thinking about something: the immediate presence of an object is not required, nor is it clear that an object independent of the thought is required. In short, it looks as though thinking can be satisfactorily described as just a state of the subject, whereas perceiving consists in a genuine relation between two independent entities. If this were correct then it would help to explain why cases of delusion and hallucination are a serious matter, and why they provide the best opening for someone who wants to postulate the existence of non-physical objects of perception. It would also help to explain why cases of illusion are less well suited to that purpose. In the latter cases we take the perceived object to have a different character from its real one, but at least there is already an object there for us to stand in relation to, something in which to anchor our mistakes.

It goes without saying that these considerations are less than compelling, and it may well be that cases of seeing where there is no material object are better characterised as states of the subject than by postulating any non-material entity. But to raise these points at all is to go beyond Austin's discussion. In his dogged insistence on describing the obvious and resisting the introduction of any new terminology, he effectively rules out the possibility of this kind of debate.

5. Senses of 'see'

The question 'Are there different senses of "see"?' appears to be a question exclusively about language. In fact, in the context we are concerned with, it is a transposition into linguistic form of a far wider and more substantial question, a procedure the value of which I argued for in Chapter II. In its non-linguistic form the question is whether all the types of experience we call 'seeing' can usefully be characterised in the same way, or whether we should divide them into different types. Ayer had argued for the latter view, and in Chapter IX of *Sense and Sensibilia* Austin sets out to refute it.[3] The general character of such an issue is familiar enough by now. We begin from a range of particular situations which we describe in a certain way for certain reasons. The problem is then to arrive at an analysis of the concepts embodied in those descriptions in such a way as to determine whether they are adequate and where they have application. The aim will be to achieve a unified account of any concept, i.e. to assume that a given term has one sense, but this is an aim which may sometimes have to be abandoned.

Perception, I suspect, is a case in point. Certainly the grounds for multiplying sense of 'see' are much stronger than for multiplying senses of 'know', for example. One source of pressure to do so is the variety of cases of perception mentioned in earlier sections – hallucinations, seeing after-images, phenomena like the Müller-Lyer diagram, and also the possibility of giving alternative, incompatible descriptions of one and the same perceptual experience, as when we speak of 'seeing a huge star' and 'seeing a tiny speck'. These might prompt the following move. It is reasonable to suppose that at least sometimes a perceptual judgment of the form 'X sees Y' requires for its truth that there be an appropriate object satisfying the description Y — at least sometimes it cannot be a fact that John saw a table unless there was a table there. What the cases cited suggest, in their various ways, is the less truistic possibility that we sometimes count a case as one of perception by virtue of a certain experience which the subject has, regardless of whether there is any appropriate object in the appropriate position. It might be argued, in other words, that we should distinguish a *relational* and an *experiential* sense of 'see'. (The postulation of an experiential sense would be an alternative to the move, considered at the end of section 4, of postulating non-material objects of perception.)

However, there is room for dispute over the range of experiences which the notion of perception should be expected to cover. It is sometimes said that hallucinatory experiences are not really cases of perception, and that view might be espoused here in the interests of retaining a univocal account of 'see' and rejecting the idea of a merely experiential sense. It might be suggested that when someone undergoes hallucination he does not perceive but merely thinks that he perceives, *in the relational sense*, and of course thinking that you perceive is not perceiving, any more than thinking that you are clever is being clever. In this spirit Austin says, 'If I do want to insist that ghosts don't exist *in any sense at all*, I can't afford to admit that people ever see them — I shall have to say that they think they do, that they seem to see them, or what not' (SS, p. 95n.; Austin's italics).

Now it may or may not be right to regard hallucinations as not really cases of perception, but it is certainly wrong to reclassify them in the way suggested here. This is because it is just not, as a matter of fact, true that someone who is undergoing hallucination necessarily thinks that he is perceiving in the relational sense. In some cases, at least, he will be able to discriminate the unreal 'objects' of his hallucination and will not be at all disposed to think that he is really seeing, in the relational sense, a pink rat, though he may still be disposed to say that he is having a visual experience (cf. Dretske, *op. cit.*, pp. 44–5). This is a good example of the importance which contingent facts have for an adequate philosophical analysis. Given this fact about the nature of hallucination, if it is regarded as distinct from perception then it will have to be accounted for in some way other than that suggested in the previous paragraph.

For the most part, however, Austin does not argue for discounting purported cases of perception where there is no perceived object. His suggestion is rather that such cases are quite exceptional and thus only require a stretching of the ordinary, relational sense of 'see', not the postulation of a different sense. With regard to double vision, where we might want to say that I see two pieces of paper, though there is only one piece of paper in the world, he says this:

'Since, in this exceptional situation, though there is only one piece of paper I seem to see two, I may want to say, "I am perceiving two pieces of paper" *faute de mieux*, knowing quite well that the situation isn't really that in which these words are perfectly appropriate. But the fact that an exceptional situation may thus induce me to use words primarily appropriate for a different, normal situation is nothing like enough to establish that there are, in general, two different, normal ("correct and familiar") *senses* of the words I use, or of any one of them. To produce a rather baffling abnormality like double vision could establish only, at most, that ordinary usage sometimes has to be stretched to accommodate exceptional situations.'

(SS, p. 91; Austin's italics)

Though the circumstances are different in cases like this, Austin insists that the meaning of the perceptual statements is not:

'It is, I suppose, true that, if I know that I am suffering from double vision, I may say "I am perceiving two pieces of paper" and, in saying this, *not mean* that there really are two pieces of paper there; but for all that, I think, my utterance does imply that there are, in the sense that anyone not apprised of the special circumstances of the case would naturally and properly, in view of my utterance, suppose that I thought there were two pieces of paper.'

(SS, p. 89; Austin's italics)

He takes a similar line over the case where we describe a hallucinatory experience as 'seeing pink rats' (SS, p. 97), and to drive home his claim that it is not necessary to multiply senses we are offered an analogy — a singularly unfortunate one, as I shall go on to explain:

'I might say, while visiting the zoo, "That is a lion", pointing to one of the animals. I might also say, pointing to a photograph in my album, "That is a lion." Does this show that the word "lion" has *two senses* — one meaning an animal, the other a picture of an animal? Plainly not.'

(SS, p. 91; Austin's italics)

As for cases where we offer two completely different descriptions of what we see — 'a huge star', 'a tiny speck' — Austin sees even less of a problem here, for after all the tiny speck just *is* the star (SS, p. 92). He then hazards the suggestion that we may feel uncomfortable about these cases because we realize that the question 'What does X perceive?' can be given different answers, all correct, and we mistakenly assume that the question itself must therefore have more than one sense. 'But the proper explanation of the linguistic facts is not this at all; it is simply that what we "perceive" can be described, identified, classified, characterized, named in many different ways' (SS, p. 98).

Austin's case here seems to me to be fairly weak. First of all, he underestimates the number of occasions when we have an interest in the content of someone's perceptual experience, without regard to the question how accurately that experience reflects the contents of the material world (cf. Anscombe, 1965, pp. 169–70 for a wealth of interesting examples of the relevant kind). This is a fair *ad hominem* point to make, when Austin himself rests so much of his case on the unusualness of non-relational cases of perception, and it is also an important point in its own right. Given that there is a fairly common, clearly-defined type of context in which it is only the content of the perception which is relevant, we have strong grounds for accepting a 'two-senses' theory. The more cases there are where an essential feature of the relational sense (the existence of an object of the appropriate kind) need not be fulfilled, the less plausibility there is in saying that we are still using that sense but just 'stretching' its application.

The analogy of the two uses of 'That is a lion' is unfortunate because Austin does not consider the most obvious possibility, *viz.* that although 'lion' is not ambiguous, the term 'is' is, being construed in one of its uses as 'is a representation of'.[4] This is relevant to Austin's reaction to the fact that 'What do you see?' can be given many different answers. After all, says Austin, we can say that I kicked a piece of wood or that I kicked Jones' front door, and no one is tempted to say that 'kick' has two senses, for the piece of wood just *is* Jones' front door (*ibid.*). But the 'is' in the last sentence signifies identity (or possibly constitution — cf. Wiggins, 1967, pp. 10–11), and for that reason the example here will not work as an analogy for understanding the case of perception. The descriptions 'piece of wood' and 'front door' are, to say the least, compatible whereas this is often not true in perceptual cases. The statement that a tiny speck *is* a huge star is one which stands in need of explanation, and it is significant that we cannot say, as Austin realizes, that the huge star is a tiny speck (SS, p. 98n.). One explanation would be that we experientially see a tiny speck (though there is no tiny speck to be found in the world) and simultaneously relationally see a huge star (whether we realize it or not).

The last point may suggest yet another way of accommodating these cases which stops short of multiplying senses of 'see'. This would be to make use of the *seeing as* formula. We could avoid talk of seeing things which do not exist by saying that I do not see a tiny speck but rather that I see a huge star *as* a tiny speck, that I do not see two pieces of paper in double vision but rather that I see one piece of paper *as* two, and so on. This is a move which Austin briefly considers, and one which he appears to have some sympathy with (SS, pp. 100–2). Its drawback, however, is that it can be utilized only in situations where there is *some* object which can be seen as something or other. In cases of hallucination there is not, and we are therefore still left without any general way of accounting for all the initial cases. So once again the pressure is to distinguish senses of 'see'.

6. Incorrigibility

Suppose that it is conceded that there are two senses of 'see' of the kind indicated. In one sense 'seeing' applies to the having of a perceptual experience, in another sense to the standing in a certain relation with something else. Many questions remain which would need to be answered in a full theory of perception. Can an acceptable analysis be given of the conditions governing the use of 'see' in each sense? How are the two senses related? For example, if I see an object in the relational sense does it necessarily follow that I see in the experiential sense? Is one sense in any way more basic than the other?

There is some reason for saying that the experiential sense is in one way more basic. When I make a statement about experiential perception I may well use terms which have their primary application in relation to independent objects — I may say, for example, 'I saw a dagger' meaning by this that I had a visual experience *as if* there were a dagger before me. But despite this, in making such a statement I make a claim which is confined to a description of my experience itself and is not a claim about any independent objects. To that extent it may be said that, in making this type of perceptual statement, I stick my neck out less than when I make a statement claiming a relation between me and a perceived object. This is a point which may be made simply as part of a total account of the nature of perception, but as Austin notes, it is very commonly tied in with a further epistemological point, about the way we come to have knowledge of the world through perception:

'In a nutshell, the doctrine about knowledge, "empirical" knowledge, is that it has *foundations*. It is a structure, the upper tiers of which are reached by inferences, and the foundations are the *data* on which these inferences are based.'

(SS, p. 105; Austin's italics)

The picture which may then emerge — and it is one which Austin emphatically rejects — is that of an individual beginning with his own neutrally described perceptual experiences, and building upon these to reach conclusions about the nature of the world external to those experiences, the world which they are experiences of. It is part of the same picture to suppose that those conclusions will stand in need of verification, since they will involve assumptions, inferences and a substantially greater risk of error. In contrast, statements about one's experience provide the incorrigible foundations. About this aspect of myself I can make no errors, except those of a 'merely verbal' kind (cf. Ayer, 1940, p. 82).

In rejecting this picture, Austin makes some astute points against the idea that my knowledge of my own experiences is incorrigible. We may say, if we like, that a claim about my experience involves less risk than a claim about an object in the world; but Austin points out that it is futile to attempt to define a kind of sentence in the utterance of which I take *no risk at all* (SS, p. 112). Why is it? Because no matter how tentative my statement, and no matter how restricted its subject matter, it will involve the use of descriptive words, words which *classify*, and therefore bring in memory and recognition (PP, p. 92). But I may misremember or fail to recognize, and hence there is room for error, even if what I am describing is only my own experience. More simply, I may just fail to attend sufficiently to my experience, and for that reason run a risk of error in describing it (SS, p. 113). Moreover, if these sources of possible error exist in the case of relatively straightforward *perceptual* experiences, they will apply even more obviously to one's knowledge of more complicated matters such as one's emotions and feelings; over the question whether I am experiencing anger, or even pain, I may make sincere mistakes and need to be corrected by others (PP, p. 110).

These are valid and important points to make against a view which was and probably still is thought to be correct by many philosophers. But where does this leave the original picture? If it is true that my opinions about my own experience are not impregnable, can any part of that picture be salvaged? Certainly it can still be insisted that there is a very great difference between my relation to my own experiences and my relation to the physical world. Even if I may make mistakes about my experiences and even if I may be corrected by others about their nature, at least where I do give an accurate description of an experience it is not necessary for me to be able to cite evidence for it, beyond the fact that I am having the experience itself. This, it may be thought, marks an important contrast with my claims about objects in the world, and allows the other half of the original picture to be retained. If I claim for example to see a pig, in the relational sense, then I do need evidence. And then given the possibilities of deception discussed earlier, there will be a permanent possibility of error, a permanent hiatus between my evidence and a conclusion about any object in the world which I take myself to be perceiving.

Austin's argument against this lapses into familiar style:

> 'The situation in which I would properly be said to have *evidence* for the statement that some animal is a pig is that, for example, in which the beast itself is not actually on view ... But if the animal then emerges and stands there plainly in view, there is no longer any question of collecting evidence; its coming into view doesn't provide me with more *evidence* that it's a pig, I can now just *see* that it is, the question is settled.'
>
> (SS, p. 115; Austin's italics)

Moreover, even in those cases where it may be appropriate to talk of requiring evidence for my conclusion, he does not allow that any hiatus can remain between the two:

> 'If, for instance, you tell me there's a telephone in the next room, and (feeling mistrustful) I decide to verify this, how could it be thought *impossible* for me to do this conclusively? I go into the next room and certainly there's something that looks exactly like a telephone. But it is a case perhaps of *trompe l'oeil* painting? I can soon settle that. Is it just a dummy perhaps, not really connected up and with no proper works? Well, I can take it to pieces a bit and find out, or actually use it for ringing somebody up — and perhaps get them to ring me up too, just to make sure. And of course, if I do all these things, I *do* make sure; what more could possibly be required?'
>
> (SS, pp. 118–19; Austin's italics)

I have little sympathy with the position which Austin is attacking here, but equally little with his chosen method of attack. Once again, in the first of these quotations, he rejects a comprehensive doubt by adverting to what we ordinarily say and think; and once again my objection to his procedure would take the same general form. One way in which the doubt can be expressed is as questioning whether we should use the concept of evidence as we ordinarily do in this context; and even if such a doubt is to be rejected, this can hardly be done satisfactorily merely by pointing to the way we do use the concept. But it may be thought that the second quotation covers this. The doubt rests, to a large extent, on fears about the possibility of deceptive perceptions, and surely Austin here shows that such fears are groundless? Not really. He reminds us, in entertaining style, that there are ways of checking on *known* sources of error, but, as in the context of the problem of other minds, this is not sufficient to neutralise the fear that there may be new, unrecognized sources of error. The bluff assurance that we can make absolutely certain, by a fairly short process of elimination, is more bluff than assurance.

7. Reality

Our perceptual experiences give a major source of information about the real nature of things, but when our perceptions are flawed in some way then we may end up with a mistaken idea about some part of the real world. As a result of this we may come to reflect in a general way on the distinction between appearance and reality, and wonder what it is for something to be real, as opposed to not-real. In an analytical approach this will entail an investigation into the concept of reality, and in Austin's approach, as we have come to expect, it will entail considering the ordinary use of terms like 'real', 'really', etc., in an attempt to analyse their meaning. The remarks which he makes in this connexion prompt the question which has already been raised in other contexts. By examining the language of reality in the way he does, does he tell us anything about reality, or only something about language? I shall let the answer to this emerge from an exposition of the particular points which he makes.

First, he stresses the peculiarities of a term like 'real' which any analysis will have to cope with. The term 'does not have one single, specifiable, always-the-same *meaning*. (Even Aristotle saw through this idea.) *Nor* does it have a large number of different meanings — it is not ambiguous, even "systematically" ' (SS, p. 64; Austin's italics and parenthesis). The first part of this remark is reiterated in the contention that 'there are no criteria to be laid down *in general* for distinguishing the real from the not real' (SS, p. 76; Austin's italics); and the latter part of the remark is backed up by Austin's own claim to say some general things about the use of the term 'real', which we shall come to in a moment.

Consider a sample of the way in which Austin

attempts to establish that no general analysis of the concept of reality is possible. People sometimes wonder whether colour is part of the real world, or whether it is something 'subjective' or mental which we, being the kind of sentient creatures we are, wrongly project on to the physical world. Leaving aside this question, and supposing that such 'subjective' views are mistaken, attempts are sometimes made to say what, in general, determines that an object in the world has one colour rather than another. One answer frequently given is that we are to take as the real colour of an object that colour which it appears to a normal observer to have in standard conditions of light. Austin objects to this that when I say of someone, 'That isn't the real colour of her hair', I may not mean anything about its appearance in standard conditions but simply that it is dyed (SS, p. 65). 'As so often' he suggests, 'you can't tell what I mean just from the words that I use ... ' (*ibid.*). Clearly he hopes to discredit the idea of giving a general account of real colours by supplying an accretion of such embarrassing counter-examples. What is the real colour of the sun? The moon? A chameleon? (SS, p. 66). And similarly for any attempt to give a general account of the real shape of objects — what is the real shape of a cloud? a cat? (SS, p. 67).

Yet Austin himself, in apparent contradiction of this, goes on to make some general claims about 'what might be called the salient features of "real" — though not *all* these features are equally conspicuous in all its uses' (SS, p. 68). He makes four points, as follows:

(1) The term 'real' is *substantive-hungry* (*ibid.*). That is to say, no definite sense attaches to the idea that something is real until we have answered the question 'A real *what?*' Closely connected with this is the fact that something may be a real *X* but not a real *Y*. I may have an object which is a real painting, but not a real Vermeer. Austin suggests that this property is shared by certain other philosophically interesting terms, such as 'good' (SS, pp. 69–70). A man might, for example, be a good father but a bad husband.

(2) 'Real' is what Austin calls a *trouser-word* (SS, p. 70):
'That is, a definite sense attaches to the assertion
that something is real, a real such-and-such, only
in the light of a specific way in which it might be,
or might have been, *not* real. "A real duck" differs
from the simple "a duck" only in that it is used to
exclude various ways of being not a real duck —
but a dummy, a toy, a picture, a decoy, &c.; and
moreover, I don't know *just* how to take the
assertion that it's a real duck unless I know *just*
what, on that particular occasion, the speaker has
it in mind to exclude.' (*ibid.*; Austin's italics. Cf. PP,
p. 87)

(3) 'Real' is a *dimension-word*. That is, it is the most
general and comprehensive term in a whole group of
terms of the same kind, terms which fulfil the same
function. Others in the group would be 'proper', 'live',
'true', 'genuine' (SS, p. 71).

(4) 'Real' is an *adjuster-word*. In fact, Austin explains
what an adjuster-word is by reference to 'like'. There
are occasions when we come across an object which
does not quite fit the conception we have held hitherto
about objects of that type — say, something which
shares many, but not all, of the features which a
normal pig has. Rather than saying that it definitely *is*
or *is not* a pig, we can then introduce flexibility into our
descriptions of the world by saying it is *like* a pig. And
we may then add to this that it is not a *real* pig (SS, p.
74. Cf. PP, p. 89).

Many objections can be made to Austin's account.
As points of comparative detail, for example, he does
not tell us in connexion with (3) *what* common function
the different terms are supposed to have (cf. Bennett,
1966), or in connexion with (4) why we should need the
expression 'not a real *X*' as well as 'like an *X*' — and it
seems in any case that '*not* real' would have the
function of adjusting, rather than the unqualified
'real' (cf. Coval and Forrest, 1967). But more
importantly, the whole approach may be questioned

(cf. Bennett, *op. cit.*). It may be said that his conclusions do indeed add up only to conclusions about language, that he says something about the rationale for *saying* that something is real, the context and reasons which must obtain if there is to be any point in my mdking a remark which makes use of the concept of reality; but the conditions for saying that something is real are not necessarily the same as the conditions for that thing's *being* real. This might also explain why Austin is able to make the general observations he does about 'real', even though he believes that the term does not have one meaning. He may feel that there is nothing of interest in common between different cases of a thing's being real, but that there is between different cases of saying that something is real, *viz.* a certain constancy of intention, or whatever, on the part of the speaker, to which there need not correspond any constancy in the world of which the speaker speaks.

Further support can be gained for this interpretation of Austin by noting the confusion under his point (2) between statement-meaning and speaker-meaning. Perhaps I do not know what *you* mean, what you 'have in mind' when you say, 'It's a real duck' unless I know what possibility you intend to exclude; but your utterance has a meaning of its own, regardless of what is in your mind, and the line of dependence may easily run the other way, so that it is the meaning of what you say (together with the circumstances in which you say it) which may help me to determine what *you* mean. And then Austin's approach serves to leave the 'what you say', the statement-content, unexplained. I have argued in general in favour of making distinctions of this kind in dealing with meaning (cf. Chapter IV, section 3), and the distinction between statement-meaning and speaker-meaning is made all the more evidently necessary in the present context by the fact that a different truth value may attach to each. Suppose that you say of some object, 'It's a real duck', meaning thereby to exclude the possibility that it is a toy one, and suppose that the object is indeed not a toy but a decoy duck. Then the statement which you have in mind — *that it is not a toy duck* — is true. But for all that, the statement expressed by what you say — *that it is a real duck* — is false. Moreover, if we pursue this it helps to throw some light on the concept of reality in a more general way, not being confined to speech situations like Austin's remarks. In the example, what you have in mind is a specific and limited possibility, whereas the content of what you say involves a claim which is general and unlimited. For an object to be a real X it is not sufficient that this or that particular way of failing to be an X should be ruled out — *all* such possibilities must be ruled out. It is this which remains constant, across contexts and for different values of X, in the content of actual and possible assertions, questions, thoughts, etc., about the reality of something. Nor does this make the idea of reality a particularly negative one, as some of Austin's remarks tend to suggest. On the principle that two negatives serve to cancel each other out, an assertion which has the function of *excluding* all possible *failures* in meeting the conditions for being an X has the positive function of emphasising success and fulfilment of the conditions for being an X. In other words, to be a real X is to satisfy the conditions for being an X as opposed to being a toy X, an imaginary X, a Y which looks like an X, *and so on without limit* (cf. Coval and Forrest, *op. cit.*).

Now Austin points out that the Greeks had only one word to do duty for the English words 'real' and 'existent' (SS, p. 68n.), and he says that for this reason amongst others we do not have their excuse for confusion on the present topic. But perhaps it is the very wealth of distinct expressions which misleads us here. Critics have taken Austin to task for paying scant attention to that sense of 'real' which is synonymous with 'existent'; I should be inclined to doubt whether there is any other sense of 'real' — always with the proviso that this meaning can be exploited by a speaker in a particular context to carry some other, perhaps more specific, message (a point which occupies the major part of Austin's attention, but which he misunderstands). Can we, then, simply settle for an analysis of reality in terms of existence? I do not think we can, and I shall now consider some objections to it, of varying degrees of force. One interesting upshot of the discussion will be that the by now standard criticisms which I have levelled against Austin's account in view of his preoccupation with speech, while not being in error, carry rather less bite in the present context than elsewhere.

First, there is the fairly Austinian-sounding objection that the proposed analysis would fail to explain or exclude altogether cases where we do as a matter of fact say of some object that it is a real X. The objection need not rely on the type of case already disposed of, where the speaker can be said to exploit the statement-meaning in order to convey some further, more specific message. Consider Austin's example, where someone says, 'Now this is a *real* carving-knife!' (SS, p. 73). This is one way of saying it is a good carving-knife, and it is difficult to see how that particular point could be made if the meaning of my statement were simply that the object existed as, or met all the conditions for being, a carving-knife. In the earlier case, being a real duck would, on the proposed analysis, *entail* not being a toy, and in that case we can see how I can convey the latter information by saying the former. But being a real X, on the proposed analysis, does not entail being a good X. Hence, it remains a mystery how I can convey the message I do by saying, 'This is a real carving-knife'.

It is important to see why an objection like this is misguided.[5] We are familiar by now with the idea that if an analysis of some concept is sufficiently powerful, explanatory, etc., then this can itself be used as an argument against employing that concept in some situation which is not consonant with the analysis — even if, prior to formulating the analysis, people would be disposed to. But something ought to be said to temper the picture which has been presented so far, as though we were confronted with the stark choice of either finding an analysis which accounted for all contexts where the concept was in fact applied, or else finding an analysis which accounted for some and then ruling decisively against the employment of the concept in any others. The choice is not as stark as that because, having arrived at an acceptable analysis, we may decide that some particular case which strictly falls outside it is permissible, although peripheral or involving an extension of the concept or being a metaphorical use of it. These are themselves, of course, all distinct possibilities. Each could be explored in accounting for an idiom like 'This is a real carving-knife'. Certainly it would be very flat-footed to object to the use of the remark on the grounds that the decrepit, rusty old knife lying next to the one I am enthusing about is also, strictly, a real carving-knife. But everything in its place. It does not devalue imaginative, exaggerated or metaphorical uses of language to point out that that is what they are. On the contrary, it devalues them to treat them as if they were on a par with central, standard, literal uses of language. There is a permanent tendency for a philosopher like Austin to succumb to this latter temptation, in view of his prior commitment to the idea that any actual usage is, merely on that account, to be taken as acceptable. This affords no insight into the connexions between usages and the ways in which some uses may have priority over others.

However, the particular example we have been dealing with would need to be considered further only if the proposed analysis of reality were itself accepted as adequate. The fact is that it should not be. Any progress made by analysing reality in terms of existence is merely illusory, when the idea of existence is itself surrounded by philosophical difficulties. We cannot in this way even settle the question whether there are different senses of 'real' when it is equally a matter of dispute whether there are different senses of 'exist'. Hence, it is unlikely either that the proposed analysis affords much of an insight into the idea of reality or that it will enable us to decide in particular cases what things are real so-and-so's. The idea of reality, if we step back and consider it, *is* a peculiar one which it is difficult to re-express in any more enlightening way. The peculiarities of the idea run at least partially parallel to those in the idea of existence, and that is why it is unlikely that we can use one idea to explain the other.

One such peculiarity is this. On the one hand, reality is of a very different order from, say, redness. If I am told that something is a real X, this information is in one way far less specific than knowing that it is a red X. Yet, looked at in another way, the information that something is a real X involves the fullest possible characterisation of it, since (as I have argued) to be a real X requires the fulfilment of *all* conditions for being the relevant X. Now this can be explained partly by reference to Austin's point that 'real' is substantive-hungry. If the information that something is a real X is specific, it will be the term X which is responsible for this, rather than the term 'real'. For example, if you tell me there is a real Chippendale table in the next room, then I know far more than if you merely tell me there is a real material object there, and this is clearly because of the difference in specificity of the ideas of a material object and a Chippendale table.

If the idea of reality is, in the suggested way, incomplete and if the characterisation of something as real is on its own account a minimal and general characterisation, then we shall meet with limited success in trying to extract an analysis of reality from a scrutiny of the situations where we feel an ascription of reality would be in order. Indeed, I believe the limit is reached with my earlier suggestion that reality is to be equated with the satisfaction of conditions for existence, and that is obviously an intolerably low limit. The alternative, if we continue to look at the objective features of the appropriate contexts, is to diversify the analysis of reality, to say that reality for objects of type X consists in the satisfaction of conditions C_1, C_2, C_3, whereas for objects of type Y it consists in the satisfaction of conditions C_4, C_5, C_6, and so on. But if we feel that the first alternative produces results which are too thin, and the second alternative results which are too paradoxical (since 'real' would change its meaning each time it was applied to a different type of object), we may choose a different avenue altogether. Where the application of a concept carries a characterisation of the world which is minimal, then a correspondingly larger part may be played in the analysis of that concept by reference to the contribution which *we* make in applying it — that is, by reference to the point, interest and motivation in making the discrimination implied by the use of the concept. It is at this point that we can see why my criticism of Austin for giving the rationale for the *saying* that something is real, rather than the rationale for what is said, carries less force here than in other contexts. It is not that those criticisms must be withdrawn, nor is there any doubt that Austin proceeds in a way which is intolerably narrow. It is simply that on this occasion at least he is proceeding in the right direction. We need the concept of reality because in any domain entities may not only fulfil some of the conditions for being entities-of-a-certain-sort, but also sufficient of such conditions for us to be deceived into thinking that they fulfil them all. In short, it is the enormously important contingent fact that we live in a world where mistakes in classification are possible which gives point to the concept of reality, and it is the need to avoid such errors which justifies and gives shape to the marking of the distinction between reality and appearance (cf. Coval and Forrest, *op. cit.*). It is the need to express this point in many otherwise very different contexts which gives the concept of reality its unity.

However (and this may again be to follow the spirit of Austin's argument), it may be that not much more than this can be said in a completely general way about the concept of reality. To ask 'What is reality?' or 'What is the difference between reality and appearance?' is to ask questions which sound large and impressive, but it may have to be accepted that, at least in that form, they cannot be given very exciting answers. This will not be because there is anything wrong with asking general questions as such but because the particular concept of reality is incomplete in the ways already discussed. We should therefore have to meet such questions with further questions. What is the reality *of what kind of thing?* What is it for *what type of state of affairs* really to be the case? We need, that is, to return to a more concrete and specific level, to consider the particular fields in which error is possible, to decide what constitute error and the avoidance of error, and so on. The whole of our perceptual experience and activity is one such area. It is unfortunate that Austin should have half-seen, in his discussion of the idea of reality, that this is how we should proceed, and yet did not himself take seriously enough the possibility of various kinds of perceptual error and the consequences this might have for our view of what constitutes the nature of the real world.

8. Conclusion
Austin's primary purpose in his discussion of perception is the negative one of defeating the series of arguments, to do with illusion, deception, and so on, which lead to some version of a sense-datum theory. But his stated hope is that two more positive consequences should flow from this: the learning of 'a technique for dissolving philosophical worries (*some* kinds of philosophical worry, not the whole of philosophy); and also something about the meanings of some English words ("reality", "seems", "looks", &c.) which, besides being philosophically very slippery, are in their own right interesting' (SS, p. 5).

So far as the negative purpose is concerned, although I believe that the arguments Austin wishes to defeat are bad ones, which result in little useful insight into perception, it will be evident from my discussion that I view his attack on them as largely ineffective. Throughout this chapter I have had to avoid the impression of giving support to those arguments in the act of diagnosing the ineffectiveness of Austin's attack. His failure connects with his first positive purpose. Insofar as the technique in question rests on pointing to the way we ordinarily speak of our perceptual experiences and showing that this conflicts with the way of talking proposed by sense-datum theorists, then what we learn about that technique is that it is patently inadequate for dissolving philosophical worries.

What of the second positive purpose, to tell us something about the meaning of some of the terms used in talk of perception? If this is taken to be an intention to provide an analysis, then by the criteria proposed for successful analyses in chapter II, it cannot be said that Austin succeeds here either. Indeed, when he is talking about actual cases of perception, the most striking thing is the number of unhelpful tautologies he comes out with. When a proof-reader makes a mistake and sees a word which is not there, is this a case of perceptual illusion or delusion? 'Neither' says Austin, 'he simply *misreads*' (SS, p. 27; Austin's italics). What about dreams? We might wonder whether they are cases of perception at all and whether *they* constitute cases of illusion or delusion. 'Neither' says Austin, 'dreams are *dreams*' (*ibid.*; Austin's italics). Again, if we wonder how, in general, we should characterise the experience of seeing mirages, Austin cuts short the debate by reminding us that we have a word for it, namely *mirages* (SS, p. 32. For further examples, cf. SS, pp. 14, 30). Without a doubt it is possible to reproduce what is involved in these cases of perception by the use of the same terms twice over, but this hardly results in our seeing them in a new and strikingly original way.

The question what the scope of perception is is dismissed as not being the concern of philosophy early in Austin's discussion, as we saw in section 2, above. The question what the nature of perception is is one which he does not, properly speaking, come to grips with. It does not follow from this that his own second positive purpose is entirely unfulfilled. As we saw in the remarks he makes about 'real', for example, he has much to say about the meaning of such words, *if this is taken to refer to the role they may play in spoken communication.* Here Austin provides interesting facts, and at least the beginning of a theory. But that contribution must be recognized for what it is: a contribution to the philosophy of speech, not a theory about extra-linguistic reality.

VII

Philosophical Problems: Truth

1. Introduction

Outside philosophy, an interest in truth would normally be an interest in what particular things are true — a concern with *the* truth. The more general enquiries characteristic of philosophy are, once again, dual enquiries into both the nature and the scope of the concept. The two fundamental questions are accordingly (*a*) what truth consists in, what conditions must be met for something to be true, and (*b*) what kinds of things are true.

In the context of truth, this second question is susceptible to two interpretations, both of which give rise to philosophical controversy. In the first place, it may be construed as asking what sort of thing truth is primarily and properly ascribable to — whether, for instance, it is to be located in people, in the form of their beliefs or judgments, or in language, in the form of sentences, or in some other less clearly defined realm such as that of the logicians' 'propositions'. For the tradition to which Austin belongs, the choice will have to be made in something like these areas. It is assumed, that is, that truth is to be ascribed to something 'judgmental' in form, i.e. something of the form *that so-and-so is the case*, and there is comparatively little interest in the way truth attaches to such non-judgmental objects as symphonies. For the moment, then, I shall use the term 'judgment' in a stipulatively neutral way, to refer to whichever of these things truth is primarily ascribable to.

The second interpretation of the question what

kinds of things are true can now be drawn out. There are various ways of classifying judgments, either by subject matter into scientific, moral, historical, etc., judgments, or by form into categorical and hypothetical judgments, or judgments about the past, present and future, and so on. So which judgments, under these various classifications, can properly be said to have a truth value? Here again there is material for controversy, some people contending, for example, that moral judgments cannot be true or false, others that hypothetical judgments cannot. We should obviously expect the usual mutual influence between views on these questions and views on the first question, what truth consists in (cf. Mackie, 1970, p. 333).

It is principally that first question which occupies Austin's attention in his paper 'Truth' (PP, pp. 117–33), part of a symposium given with P.F. Strawson (1950b). But, as might be inferred from his general theories of the nature of language which we examined in Chapters III and IV, he also has definite views on what to ascribe truth to and the types of judgment which have a truth value. He defines his own position in relation to some well-entrenched alternative theories of truth, and, as in previous chapters, I mention the relevant ones here, briefly and without critical comment.

On the face of it, probably the most appealing answer to the question what makes a judgment true is 'correspondence with the facts'. Any judgment, it might be said, aims to say something about the world, to state some fact about it, and if there is a fact in the world of the appropriate specification, then that judgment is true. Thus the *correspondence theory*. Implicit in this theory is the claim that statements of the form 'it is true that John is here' stand in positive need of analysis because their surface appearance is misleading. In making the statement I may seem to ascribe the simple property of truth to the judgment 'John is here', and this suggests, by its form, that to verify what I say you would have to examine that judgment itself to see whether it had that property or not. What the correspondence theory implies is that truth is not a simple but a *relational* property, that the truth of a judgment is not something 'internal' to it, but rather that its truth consists in its standing in a particular relation to something else, roughly a chunk of the world. This may seem unexceptionable, if not very exciting, but we shall soon learn otherwise.

One way of understanding the *coherence theory* is as a reaction to some of the alleged difficulties in the correspondence theory. It may be objected that the kind of naked confrontation between judgment and the world implied by the correspondence theory is an illusion. If I want to test the truth of the judgment that John is here, then anything about the world relevant to it will already have to be expressed in something like judgmental form — that there is a person of a certain description in a certain place, that I shall see certain things if I look in a certain direction, and so on. It may then seem to follow that the truth of a judgment is best understood not as a relation between the judgment and something of a quite different order of existence, but rather as a relation between the judgment and something of its own size, *viz.* other judgments. The truth of a judgment may then be said to consist in its *coherence* with other judgments.

Each of these two theories implies that the analysis of any statement such as 'it is true that p' or 'p is true' involves an elaboration of it. The implication of the superficial grammatical form must be removed by replacing it with a more appropriate form for making clear that truth is relational. A third theory, the *redundancy theory*, involves a drastic move in the opposite direction. Here the suggestion is that in 'p is true' the words 'is true' are 'logically superfluous'. The information conveyed by 'p is true' is no different from, and no greater than, that conveyed by 'p'. In that sense truth is a logically redundant concept, and that is what would need to be made clear by analysis.

The redundancy theory immediately prompts a question. If, say, 'it is true that John is tired' is no different from 'John is tired' in terms of the information it conveys, how do we come to have the concept of truth, and words like 'true', in the language at all? Is it simply that an unnecessary reduplication of effort has taken place, and in numerous languages too? An attempt can be made to meet this query by giving the concept of truth a role to play and yet at the same time staying within the terms of the redundancy theory. In this spirit it may be said that although, when I say, 'It is true that John is tired', I make no new assertion over and above 'John is tired', nevertheless I am making that assertion in a particular way which requires a particular context. I am really reaffirming that John is tired by way of agreement, concession, confirmation, etc. In short, I am making the assertion 'p is true' in a context where 'p' has already been made or is envisaged as having been made (cf. Strawson, 1949). In the terminology familiar from chapter IV, we might say that assertions involving 'true' have a certain characteristic illocutionary force, viz. that of agreeing, conceding, etc.

2. Austin's theory

The modifications just discussed result in what we might call a supplemented redundancy theory. With its use of familiar Austinian terminology and talk of 'assertions made in a particular context' (rather than 'judgments' used in an expressly neutral way), it is a theory which Austin ought to find congenial. We should certainly expect such an illocutionary analysis of the concept of truth to appeal to him if we recall his views on the concept of knowledge, discussed in chapter V. At first sight, therefore, it is a curious fact that Austin rejects the supplemented redundancy theory in favour of a version of the correspondence theory. This is an anomaly which I shall try to account for later. I believe the case of truth is one where two different sides of Austin's philosophy pull him in two different directions. First, however, we must examine the theory which he does adopt.

A judgment is true if it corresponds to the facts. This is not so much a theory as the promise of one, and if the promise is to be redeemed then one thing which must be done is to explain *in what way* a judgment corresponds to the facts when true. Undoubtedly the most natural way to interpret the idea of correspondence is as some 'mirroring' of the world. Thus, I have spoken in earlier chapters of the function which language and thought have of reproducing the structure of the world, or of mapping and reflecting its character. I have already warned, however, that these are no more than metaphors, and it is a commonplace objection to the correspondence theory that it takes the metaphors too seriously and makes a metaphysics out of a mere *façon de parler*. Clearly a map can map the structure of some part of the world and a diagram can reflect things as they are in reality, but this is because in these cases the idea of resemblance can be taken at its face value. Each constituent of the world (or at least each one relevant to our concerns) will have its symbol on the map or diagram, and the spatial and similar relations holding between those constituents will be reproduced in the distribution and arrangement of the symbols. But, it will be objected, this is precisely not so with language, which is what any judgment must ultimately be embodied in. None but the most rudimentary languages can truly be said to be ideographic, and in a developed natural language such as English there is, generally speaking, no structural resemblance at all between a judgment and that which it is a judgment about. If the cat is on the mat and I draw a picture of a cat on a mat, then the picture will reproduce a part of reality in representative form by virtue of a visible structural resemblance between the picture and reality (though, notoriously, nothing in the picture itself carries the message that it reproduces reality in this way. Pictures are not by their nature assertions). Nothing similar is true of the judgment which I express in the words 'the cat is on the mat'. My judgment may stand in some relation to the relevant part of reality — indeed, it *must* do so if we are ever to be led from words to the world — but here there is no relation of resemblance.

Against a version of the correspondence theory which postulates a point-by-point correlation between language and the world, such as that advanced in Wittgenstein's *Tractatus*, this objection is well taken. But it does not follow immediately that truth cannot be explained via the idea of correspondence. What does follow is that some new interpretation of the idea will have to be found, and the metaphors of mirroring, mapping, and so on, will have to be acknowledged as potentially misleading. This is where Austin comes in. The most original part of his theory is the suggestion that the correspondence which obtains between a true judgment and the world is '*absolutely and purely* conventional …. There is no need whatsoever for the words used in making a true statement to "mirror" in any way, however indirect, any feature whatsoever of the situation or event …' (PP, pp. 124–25; Austin's italics). So far, of course, this is purely negative. If there is no need of any 'mirroring', the question remains what there *is* need of.

The answer to this, the account of what correspondence does consist in, is bound up with Austin's views on another of the questions I have mentioned, the question what kind of thing it is which corresponds to the world, what kind of thing it is which is the primary truth-bearer. Here Austin is true to that feeling for concrete phenomena which, as we saw, characterises his approach to the philosophy of language as a subject. It is *statements*, construed in the concrete sense of statement-acts, which Austin nominates as the primary truth-bearers (PP, p. 118). 'A statement is made and its making is an historic event, the utterance by a certain speaker or writer of certain words (a sentence) to an audience with reference to an historic situation, event or what not' (PP, pp. 119–20).

The concrete speech act is therefore chosen as the first term in the correspondence relation; and whether we use the favoured expression 'statement' or alternatively 'assertion' to pick this out, what is important is that the expression we use should 'have the merit of clearly referring to the historic use of a sentence by an utterer' (PP, pp. 120–21).[1]

This preference for the concrete is one reason why Austin chooses statements as primary truth-bearers. But there is a second reason why he nominates statements rather than, say, sentences at this juncture, and it is a reason which brings us nearer to an understanding of the idea of conventional correspondence. Some philosophers argue that truth is primarily a property of sentences. Austin argues that it is always a sentence *as used by a certain person on a certain occasion* which is true or false (PP, p. 119). People may use one and the same sentence to make different statements. For example, you and I may use the same English sentence, 'my hands are cold', and one of us may speak truly and the other falsely despite using the same sentence. Equally, I may say, 'It is raining outside' on two different days and speak truly on one occasion and falsely on another. This indicates that what partly determines the truth or falsity of what I says is the particular statement which I make in using a certain sentence. To cope with this in answering the question what are the primary truth-bearers we can say *either* that truth attaches to sentences as used to make a certain statement (rather than just 'sentences') *or* that it attaches to statements. It is probably simpler to follow Austin in adopting the latter terminology.

Taking that question as settled, we now return to the question what it is for a statement to be true. In what way must it 'correspond to the facts'? Here the significance of the distinction between sentences and statements, and its bearing on this question, become known, explicit. Austin says that in order to achieve the kind of communication which we do about the world,

' ... there must be two sets of conventions:

Descriptive conventions correlating the words (=
sentences) with the *types* of situation, thing, event,
&c., to be found in the world.

Demonstrative conventions correlating the words
(= statements) with the *historic* situations, &c., to be
found in the world.

A statement is said to be true when the historic
state of affairs to which it is correlated by the
demonstrative conventions (the one to which it
"refers") is of a type with which the sentence used
in making it is correlated by the descrip:ive
conventions.'

(PP, pp. 121–22; Austin's italics and parentheses)

The position, then, seems to be this. When I say
something about the world, I make use of a stock of
symbols with conventionally fixed meanings, symbols
which are essentially re-applicable, capable of being
used on more than one occasion. The symbols of
language, whether individually or in combination into
some form of judgment, may correlate by virtue of
their meaning with types of object, state, situation, etc.
That essential generality or re-applicability of language
is something I have had occasion to stress. But the
other side of the coin is that if we are ever to say
anything particular about the world as it is on a
particular occasion, then it must also be possible to use
such symbols so as to isolate some single, definite state
of affairs, not just a *type* of state of affairs. That is, it
must be possible to use context so as to correlate with a
particular state of affairs. The sentence 'The man on my
left is wearing a green shirt' correlates with a certain
type of situation by virtue of its meaning, and can be
used on innumerable occasions to apply to particular
instances of that type. When and only when the
sentence is used in that way, i.e. to apply to a situation
of the appropriate type, is the statement which is made
true. It is this, rather than any structural resemblance
between the statement and state of affairs, which

explains the idea of a statement's corresponding to the facts.

As far as positive doctrine is concerned, this is all Austin has to offer (though he has additional things to say in criticism of alternative theories and in defence of his own against possible objections). Someone who has raised the question 'what is truth?' might well feel that he had been given an inadequate answer, if this is all he gets. It may therefore be necessary to make two preliminary points in Austin's defence, before moving to a more detailed examination of his theory. First, if Austin does fail to give an analysis of truth which is lengthy, profound and interesting, and at the same time plausible, then this is only a failing which he shares with almost every philosopher who broaches the subject. The point is well taken that truth is an area 'where it seems even easier than usual to fall into error but where, if one avoids error, the conclusions that one can reach are almost trivial' (Mackie, *op. cit.*, p. 323). The second point is that Austin himself may have made no grandiose claims on behalf of his theory. He announces that 'the theory of truth is a series of truisms' (PP, p. 121), and ends his paper by asking rhetorically why we should not accept the analysis of truth in terms of 'the rather boring yet satisfactory relation between words and world which has here been discussed ...' (PP, p. 133). Now the paper 'Truth' is not devoid of Austin's heavy donnish humour (it is already well under way in the first paragraph), and it might be prudent to take these disclaimers with a pinch of salt. All the same, there is some reason to give him the benefit of the doubt and suppose that his disclaimers are intended seriously. In the course of criticising the redundancy theory he comments:

'There are numerous other adjectives which are in the same class as "true" and "false", which are concerned, that is, with the relations between the words (as uttered with reference to an historic situation) and the world, and which nevertheless no one would dismiss as logically superfluous. We say, for example, that a certain statement is exaggerated or vague or bald, a description somewhat rough or misleading or not very good, an account rather general or too concise. In cases like these it is pointless to insist on deciding in simple terms whether the statement is "true or false". Is it true or false that Belfast is north of London? That the galaxy is the shape of a fried egg? That Beethoven was a drunkard? That Wellington won the battle of Waterloo? There are various *degrees and dimensions* of success in making statements: the statements fit the facts always more or less loosely, in different ways on different occasions for different intents and purposes.'

(PP, pp. 129–30; Austin's italics)

 The implication is that even where it is the use of language to reflect reality which is in question, truth may not be the most important consideration. 'We become obsessed with "truth" when discussing statements, just as we become obsessed with "freedom" when discussing conduct' (PP, p. 130), whereas in fact, in both cases, we should be concerned with other dimensions of assessment. Moreover, we saw in Chapters III and IV that Austin's chief preoccupation with language concerns not its function in reflecting reality, but the various ways in which it may be used creatively, and we find echoes of this in the present context with the observation that many uses of language do not in any case have it as their aim to say anything true or false (PP, pp. 131, 132). All these factors combine to suggest that Austin may have seen problems of truth as something less than the most vital ones. This gives a further reason for wondering why he did not take the shortest cut and embrace the supplemented redundancy theory himself.

3. Statements and facts

If Austin's theory were a series of truisms based on

explaining truth in terms of a boring relationship it would on those grounds alone fail to meet the criteria for a successful analysis, since it would shed no new light on the concept of truth. But the compressed account offered in his original paper has given rise to a long debate and it has been claimed that, far from being truistic, the account is mistaken. The terms between which the truth-relation is supposed to hold — statements and facts — provide one locus of difficulty, and Austin's account of the relation itself provides another. Both are well probed by Strawson (1950b and 1965). I shall consider some of the criticisms of the theory at these different points, and include in my assessment of their validity a consideration of what Austin has to say in his later reply to Strawson (1950b), 'Unfair to Facts' (PP, pp. 154–74).

In one part of his criticisms Strawson conducts a pincer movement and argues that neither statements nor facts are independent entities, so that truth cannot consist in any relation between them. Making use of the distinction between statement-act and statement-content (though he does not himself use those labels), he suggests that whereas the statement-act is a concrete thing in the world which may stand in relation to other things in the world, it is not this but the statement-content which is properly true or false. And he suggests that, in contrast, the statement-content is *not* something in the world: terms like 'statement' when used in this way are 'convenient, grammatically substantival devices', but we should be wrong to infer from this that they actually name anything (*op. cit.*, pp. 33–4). In short, it is what I say, not my saying it, which is true or false, but it is only my saying something which can be located in space and time, and stand in relation to something else. As if this were not bad enough, Strawson also argues that *facts* are not part of the world, capable of standing in relation to other parts of the world: 'Facts are what statements (when true) state; they are not what statements are about. They are not, like things or happenings on the face of the globe, witnessed or heard or seen ...' (*op. cit.*, p. 38). He accepts that there are two sets of conventions as described in Austin's definition and also that at least sometimes stating involves using both. But the only things in the world, he seems to say, to which our words can correlate via these conventions are objects and people. These may provide a material correlate for a referring term, such as 'table' or 'boy', but for descriptive terms such as 'red' or 'fat', and for statements themselves there are only *pseudo*material correlates (*op. cit.*, pp. 36–7). In short, facts and statements (in the relevant sense) are in their different ways abstractions, not things. And finally, they are in any case too nearly the *same* abstraction for it to be possible that they should stand in relation to each other (*op. cit.*, p. 39).

Although Austin's general orientation leads him to ascribe truth to statement-acts, his original paper contains arguments which might easily have led him to Strawson's conclusion that it is a property of statement-contents. He considers the suggestion that truth should be ascribed to *beliefs*, and rejects it for two reasons: first, on the grounds that 'it may be doubted whether the expression "a true belief" is at all common outside philosophy and theology ...' (PP, p. 118); secondly, because 'it seems clear that a man is said to hold a true belief when and in the sense that he believes (in) *something which* is true, or believes that *something which* is true is true' (*ibid.*; Austin's italics). Now the first reason follows directly from Austin's normative commitment to the adequacy of existing usage, and it is in consequence a feeble reason. Even if it happened not to be common for people to speak of true beliefs — and Austin cites no evidence for what I should have thought was a dubious claim — this is not crucial. There might be compelling theoretical grounds for recommending that people *should* talk in that way. But it is the second reason which might have led Austin to Strawson's view. *If* this shows that it is not beliefs which are the primary vehicles of truth and falsity, it shows equally well that statement-acts are not: for here, too, if someone makes a true statement then he states *something which* is true. It then looks as though truth will have to be ascribed to statement-contents, if to statements at all.

However, though the argument can be mounted with regard both to beliefs and to statements, it is less clear how powerful an argument it really is. Mackie, for instance, has argued that although it is natural to regard *what* is said as true or false, still the statement-content is an abstraction which can exist only as the content of a speech episode. He therefore suggests that there is no obstacle to regarding the statement-act as true or false, though we shall have to recognize that the aspect of it which matters for truth or falsity is its 'propositional content' rather than any other more concrete features which it may possess *qua* event in the world (*op. cit.*, pp. 323–24). This represents a compromise solution which would enable us to retain a first term for a correspondence-relation. But Mackie's own argument can be questioned in turn, and we shall have to return to the question of the dependence of statement-contents upon actual linguistic utterances. This will connect with the need we have for what I shall call the idea of *independent truth*, truth which does not rest in any way on the existence of human action, intervention or language, and it will be the locus of an intertwining of statement and fact which serves to cast doubt on the usefulness of the correspondence theory.

If we turn our attention to the argument about facts, two general difficulties confront us. One is that it is not easy to see just what is at issue in the disagreement about whether facts are 'part of the world' (cf. PP, p. 156). Much of Strawson's argument, for example, seems to rest on claiming — what is in any case obvious — that we do not always speak of facts as *things* in the world (cf. *op. cit.*, pp. 35–43). Connected with this is the second point, that the debate provoked by Austin's original paper has been heavily influenced by the assumptions of Austinian ordinary language philosophy.[2] Strawson suggests that his own claims about the dubious status of facts are 'reflected in the behaviour of the world "fact" in ordinary language; behaviour which Mr. Austin notes, but by which he is insufficiently warned' (*op. cit.*, p. 37). Not to be outdone, Austin, in his later defence 'Unfair to Facts', argues that it is on the contrary Strawson's own position which is 'unplausible and based on insufficient consideration of ordinary usage' (PP, p. 155). The same background assumptions extend to the debate over possible alternatives to facts as the second term in the correspondence-relation. Thus, although Austin says that truth consists in correspondence with the facts, in his analysis of correspondence he speaks not of facts but of states of affairs (PP, p. 122. Cf. PP, p. 154). Strawson points out that in ordinary language we speak differently of facts, situations and states of affairs (*op. cit.*, p. 39), and his point has been taken up elsewhere (e.g. by Warnock, 1964, pp. 12–13).

Now it may or may not be profitable to investigate the differences between the expressions 'fact', 'state of affairs', etc., but merely reporting on ordinary usage will be of no use. We shall need to consider *why* we say the things we do, and how they are to be interpreted. Consider, for example, Austin's own attempt to establish that facts are part of the world. Strawson had said, obscurely enough: 'What "makes the statement" that the cat has mange "true" is not the cat, but the *condition* of the cat, i.e. the fact that the cat has mange … but the fact it states is not something in the world' (*op. cit.*, p. 37; Strawson's italics). Austin is probably right in objecting to this, but the way in which he does so is itself open to doubt. He claims

'(1) that the condition of the cat is a fact;
(2) that the condition of the cat is something-in-the-world — if I understand that expression at all.'

(PP, p. 156)

Although it is not entirely clear from the text,

presumably Austin wishes to conclude from these two premises

(3) that facts are something in the world.

A parallel argument might be:

(4) the tail of the cat is an object

(5) the tail of the cat is something in the world

(6) therefore, objects are things in the world.

But, apart from any other defects in the argument (4)-(6), Austin's argument cannot be construed on analogy with it, and this illustrates precisely the danger of basing any claims on uninterpreted ordinary idioms. Premise (4) states the category to which something belongs. What would be analogous to this in Austin's argument would be, not his premise (1), but rather 'the condition of the cat is a *property*', and then no conclusion about the status of facts would follow. Although we may *say* that the cat's condition is a fact, the only way of construing this in such a way that it states a truth is as the claim that the cat's *being* in a certain condition is a fact. 'The cat's condition is a fact' must be taken to mean 'It is a fact that the cat is in a (certain) condition'. And this is not a categorical statement parallel to (4). So whereas Strawson seems to keep facts out by showing they are not things, Austin tries to smuggle them in by an impossible identification of facts with conditions.

It is probably foolhardy to pursue a question whose precise import is unclear, but on the assumption that some definite sense can be attached to the claim that facts are part of the world, I am inclined to present one more consideration to make it easier to accept that they are. Given the kind of creatures we are and the kind of world we live in, we need to distinguish between *dependent* and *independent truth*. Consider the following statements:

(a) I promise to be there on time.

(b) The sergeant ordered Jones to shut the door.

(c) Jones hit the sergeant.

(d) The moon has mountains over 20,000 feet high.

Doubtless there are many differences between them,

but one distinctive feature of (a)-(c) is that their truth depends, each in a different way, on the existence of human beings. They illustrate that human beings can *create* truth, by action, by language, by convention and so on. In these respects (d) is quite distinct from the others, since it does not depend for its truth on the existence of a human race at all. Its truth is something we discover, not create. Mountains on the moon exist, and have the character they have, independently of us. That is to say, both their existence and their nature is independent. We not only discover (rather than create) the mountains: we also discover *what* they are like, *that* they are of such and such a kind. In short, we discover *facts* about the moon. And only what is already there can be discovered.[3]

Someone might now point out that I began by speaking of independent *truth*, and suggest an extension of the argument. Equally, it might be said, we discover *truths* which exist independently of our discovering them or indeed thinking about them at all. It was true that the moon had mountains over 20,000 feet high before there was anyone around to say so. But this brings statements back into the picture. If truth attaches to statements then it looks as though we have an argument for the independent existence of statements — not, of course, statement-acts, which do require the existence of a language and an utterer, but of statement-contents. If this is correct, it casts doubt on Mackie's claim that statement-contents exist not on their own but only as the contents of speech episodes: at most we should concede that they are the contents of *possible* speech episodes. Further, we now have a reason for saying that truth is primarily a property of statement-contents rather than statement-acts. There are statements which are true in advance of anyone's saying anything and there are presumably true statements which no one ever will utter — and 'statements' here *must* mean statement-contents.

4. Correspondence

These arguments about statements and facts are nothing if not provisional. Moreover, even if they could be taken to show that statements and facts are something more than abstractions, there is still the objection that 'true statement' construed in the relevant sense (i.e. statement-content) and 'fact' are two names for the *same* category. It may be possible to avoid that conclusion by suggesting that we have each category for a different purpose: that of facts to describe the way the world is, and that of statements to describe what can be said about the world, though not necessarily what *is* said about it (cf. Mackie, 1973, pp. 54–56). But even if we can, in this way, prevent the notions of fact and true statement from collapsing into each other, it does not follow that truth can be satisfactorily and informatively explained as consisting in some relation between them. It may well be, as Strawson implies, that the three ideas of truth, fact and statement all stand too close together and share too many of each other's problems for the first to be given a satisfactory analysis in terms of the other two (cf. *op. cit.*, pp. 37–8, 42). Indeed, I believe that this is so, and I shall try to draw out some of the difficulties facing the correspondence theory as a result of the intertwining of the three ideas.

Austin draws an interesting parallel between the idea of a fact and the idea of existence:

'It seems to me ... that to say that something is a fact *is* at least in part precisely to say that it is something in the world: much more that than — though perhaps also to a minor extent also — to classify it as being some special kind of something-in-the-world. To a considerable extent "being a fact" seems to resemble "existing" in the sorts of way that have led it to be held that "existence is not a predicate". One might compare:
Cows are animals   with Fevers are diseases

Cows are things	with	Fevers are conditions
Cows exist		Fevers are facts
There are such things		There are such
as cows		conditions as fevers'
		(PP, p. 158)

Now when 'fevers are facts' is construed in the way I suggested that something of this form must be, namely as elliptical for 'it is a fact that there are fevers', then there does indeed seem to be a close parallel between this and assertions that something exists. But the series of comparisons made by Austin suggests a problem. Facts are most naturally and informatively specified in judgmental form; but this is a form which is natural to other things besides facts — beliefs, expectations, regrets, possibilities, etc. So the form of words 'John's being in the room' or 'that John is in the room' may express a fact or a possibility. How, in general, should we distinguish the two? When it is objects which are in question, we distinguish by means of the notion of existence (horses exist, unicorns do not). When it is states of affairs which are in question, it is difficult to resist the suggestion that we should mark the parallel distinction between actuality and possibility by means of the notion of *truth*. 'John's being in the room' expresses not merely a possibility but a fact when it is *true* that John is in the room. But if we succumb to that suggestion, it is obvious what the problem will be. We shall have decided that the most natural and satisfactory way of explaining the general category of facts is in terms of truth. The only progress we make will be circular if we then go on to explain truth in terms of, amongst other things, facts.

Related difficulties arise in the specification of *particular* facts. When Strawson first says that 'fact' is wedded to 'that-clauses' (*op. cit.*, pp. 37–8) it is not clear whether he is making the point I have been making.[4] Austin interprets his claim as 'a statement about English usage' to the effect that whenever the expression 'fact' occurs it can be supplemented with a 'that-clause' without offending against idiomatic English (PP, p. 163). The truth is probably that, as with some of Austin's own claims, Strawson intends his point to be both one about English usage and about much more than that. No doubt it is very easy to refute the claim in just that form: it will very often *not* be consonant with idiomatic English to tack a 'that-clause' on to the end of the expression 'fact'. But for reasons which are familiar enough by now, the philosophical value both of the claim and of its refutation may be very low. On the other hand, Austin makes a concession to a potentially far more damaging interpretation of Strawson's claim when he allows that

> 'the expression "The fact that S" *means* "a certain fact [or actual occurrence, &c.], *viz.* that correctly described [or reported, &c.] by saying now 'S' [or at other times 'S' with change of tense]." ... It is a usage grammatically *like* (not of course in all ways the same as) the *apposition* usage with proper names, as when we say "The person Caesar" which we should interpret as "a certain person [or actual man, &c.], *viz.* the one designated by the name 'Caesar' " '.
>
> (PP, p. 165; Austin's italics and parentheses)

Once again the parallel is partly instructive and partly damaging to Austin's overall case. One central way of picking out a person in the world is by the use of that person's name, and what answers to this in the case of picking out a fact in the world is the use of some statement 'S'. In both cases there are, of course, other possible ways. I may pick out a person by the expression 'The only person who bought me a drink last night' instead of using the name 'Kate', and I may pick out a fact by referring to it as 'The fact which caused him to lose the bet' instead of 'The fact that he was too drunk to stand'. But there can be little doubt that it is the latter which gives the essence of the fact. This, to repeat, does not show that facts and true statements are one and the same thing, but it does raise the question whether truth can usefully be defined in terms of a relation between them.

A similar question arises when Austin extends the comparison and asks whether there is a parallel between the following two trios:

1. 'Cicero'	2. 'The cat has mange'
Cicero	The cat's having mange/the mangy condition of the cat
The person Cicero	The fact that the cat has mange.

(cf. PP, p. 166)

Doubtless there are parallels of various kinds between 1. and 2., but for anyone who advocates a correspondence theory of truth it is the differences which are more important. If the relation between a statement and a fact were just the same as that between a name and the person named, there would be no need for any idea of correspondence at all: it could simply be said that a statement is true if it names a fact. Now the instinct to reject such a complete parallel is a sound one. Both in Austin's discussions of language as a subject and in our discussions of philosophical analysis we have seen ample reason for supposing that statements do not stand in the same relation to what they are about as a name does to the object which it names. But then the onus is on Austin, as a correspondence theorist, to say something informative about what is special and peculiar in the relation between an entire statement and whatever it relates to. In other words, we come back again to the question of correspondence.

Unfortunately, in 'Unfair to Facts' Austin takes up a defensive stance on this question, and one which leads to a loss of the insight which the paper 'Truth' contained.[5] In the later paper he does not, indeed, profess to say anything about the *nature* of the correspondence-relation (cf. PP, p. 154), but all the

PHILOSOPHICAL PROBLEMS: TRUTH 205

same in the course of arguing for the existence of some such relation he manages to commit himself to a particular, and unacceptable, view of it. 'Corresponds with the facts' he reminds us, is 'a wholesome English expression', and he objects to the idea of treating it 'as though it were a philosopher's invented expression' (PP, p. 159). Moreover, if we allow that there is a relation of correspondence between a map and the topography then so ought we to also when we say that a statement corresponds with the facts (PP, p. 160). The existence of this and related idioms in the language Austin takes as particularly significant:

> 'The expression "fitting the facts" is *not* by any means an isolated idiom in our language. It seems to have a very intimate connexion with a whole series of adverbs and adjectives used in appraising statements — I mean, 'precise', 'exact', 'rough', 'accurate', and the like, and their cognate adverbs. All these are connected with the notion of fitting and measuring in ordinary contexts, and it can scarcely be fortuitous that they, along with fitting and corresponding, have been taken over as a group to the sphere of statements and facts. Now to some extent the use of this galaxy of words in connexion with statements *may* be a transferred use; yet no one would surely deny that these constitute serious and important notions which can be, and should be elucidated .... Yet all these terms are commonly dismissed along with the supposed useless "fitting the facts".'
>
> (PP, p. 161; Austin's italics)

Here the unacceptable general assumptions behind Austin's philosophical method confront us again. An existing expression is presumed superior to any invented ones, the more so since it is one of a whole cluster of similar expressions. But both an existing and an invented expression would need to be judged in the same way — in terms of what they mean and imply, whether the criteria for their application are clear, whether they are adequate for describing the world or expressing a response to it, and so on. Mere longevity will not guarantee any of this, though doubtless there will be *some* explanation for the survival of an existing idiom. For that matter a 'galaxy' of related idioms will not guarantee adequacy either. Indeed, it will not even guarantee that the expressions are being used non-metaphorically, for we should expect that the use of one striking metaphorical expression is likely to attract others. This is an occasion, therefore, when we need to keep distinct the idea that there is a reason why we speak in certain ways and the idea that there are *good* reasons for speaking in those ways. Consider an example which illustrates the pitfalls. Beginning with such expressions as 'making a pile' and 'rolling in it', I can think of at least a dozen idiomatic English expressions whose use carries the implication that we stand in the same relations to money as we do (or might) to our own excreta.[6] No doubt there is a reason why such idioms occur, and their use may reveal much about people's attitudes towards money; but I take it that no one would regard this as showing something about the literal relations which obtain between people and money. What we have here is a psychologically revealing façon de parler. So it is, one can plausibly argue, with 'corresponds' and the rest when they are applied to statements. We saw in section 2 above that there are good reasons for resisting a literal interpretation of 'correspondence', etc., and this was precisely what led Austin to say that the relation between a true statement and the reality it relates to is absolutely and purely conventional (PP, p. 124). He is quite right in saying that all these expressions require elucidation, but he should not have abandoned his original inclination to avoid any *literal* interpretation.

Let us return to his original analysis of the idea that truth consists in correspondence with the facts:

'A statement is said to be true when the historic

state of affairs to which it is correlated by the demonstrative conventions (the one to which it "refers") is of a type with which the sentence used in making it is correlated by the descriptive conventions.' (PP, p. 122)

Here there is no hint that all the 'fitting' idioms need be taken literally — rather the reverse — and thus this original analysis is not open to objection on that account. But it may still be open to objection on other grounds. Austin presents the truth of a statement in two stages. First, the demonstrative component in the statement leads us to some particular fact or state of affairs; and secondly, if that fact or state of affairs has a character consonant with the descriptive component of the statement then the statement is true. There is more than one reason for thinking that these two stages must collapse into each other. For example, the idea of 'pure reference' is a dubious one, and it may well be a misunderstanding of the way language works to suppose that demonstrative conventions alone could lead me to some state of affairs. Doubt can be cast, indeed, on the whole idea of making a separation between demonstrative and descriptive conventions in language (cf. Strawson, 1965). The difficulty I should focus on, however, derives from the intertwining of the notions of fact and true statement which I have sketched in the preceding pages. You cannot isolate a fact as (perhaps) you can an object, by pointing to it; its essence can only be given in judgmental form. The consequence of this is that if we are to be sure of comparing our statement with the right fact then that fact will itself have to be expressed either in the same terms as the statement or in synonymous terms. It is no good comparing a statement, e.g. that John is in the room, with one fact after another in order to see whether it corresponds to one of them. Obviously if the statement is true it must correspond specifically to the fact *that John is in the room*. But this is to fix the nature of the fact in all respects. It therefore gives a false picture to suggest that we could, even metaphorically, hold up the statement and hold up the fact but yet *leave open* the question whether they fit each other. There is no stage of homing in on to the world from a given statement in such a way that some particular fact is picked out but yet the character of the fact is left indeterminate. And this means that the idea of correspondence is left with no role to play. We can say if we like that truth is correspondence with the facts; but all that means is that a given statement S is true if it corresponds to the fact that S. And all *that* means is that the statement S is true if *it is* a fact that S. When this version of the correspondence theory is probed, therefore, it turns out not to yield any more original way of seeing the concept of truth than we possessed already.

Two possible defences of Austin against this charge should be mentioned. Both rely on picking up a point referred to earlier, that of differentiating between different possible candidates for what, in the world, a statement must correspond with. The first is to propose that the world correspondent in Austin's theory should be, not a fact, but an object. Certainly I can make a statement which picks out an object in the world without fixing its nature in all respects: I may identify the watch in my pocket by stating, 'The watch in my pocket is made of gold', even if the object in question is not made of gold. On this interpretation, then, there would be room for the two-stage process envisaged in Austin's account of the correspondence between statement and something else (although here there would be no plausibility at all in saying that it is demonstrative, and not descriptive, conventions which lead to the picking out of the object). We could say that a statement of this kind is true when the object picked out by it also has the character ascribed to it in the statement. But if Austin's theory is interpreted in this way, it falls prey to an objection made by Strawson, that it becomes excessively narrow (1950b, pp. 51–2). There are many different types of statement which are true or false, but which do not involve ascribing a property to a previously picked-out object in the simple way required, e.g. 'All mules are sterile', 'There are no one-legged dogs', 'If John has gone out, he will be soaked'. Austin tries at the outset to answer the completely unrestricted question what it is for *anything* to be true, but for statements like these the amended Austinian theory offers no account at all.

It could be argued that 'true' is used in a basic sense in relation to the basic statements which do make straightforward reference to some particular object, and that further, more complex senses of 'true' involved in more complex statements are in some way reducible to the basic one. This seems to me an unacceptable suggestion, even if it were one which could be expanded in any detail. It is unacceptable for a higher-order reason which I have invoked elsewhere: it would lead us to conclude that some kind of play on words is in operation when I say that two things are true, namely (1) that my watch is made of gold and (2) that if my watch is made of gold it must be worth a lot of money. *Of course* the conditions for the truth of (1) and (2) differ, but that is because of the different (and different types of) content of each. 'True' itself does not mean something different when applied to each, any more than 'possible' would if we said instead that both (1) and (2) were possible. Even if there were nothing else wrong with the amended version of Austin's theory, it would fail on these grounds.

The second defence, proposed by Warnock (*op. cit.*), is to point out that Austin speaks of a state of affairs, rather than a fact, in his definition, and to insist that the distinction between the two is important. Thus, Warnock recognizes the need to avoid the narrowness which results from taking objects to be the world correspondents, and argues that we also avoid the trivialisation which results from giving the role to facts if we give it instead to states of affairs (*op. cit.*, pp. 14–15). For, he suggests, if someone says 'The corn is green' then I may understand that he is referring to the state of affairs obtaining in my field, but I can then as a separate step go and see whether that state of affairs is of the character which he says it is (*ibid.*). This, however, seems to me to be an equally unsatisfactory way of trying to meet the difficulty. The idea is that the statement leads us to a state of affairs which can be described in some way such that it is obviously that state of affairs which is relevant for the truth of the statement, but also such that the description of the state of affairs does not of itself *settle* the truth or falsity of the statement. One danger here is that a particular state of affairs can itself be picked out only via some reference to a particular object or a particular time and place ('the state of affairs *obtaining in my field*'). If that is correct, then the theory will again fail on grounds of excessive narrowness: any statement which does not include particular reference of that type will fall outside the scope of the theory. A more general weakness, however, is this. We cannot simply say that my statement 'The corn is green' is true if it corresponds to *the* state of affairs in my field, for many states of affairs obtaining in my field (the corn's waving in the wind, etc.) will be *irrelevant* to its truth. I see only two ways round this. One is to say that the statement is true if it corresponds to the state of affairs *consisting in my corn being green* — which is open to exactly the same objection as that originally raised against that version of the theory which speaks of correspondence with a fact, instead of a state of affairs. The other is to say it is true if it corresponds to the state of affairs regarding the colour of my corn. But then I see no way of generalising that so as to account for the truth of *any* statement, except in such terms as 'the statement is true if it corresponds to that state of affairs which *determines the truth* of the statement'. And the circularity of that is obvious.

There is one further problem about how generally applicable Austin's theory could be (cf. Warnock, *op. cit.*, pp. 18–20). Throughout this chapter we have concentrated exclusively on statements about the empirical world. But these are not the only statements which we should regard as true or false — there are also, for example, the statements of logic and mathematics. It is evident that some statement such as 'two plus two equals four' does not pick out some particular state of affairs, fact or object in the world, etc., in the manner Austin's theory would require. If the theory had proved adequate elsewhere, we should then have to decide whether a distinct sense of 'true' was in use in relation to non-empirical statements, or whether, on the contrary, this showed a failure of generality of Austin's theory at another point. But I hope I have said enough to show that his theory fails before we even get as far as this particular issue.

5. Conclusion

The problem of truth provides an interesting point of tension for Austin's philosophy as a whole. In some problem areas the different aspects of his general method combine well in a kind of mutual support system. Thus, for example, we saw that he offers an illocutionary analysis of knowledge, an analysis of concrete speech acts involving the use of 'know', and this is underpinned by a description of the situations in which we should ordinarily say 'I know' and an account of the difference between these and situations where we ordinarily use related terms such as 'believe' and 'am sure'. In the problems connected with perception Austin's uppermost purpose is to preserve from sceptical attack the things which people ordinarily say, and in several places this is buttressed by drawing attention to the remarks people would actually make in the situations which the sceptic calls attention to, and by emphasising the point and interest behind such statement-acts.

Now one can hardly begin to consider problems of truth without giving thought to the nature of language, and Austin's stress on the illocutionary aspect of language might naturally be thought to suggest, as I said earlier, a theory of truth similar to Strawson's (1949). That is, we might naturally suppose that he would favour explaining the concept of truth by reference to the need we frequently have verbally to reaffirm, in a concrete speech situation, what others have said. I have argued that in general illocutionary theories are inappropriate for answering classical philosophical problems, and so it might be thought in any case all the better for Austin that he here abandons an approach which consistency would demand that he follow. There is more to the matter than this, however.

For one thing, Austin explicitly recognizes here, as he does not elsewhere, some of the weaknesses in an illocutionary analysis of a concept. First, he recognizes that illocutionary force is only one aspect of a statement: to perform a statement-act may be to do something to which some general label, such as 'insulting' or 'confirming', may be affixed, but this is quite compatible with simultaneously saying something which is itself capable of truth or falsity (cf. PP, p. 133). I should want to strengthen this point by noting that at least very often the illocutionary force of a statement-act is partly a *result* of the particular content expressed in it. If we give an analysis of a concept, therefore, in terms of the illocutionary force of statements which contain it, we are putting the cart before the horse, and leaving ourselves no room to explain *how it is* that statements embodying the concept can be used in that way. We have lost the chance of explaining the contribution which the internal content of a speech act may make to its concrete social aspect. Secondly, Austin recognizes that an illocutionary analysis is likely to yield the rationale for applying the concept *in speech*, but that this tells us nothing about contexts where, for example, I *see* that the concept applies but do not say anything (*ibid.*). Had Austin borne these points in mind elsewhere he would have made far fewer errors.

However, I do not think his refusal to espouse an illocutionary theory of truth rests merely on the recognition that such theories are in general inadequate. In my discussion of the theories of performatives and illocution I pointed out that for the most part Austin abandons his general philosophical method when dealing with language as a subject. If he shared the view I expressed a moment ago, that problems of truth inevitably raise problems of the nature of language, then this too would explain the abandoning of his normal procedure. *The discussion of truth is a continuation of the discussion of language as a subject,* for Austin. Why, then, does he not speak here of the theory of illocution, which is after all a theory about language? Because he is not speaking here of the various creative uses of language, for which the theories of performatives and illocution are formulated. He is speaking of what was traditionally taken to be the only use of language, its use to reflect the nature of pre-existing reality. Hence, a theory complementary to those other theories is required, not something which itself makes use of them.

This explains the nature of the arguments in the 'Truth' paper,[7] and it explains why, in my opinion, it is by far the most interesting attempt made by Austin to deal with a classical philosophical problem, even if it is ultimately a failure. In this paper he does not simply accumulate idioms and give a descriptive account of what people ordinarily say. His account of the different kinds of linguistic convention and the role they play in the making of statements is a clear attempt to say *why* people talk, for example, of something's 'fitting the facts'. It is a serious and worthwhile attempt to say something about how, in general, we are able to move from language to the world, how we can use arbitrary symbols in the representation of brute reality. It is all the sadder, in the light of this, that when critical pressure is applied to this theory he retreats to the stultifying methods of ordinary language philosophy in 'Unfair to Facts'.

VIII

Philosophical Problems: Action

1. Introduction

I have already drawn attention to the central part played by *agency* in human nature. The fact that we act in and on the world is probably the most important single fact in determining what kind of creatures we are. In Chapters III and IV we considered how the range of actions we can perform is itself increased and extended by virtue of the fact that we are also social creatures, possessed of a language. The act of striking another person can be performed in more or less any set of social conditions, but it takes a particular set of social conventions for acts such as ordering or promising to be a possibility. In the present chapter we shall delve a little more deeply into the idea of agency itself.

We shall also consider one of the most important ramifications of the fact that we are agents, which again stems from the fact that we are at once agents and social creatures. We act not only upon the world but upon one another, and at different times we all suffer the consequences of other people's actions and cause them to suffer the consequences of our own. Now of course I may suffer the very same consequences either as a result of human action or as a result of some natural process. For example, I may sustain a broken arm either from falling rocks or from a carefully delivered karate chop. In the two cases the degree of pain which I suffer may be identical, but only in the latter case am I likely to react by adopting a certain kind of attitude, such as bitter resentment towards the creature immediately responsible for my injury. To put it more generally, there is a range of attitudes such as resentment, gratitude, admiration, disapproval, etc., which are appropriate exclusively in relation to human actions. Intimately connected with these attitudes is the idea of *moral responsibility*. The difference we feel between human agents and mere things is that agents bear a responsibility for what they do, which licenses criticism, praise and blame, perhaps even punishment.

Where consequences as important as these follow from the application of a concept, we have ample reason for exploring it, deciding whether it is a coherent and acceptable one, and if so under what conditions it applies to someone and his actions. This last question is necessary because we do not normally suppose that an agent can be held morally responsible for absolutely everything which could be called an action of his. We should not normally think this was true, for example, of actions performed under duress or as a result of an honest mistake (e.g. if I administer arsenic thinking in good faith that it is a mild sedative, and where there has been no negligence on my part). If possible, then, we ought also to be able to give some rationale for excluding such actions from the area of moral responsibility.

We also arrive at a cluster of problems about responsibility by another route which has as its point of departure certain questions about the nature of human action. To be a human being is, amongst other things, to be an agent. But as well as the actual performance of actions this includes the *power* to perform actions which, it may be, one does not choose to perform. That is to say, central to the idea of a human being is the idea of a being with a repertoire of capacities, skills, dispositions, and so on, which that being possesses as an abiding part of its nature, even at times when they are not being realised or made manifest. No picture, either of human beings in general or of some particular human being, will be complete unless it contains a specification of such powers and capacities as well as properties more obviously 'there' and open to view. Indeed, if my claims in Chapter V were correct, the idea of capacities already enters with the idea of a human being as a being with knowledge. An analysis of the concept of the capacity to act, therefore, should leave us with a better idea of what it is to be human. A further reason for exploring this idea of a capacity is provided by the *problem of determinism*, and this brings us back to the question of moral responsibility. One of our most deeply-rooted beliefs about the nature of the world is that events which happen in it are caused to happen — perhaps, even, that *all* events are caused to happen. There are some grounds for fearing that this belief will come into conflict with the conception which we have of ourselves as agents. At its most full-blooded, at least, this conception is of a being who consciously chooses between alternative possible courses of action and is responsible, as the originator, for the realisation of one possibility rather than another. But now human actions are themselves events in the world and therefore presumably find their place in whole chains of causally connected events. If so, the idea of an agent somehow standing outside such chains, yet capable of initiating or interfering with them, may well seem to be beset with difficulties. The same considerations may be used to cast doubt on the acceptability of our idea of specifically moral responsibility. Surely, it may be said, we blame a man for what he did when we feel that he made the wrong choice, that there was a preferable course of action which he could have realised but chose not to? If our conviction about this is in error, if the action which he performed was causally determined and therefore bound to occur, if the man did not perform one action rather than another of his own free will, then surely it will not be rational to blame him for what he did? A clear, explicit account of what it is to have the capacity to act should help us to decide whether the fears expressed in this line of reasoning are well grounded.

The questions outlined in the preceding paragraphs to do with action, freedom and responsibility are, in my view, some of the most important in the whole of philosophy. For one thing they touch most deeply on the conception we have of ourselves. For another, it is even more obvious here than in other areas examined in earlier chapters that these questions are not exclusively analytical. The difficulties in verifying what actions are possible, as opposed to being actually performed, are obvious enough and provide a focus for doubt and disagreement about borderline cases, just as it is a matter of common experience that people disagree over cases where it is proper to hold someone responsible for some action performed. Moreover, the contexts in which these issues arise make it clear that comprehensive doubts can be raised about whether to apply concepts such as freedom to act and moral responsibility at all. But what serves most of all to emphasise the importance of the questions is the fact that the answers we give to them have practical consequences. Depending on whether we think a concept like moral responsibility should be applied at all, where we should apply it and on what grounds, we shall not only have different attitudes towards other human beings, we shall also act differently towards them, both as individuals and collectively within various social institutions. No one should pretend that the philosophy of action is of merely academic interest.

It was this area which occupied Austin's attention in the last years of his life, notably in the papers 'A Plea For Excuses', 'Ifs and Cans' and 'Three Ways of Spilling Ink' (PP, pp. 175–232, 272–88). In these discussions, not one but all of the characteristic features of his method come to the fore — the excessive premium placed on current usage, the emphasis on spoken language, the preoccupation with minutiae, the mistrust of comprehensive questions and comprehensive attempts to answer them. In the light of this, it is not at all surprising that Austin should have chosen just these discussions as explicit examples of his advocated philosophical method. I have made it clear throughout this book that I regard that method as inadequate for dealing with philosophical problems, and I believe that it is at its most obviously inadequate in the present context. This is partly because of his explicit and conscientious adherence to it here, and partly because of the theoretical and practical importance of the issues raised. Nowhere is the gap between the results we can expect from the method and the results we need more evident.

This is a harsh judgment, and I shall try to justify it in the sections which follow. Before I do so, however, a qualification must be entered on Austin's behalf. He insists in several places that his contribution to problems of action is only a preliminary one, and it would be a misrepresentation to suggest that Austin thought he was anywhere near giving definitive answers to the questions he discusses (cf. PP, pp. 175, 273). It is therefore a matter of looking at his contribution and attempting to show that even if it were projected much further than Austin himself took it, it would simply be projected in the wrong direction.

2. Austin's approach

Austin makes some astute points about the positive need to give an analysis of the concept of human action. If an action is taken to be denoted by any verb following a personal subject, then at least its application will be clear enough (PP, p. 178). But in fact we operate with a more restricted concept of action than this. For example, 'John fell under a bus' fits the subject + verb formula, but it describes something which happened to the subject rather than something which the subject *did*. Action, in this more restricted sense, is different from mere bodily movement, and a successful analysis of action will reveal the nature of that difference. It will also enable us to determine whether certain borderline cases, such as thinking, saying something, trying to do something, are actions in this sense (PP, p. 179). The practical importance of such an analysis has already been stressed. Austin observes that in ethics we are concerned with right and wrong chiefly as they apply to conduct, and for that reason it will be desirable to have a clear idea what constitutes conduct (PP, p. 178).

There is one further point of some importance, given the connexion between action and ethics. In what turned out, sadly, to be a prophetic remark, Austin warns against assimilating all actions to very simple ones, such as posting a letter or moving one's finger (PP, pp. 179, 202). Much of the philosophy of action which has appeared since Austin wrote commits just this error. If the only difference between chickens and human beings were that human beings cross the road in order to buy some tobacco, a concentration on very simple, everyday actions would not matter. But very often in ethical contexts it will be conduct of an infinitely more complex and extended kind which is in question. If we ignore this more complex type of conduct in framing general ideas about action, then the application of those ideas in ethics will be correspondingly impoverished. Ironically, we shall see later that Austin himself was the first person to fall foul of his admonition.

These, then, are some of the reasons for seeking an analysis of action. However, Austin characteristically prefers an oblique to a frontal attack on the problem. He suggests that light will be cast on the nature of action by studying cases where terms of *excuse* and *aggravation* are used — in other words, by studying cases where we do not speak of someone's just doing something, without qualification, but of their doing something inadvertently, by accident, on purpose, and so on (PP, pp. 177, 273). Two reasons are given for proceeding in this way. First, an examination of the abnormal cases is likely to shed light on the normal ones. Different excuses, for example, will be applicable to different aspects of action, and in this way we shall be led to see something of the internal structure of action (PP, p. 180). Secondly, any given excuse will apply to certain actions but be inapplicable to others, and this will give us a means of categorising actions, sorting them into different types (*ibid.*).

Let us take the second of these two claims first. The argument is that if we take a term like 'unwittingly', we shall find that it can be conjoined with a certain range of verbs denoting action and that it cannot be conjoined with others; and so on for other such terms. In this way, we shall be able to build up a classification of action-verbs and therefore of actions.

> 'For example, take "voluntarily" and "involuntarily": we may join the army or make a gift voluntarily, we may hiccough or make a small gesture involuntarily, and the more we consider further actions which we might naturally be said to do in either of these ways, the more circumscribed and unlike each other do the two classes become, until we even doubt whether there is *any* verb with which both adverbs are equally in place.'
>
> (PP, p. 191)

Austin does allow that there may be some such verbs, but he warns against the trap of thinking we have found one when we have not. For example, I may break a cup voluntarily as an act of self-impoverishment or I may break a cup involuntarily if I cause it to break through some sudden movement. Speaking literally, we do have a verb here which can be linked with both adverbs. But Austin urges that the two acts each of which is described as 'breaking a cup' are 'really very different' and that in consequence what we have here is 'an apparent exception that really does prove the rule' (*ibid.*).

Now these last remarks are puzzling, for it is clear from the way these expressions of excuse and aggravation function that we should expect the two acts to be very different. Annexing such an adverb to an action-description is not a matter of simply adding one further property to an action which in all other respects has the whole of its nature already determined. These adverbs are, as Austin's name for them should make clear, *modifying* expressions: their presence serves to *change* what might otherwise be implied by the description of the action. In the present case, whether or not 'voluntarily' and 'involuntarily' are opposite in meaning (Austin thinks they are not. Cf. PP, p. 191), from the mere fact that they are different in meaning we should not be in the least surprised that 'breaking a cup voluntarily' and 'breaking a cup involuntarily' describe two very different actions. However, it may still be said that even if Austin is confused on this point, my criticism does nothing to threaten his main claim, that the number of action-verbs which any such modifying term can be attached to is limited, so that we can build up a classification of actions on this basis. This is fair enough, and even Austin's complete failure to indicate how such a classification might proceed can be defended on the grounds that he is, after all, proposing a programme rather than professing actually to carry it out.

This leaves the first reason for thinking that a study of excuses, etc. can throw general light on action, namely that different modifying terms enable us to discern the internal structure of action. Once again, the illustration which Austin gives of his claim is minimal. He suggests that excuses of carelessness, errors of judgment, etc. relate specifically to the *executive* stage of action, the stage where we actually carry out the action, and he distinguishes this from what he calls 'departments of intelligence and planning, of decision and resolve' (PP, p. 193). One further aspect of action on which he lays special stress is 'the state of *appreciation* of the situation' (PP, p. 194). 'Many expressions of excuse' he suggests, 'indicate failure at this particularly tricky stage', and those nominated for the position are thoughtlessness, inconsiderateness and lack of imagination (*ibid.*)

Now it is certainly worthwhile to stress that there are all these distinguishable aspects of human action. (I prefer 'aspects' to Austin's term 'stages', which is too suggestive of temporal succession.) To do so will help to combat the temptation to think of action as just what we see, the movements of a person in the world, or even movements preceded by a simple, isolatable decision to move; and this is a temptation which is certainly present if we work with very simple examples of action. If we remind ourselves of the multiplicity of its aspects then we are less likely to ignore the complexity and the continuity of human action. We shall recognize as inadequate and oversimplified the picture of a human being as making one discrete decision followed by a discrete action, the pattern to be repeated over and over again. What is less certain, however, is whether it is Austin's procedure and the concentration on excuses which enables us to do this. He does not, as one might expect, argue that different excuses link with different verbs and then suggest that the verbs themselves give evidence that action has these different aspects. He seems, rather, to rely on a prior recognition that separation of action into such aspects is possible.

But whatever we think of these general reasons for approaching action via the study of excuses and their opposite, the final test is what is actually achieved in this approach. I said that all the facets of Austin's method are apparent in his discussion, but it is perhaps the preoccupation with minute differences which first strikes the reader. It reaches levels unsurpassed in his published writings. He argues for the distinctness of doing something *intentionally*, doing it *deliberately* and doing it *on purpose* or *purposely* (PP, p. 274), and in support of this cites the different endings of 'deliber*ate*', and 'intention*al*' and 'purpose*ful*' (PP, p. 280), and the different prepositions in the expressions '*on* purpose' and '*with* the intention', arguing that this serves to make purpose impersonal in a way in which intention cannot be (PP, p. 282). He suggests it will be a remunerative exercise to consider why we say 'carelessly' but 'inattentively' (PP, p. 193), and says that in considering mistakes we should examine one by one the expressions 'by mistake', 'owing to a mistake', 'mistakenly', 'to be mistaken about', and so on, asking rhetorically why we should bother to burden ourselves with a number of slightly varying expressions unless they function quite differently (PP, p. 198).

It will be clear from my response to Austin's deployment of this argument in other contexts that I do not think the question should be allowed to pass as a rhetorical one. The reason for having a multiplicity of expressions to do with mistakes may be simply stylistic and hold no philosophical significance at all. As I have said before, we cannot make any assumptions in advance about whether these small differences in idiom will or will not have any importance, but it is necessary to keep a sense of proportion in the matter. Austin's failing is to keep neither a sense of proportion nor an open mind, a point to which I shall return. Moreover, one source of information prized by Austin, the dictionary, actually yields counter-evidence to his first claim, that there are differences between acting deliberately, intentionally and purposely. When Austin is urging the importance of using a dictionary in philosophical enquiry he suggests that quite a concise one will do. Yet if we consult the Concise Oxford Dictionary we find that it defines the adjective *deliberate* as, amongst other things, 'intentional'; that it defines the adjective *intentional* as 'done on purpose'; and that it defines the noun *purpose* as, amongst other things, 'object or thing intended'. This suggests that the three notions are not as distinct as Austin claims. However, it may fairly be said that this is merely an *ad hominem* point. If Austin himself sets great store by what the dictionary tells us, there is no reason why a critic must take the same view. There may very well be good reasons for *stipulating* distinctions between terms which the dictionary treats as equivalent. 'For example, I suppose that the terms 'avoidance' and 'evasion' are near enough synonymous, but within the framework of the present legal system it is useful to stipulate a distinction between tax avoidance, which is arranging one's affairs within the law so as to pay little tax, and tax evasion, which has the same result but involves falling foul of the law. What is important in such cases is that there should be a good rationale available for stipulating the distinctions in question. We are thus led to what might in any case be thought the most important component in Austin's approach — a consideration of concrete cases and what we should say when presented with them.

Here, too, the deficiencies in the procedure re-emerge. The method is to describe situations where we should use one of the key terms but not another, and the deficiency lies in the fact that Austin does not consider in any detail *why* we should say this or that, and what there are good reasons for saying. Only by engaging in these further deliberations shall we be in a position to resolve clashing views on what to say. Some such resolution is going to be necessary, because Austin's own claims about what to say are not uncontentious — they differ from my own intuitions, at least. I list a selection of the cases he gives (cf. PP, pp. 274-79). It should be reiterated, however, that his discussion is avowedly introductory, and his pronouncements on them are very tentative, couched as often as not in question-form.

(*a*) 'Suppose I tie a string across a stairhead. A fragile relative, from whom I have expectations, trips over it, falls, and perishes' (PP, p. 274). Here Austin implies that we should say I tied the string there intentionally, but not that I did so on purpose or purposely.

(*b*) 'As I drive up, I see that there is broken glass on the roadway outside my home; so I throw it on the sidewalk, and a pedestrian later stumbles over it and is injured' (PP, p. 275). Here he implies that we should say I threw the glass there intentionally, but normally not that I did so either on purpose or deliberately.

(*c*) When children pull the wings off flies, it is implied

that we should say they do so intentionally and deliberately, but not on purpose (PP, p. 277).

(d) 'I am summoned to quell a riot in India. Speed is imperative. My mind runs on the action to be taken five miles down the road at the Residency. As I set off down the drive, my cookboy's child's new gocart, the apple of her eye, is right across the road. I realize I could stop, get out, and move it, but to hell with that: I must push on. It's too bad, that's all: I drive right over it and am on my way' (PP, p. 278). Here, according to Austin, we should say I drove over the gocart deliberately, but neither intentionally nor unintentionally.

It would not be fair to say that Austin makes no attempt at all to provide a rationale for these pronouncements. He suggests, for example, that the case where someone does not act *purposely* is one where the agent has no interest in doing what he does (PP, p. 277), that the common factor in actions not performed *deliberately* is that there is something 'precipitate' about them (*ibid.*), and that where I do not act *intentionally*, my action is an incidental matter, incidental to some further action which I do intend to perform (PP, p. 278). Even leaving aside the fact that these are the most skeletal remarks and that Austin nowhere, as he himself points out (PP, p. 283), comes near to giving definitions of the terms in question, I should still wish to disagree with the things which he does say. For one thing, he seems to confuse acting on purpose with acting for some *further* purpose. Thus, in (a) he rebuts the possibility that I may have acted on purpose by asking, 'What could the purpose have been if not to trip at least someone?' (PP, p. 275). But this is surely a mistake on Austin's part? Just as I perform act A intentionally if I intend to do A, so I perform A on purpose if it is my purpose to perform A itself — it is not necessary that I should have it as my purpose to achieve some further result R. So, in the case in question, if it is my purpose *to tie the string*, then I performed *that* act on purpose, though it may be that I did not trip anyone on purpose. There is a similar confusion between doing something deliberately and doing it *after deliberation*. Austin says that I act deliberately 'when I have stopped to ask myself, "Shall I or shan't I?" and then decided to do X' (PP, p. 286). I should have thought that case (*d*) gives the lie to this, since it is one where Austin says that I act deliberately but where there is little plausibility in saying that I stop to ask myself whether to do what I do. Certainly there are other cases — for example, where people act in anger — which seem to me to be clear instances of deliberate action (the agent means to do what he does, it is no accident, he does not act out of ignorance or through an oversight) but where there is no question of the action's having been preceded by prior deliberation.

Instead of now giving further instances where, it seems to me, Austin is wrong in what he says we should say, I ought to anticipate a natural objection. Someone might complain that in raising criticisms of this kind I am simply accepting Austin's own assumptions: I am calling attention to small differences in idiom and resting my case on the way people do use those idioms now. The only difference between us is that we disagree on how they are used. But surely, it may be said, it is misguided to score points against him by playing him at his own game? If my objections to the method made in Chapter II were intended seriously, surely I ought to refuse to join in the game at all?

There is a measure of justice in this complaint, and it gives an opportunity to clarify further my original criticisms of Austin's procedure. My own remarks about what we should say of his various cases are remarks of a preliminary kind. To sustain them fully, it would be necessary to give a justification by way of analysing the concepts they embody, and such analyses might result in *changing* what we should say. Equally, my differentiation between closely similar idioms like 'deliberately' and 'after deliberation' is tentative. It seems clear to me that there is a difference in meaning between the two expressions, and that we may learn something about the structure of action by attending to the difference; but the onus would be on me to show that these things are so. My criticism of Austin is that his presuppositions do not allow him to keep an open mind on any of these matters. For example, his mistake about what it is to perform an action deliberately is not an isolated, fortuitous error. It stems from a *combination* of his concern with minutiae and his neo-Darwinian assumptions about language. 'Deliberate' is formed from the Latin past participle, and Austin takes this as showing that the English term signifies that something *has happened* (PP, p. 280). Why? Because 'in the long run, the expressions which survive will be such that their grammatical and morphological characteristics are of the highest significance for their meaning' (PP, p. 282). Now if this were *discovered* to be true of linguistic expressions, it would be a fact with consequences of the highest importance. For one thing, it would give a decisive answer to anyone who feared that, on the contrary, the form of linguistic expressions is often misleading as to their meaning. But Austin clearly does not regard it as a fact to be discovered, which might turn out to be otherwise. He asks us to accept it as an assumption which 'in a sense is a tautology, that *in the very long run*, the forms of speech which survive will be the *fittest* (most efficient) forms of speech' (PP, p. 281; Austin's italics and parenthesis).

It is, quite simply, begging the question to make this an assumption in philosophical investigation, and it is compounding the error to suppose that it is an assumption which is, albeit 'in a sense', a tautology, i.e. an assumption we cannot fail to make. At many points in preceding chapters we have seen reason to suppose that outward linguistic form may engender confusion, and, contrary to his stated view, Austin himself concedes as much on occasion. But even if this were otherwise, even if all the expressions which survived did wear their proper significance on their face, still there would be no justification for blocking by fiat any attempt to raise the question whether this was so or not. Moreover, this attitude will tend to lead to the exclusion of specifically analytical philosophy, at any level where such philosophy is interesting and worthwhile. For if we assume at the outset that there is nothing mysterious, misleading or suspect about the expressions we happen to operate with, then why should we feel that there is any acute need for a positive analysis of them? And then, since analysis may be the first step towards discarding a currently used concept and replacing it with a more satisfactory one, this attitude also serves indirectly to reinforce the conservative view that existing concepts and ways of looking at the world are not in need of any improvement or replacement.

My complaint against Austin, then, is not that he does wrong to discuss the ideas of deliberation, intention, etc., nor yet that he does wrong by investigating the language in which we talk of those things. An investigation of these and related ideas is essential to a proper understanding of the complexity of human action, and may well shed light on the different aspects of action which were mentioned earlier. My complaint is rather against the way in which Austin conducts these investigations, the orientation and assumptions associated with his discussion. These, I suggest, vitiate any attempt to reach important conclusions about action. It is impossible in principle that he should do so; it is not just that he only gets as far as preliminary investigations.

3. Knowledge of one's actions

Austin does, all the same, put forward views about action which, if they were true, would be important, notably in the third section of 'Three Ways of Spilling Ink'.

He suggests that we use words connected with intention when we wish to mark the fact that, generally speaking, an agent has some conception or picture or plan of 'what he is doing' as he engages in different actions (PP, p. 283). And he claims that the possession of such a 'plan' has a certain result for the agent's knowledge of his actions. 'I don't "know what I'm doing" as a result of looking to see or otherwise conducting observations: only in rare and perturbing cases do I *discover* what I've done or *come to realize* what I am or have been doing in this way' (*ibid.*; Austin's italics). Since they are the agent's own actions, and since they consist in attempting to realize some aim which he has conceived, his knowledge of them is in some sense immediate, in a way in which his knowledge of another person's actions would not be.

There is a second point which goes very naturally with this. If an agent does usually have such immediate knowledge of his own actions then it will be reasonable to grant him a special authority in describing them. This is something which Austin seems to concede, for he says that although there is some freedom in structuring the course of someone's activities, 'there is much that is arbitrary about this unless we take the way the agent himself did actually structure it in his mind before the event' (PP, p. 285). The point is of some importance, since there very often are disputes about how someone's actions are to be described, and the actions and reactions of other protagonists are likely to be different, depending on what they take the correct description of someone's action to be.

Finally, when 'intention' is used in this way to give priority to the agent's account of his actions, it has 'a most important *bracketing effect*: when the till-dipper claims that he *intended all along* to put the money back, what he is claiming is that his action — the action that he was engaged upon — is to be judged *as a whole*, not just a part of it carved out of the whole' (*ibid.*; Austin's italics).

These claims seem to me to embody a mistaken view of action, a view which underestimates the opacity of human conduct and thereby underestimates the difficulties in understanding human beings. The points about the bracketing effect of giving the agent's intention and the possibility of viewing action in a part-whole way are both important, but they can be used to argue to a conclusion which is the contrary of Austin's. The part-whole aspect, in particular, deserves far greater attention. It would be a very obvious mistake to regard a person's actions as discrete, atomic events in the world which happen to stand in temporal succession, and it would be a mistake for a number of reasons. The performance of one action will exert a powerful influence on the scope of choice in acting subsequently, and will affect the likelihood of one subsequent action as against another; there will be a detectable constancy in the actions of a rational agent, since he will have certain overall aims and ends; one action may be subsumable under another action involving a wider description; the performance of particular actions is affected by the fact of a great deal of *inter*action between agents, and any adequate description of someone's actions will need to take this into account. Arising from these considerations there is one point which is especially noteworthy, and that is that the part-whole aspect may be applicable on a far wider time-scale that Austin's own example suggests. One correct way of describing a man's action might be as pouring some whiskey into a glass, but this is also part of the more inclusive action of destroying himself by drink, or of escaping from an awareness of his own failure. Or a man needlessly reports to his superior a mistake made by a colleague, and this is part of the wider action of ruthlessly making his way to the top. If we think of these wider action-descriptions — at their widest I suppose they constitute descriptions of what a person is doing with his or her life — then I see little reason to agree that an agent nearly always knows what he is doing and that there is a question of his *finding out* only in rare cases. A great deal of imaginative literature is built around the fact that an agent can come to a *subsequent* realization of what he has, in this wider way, been doing, and the fact that regret may follow both for *what* the agent realizes he has done and for his awareness only coming *after* the action. For that matter, I should want to argue that there are many cases, both in fiction and in real life, of people who never do become aware of what they have been doing, in this wider sense, and that they therefore constitute even more obvious counter-examples to Austin's claim.

In a similar way, I should want to reject the idea that we must accord any essential priority to the agent's own way of structuring his actions in these cases. If he does not have any special immediate knowledge of his wider actions, he may be in no better a position than anyone else when it comes to structuring them in the most appropriate way. He may be lacking in self-awareness, and there may even be psychological reasons why he is in a poorer position than others. This is often true, for example, of protagonists who stand in some close personal relationship. Because judgment is clouded by the intensity of the relationship, or because of the need for self-deception, it may easily happen that good friends standing immediately outside it are in a better, more objective and detached, position to structure the protagonists' actions than the protagonists themselves. ('Didn't you realise what you were doing to him/her all those years?' they ask. And the answer may be 'No'.) Moreover, although I have focused here on actions performed over a wide timespan, since they seem to me to constitute the most obvious counter-examples to Austin's thesis, nevertheless I should say that his claims are not true of short-term actions, either, above a certain level of simplicity. An agent might structure an action by describing it as 'making a mild witticism at her spouse's expense'; given their relationship, the surrounding circumstances and their own preceding actions, it might be more appropriately structured as 'subjecting her spouse to public humiliation', and there need be nothing arbitrary about that structuring even if the agent would resist it. Clearly what happens in such a case is that a tension manifests itself between seeing the action *as a whole* and seeing it *as the agent saw it* — these do not necessarily come to the same thing.

It will be fairly clear what I think is wrong in general with Austin's claims. What he says may very well be true of actions which are not at all complex and not extended over time, but it is not true of action as such. In particular, it is not true of those actions which are, from the point of view of morality and human relations, the most important. I find it surprising, in fact, that he should lean so far in the direction of allowing the agent a privileged view of his own actions when in other areas he had pointed out the difficulties in the way of self-knowledge (cf. chapter VI section 6, above). If I can be corrected by others in the matter of knowledge of my own sensations and emotions, it is much more likely that the same will be true of my own actions, where there is so much more complexity and so much more at stake. Here I can do no better than quote against Austin his own earlier warning:

> 'We take *some very simple action*, like shoving a stone, usually as done by and viewed by oneself, and use *this*, with the features distinguishable in it, as our model in terms of which to talk about other actions and events: and we continue to do so, scarcely realizing it, even when these other actions are pretty remote and perhaps much more interesting to us in their own right than the acts originally used in constructing the model ...'
>
> (PP, p. 202; Austin's italics)

In the sections where Austin makes the claims which I have been disputing, the three examples of action which he cites are dipping into the till, striking a match, and eating my dinner. It is not easy to resist the conclusion that the philosophy of action is too serious a business to be left to the philosophers.

One further point. I have presented (and given very little argument for) a picture of human behaviour very different from that which Austin presents. It would take an enormous amount of investigation to adjudicate between the rival pictures, and not just philosophical investigation — clearly the findings of social psychology would play a major part. But whether or not Austin's picture would turn out to be defensible after investigation, I fail to see how he can defend it, as he implies he can, in the light of his own earlier investigations. How *could* his conclusions about the agent's knowledge of his own actions follow from the facts which Austin collects about adjectival endings and different prepositions? It may be thought instead that his conclusions follow from the discussion of particular cases and what we should say when they obtained, but we have seen that a discussion with Austin's assumptions will not do. And after the points made in the last few paragraphs we can add that a discussion only of the banal cases which Austin raises will not do either.

4. Responsibility
We saw in section 2 that a study of terms of excuse and aggravation is meant to help in understanding the general nature of action. The same study is meant to replace entirely any frontal assault on the concept of responsibility. Excuses are what we offer in order to avoid responsibility (PP, p. 176), and 'to discover whether someone acted freely or not, we must discover whether this, that, or the other plea will pass — for example, duress, or mistake, or accident, and so forth' (PP, p. 273). The problem of freedom is to be completely disposed of by attending to those cases where it will not do to say 'X did A' but where some modifying expression must be inserted (PP, p. 180. Cf. PP, p. 130).

I expressed reservations in section 2 about the way Austin discusses particular cases of excuse, and my reservations apply equally to his present attempt to bring those discussions to bear on problems of responsibility. His treatment of particular cases proceeds at too intuitive a level. For instance, there is the case where I perform an action knowing that a certain result will follow, but not wanting or intending that it should. I demand that you repay your debt to me, say, and I foresee that this will result in your ruin, but I do not intend that you should be ruined, only that I should be repaid. Now Austin introduces such a case in order to show that I may act deliberately and yet unintentionally, but he remarks in passing that it is an especially interesting one since 'plainly I am not responsible' for the result which I do not intend (PP, p. 279). Certainly it is a matter of the highest moral importance to decide whether we can or should hold a person responsible for that kind of result, and it may turn out that we should not. But Austin is hardly justified in saying, in a throw-away line, that this is *plainly* so. There are those who have argued that an agent *is* responsible for such results, and, whether they are right or wrong, their position at least deserves to be examined. This could be done by considering the arguments *why* someone should be held responsible here, the grounds for making that ascription, and weighing these against the corresponding reasons given on the other side. But it is just such a frontal attack on the idea of responsibility which Austin rules out. Of course, according to his own assumptions he does right to regard this as a case where I am plainly not responsible — it is, after all, a case where a term of excuse ('unintentionally') applies *ex hypothesi*. But if those assumptions lead him to pronounce arbitrarily and hastily on an important case, that gives all the greater reason for questioning them.

The study of excuses is intended to replace any direct attempt to answer the analytical question what responsibility consists in. Austin also has an argument which is intended to block the comprehensive question whether the concept of responsibility really has any application at all. This is his *doctrine of the standard case*:

'The natural economy of language dictates that

for the *standard* case covered by any normal verb — not, perhaps, a verb of omen such as "murder", but a verb like "eat" or "kick" or "croquet" — no modifying expression is required or even permissible. Only if we do the action in some *special* way or circumstances, different from those in which such an act is naturally done (and of course both the normal and the abnormal differ according to what verb in particular is in question) is a modifying expression called for or even in order.'

(PP, p. 190; Austin's italics)

Most of my actions, Austin argues, I simply perform; I do not perform them by accident or inadvertently, nor, for that matter, do I perform them deliberately or intentionally. This effectively rules out the fear that perhaps no one ever acts freely or is ever responsible for what he does. That fear could be justified only if it were possible to offer an excuse every time someone acted — 'he did it unintentionally, or accidentally, or unwittingly, or ...'. And Austin's objection is not just that there are cases where none of these things is true, but rather that in the majority of cases it would not even *make sense* to suppose that something of this kind were true.

If Austin's doctrine were sound here, it would allay fears, experienced by many people other than philosophers, about the rationality of blaming people for what they do. But the doctrine is not sound, and contains two important flaws. The first is that, like so many of the claims which Austin makes in this and other contexts, it can be sustained only as a thesis about speech. The second is that, even if this were not so, the doctrine involves the illegitimate assumption that we can read off the features of the world from an examination of the features of existing language. I shall now try to justify these charges.

When Austin says that the *natural economy of language* dictates that we may not modify most descriptions of action, he does not enlarge on what he takes that natural economy to be. But a plausible interpretation is available. A prime function of language is to communicate something to another person, and when we use it for this purpose it is in our interests to use it as efficiently as possible. Now in order to achieve this there are certain principles which we shall need to observe in our acts of communication. One such principle, which I suppose is fairly obvious, is that to communicate efficiently we should convey the maximum information consistent with what we believe to be the needs and interests of our audience. I don't say to you 'There's a man in your bedroom' if I can say to you instead 'Your husband is in your bedroom'. Clearly if I observe some such principle I am likely to save time by avoiding the need for further acts of communication ('What man?' 'Your husband'), and I am less likely to mislead. (If I just say 'a man' you might reasonably conclude that I do not know who he is.) There is a further principle, however, which may be less obvious than this and which could be taken to signify what Austin calls the natural economy of language. This is the principle that in acts of communication we should not convey *more* information than is consistent with the presumed needs and interests of our audience. Or: don't be irrelevant. There are at least the same two reasons for abiding by this principle as there were for the previous one. If I speak irrelevantly I may have to waste time in further acts of communication, and I may actively mislead my audience. The slightest infringement of this principle would be one where I include some irrelevant detail in my communication, and a major infringement would be one where the whole content of my communication is of no conceivable interest to my audience, as when I suddenly say to a colleague over coffee, 'You have two eyes, one on each side of your nose.' Now this second principle applies to contexts where we are talking of actions in the following way. Very often — perhaps most of the time

— we wish to know *whether* certain actions were performed and not *how* they were performed, because our prime interest is very often to know what the current state of the world is, rather than how it came to be. This would help to explain why neither excuse-terms nor aggravation-terms would be found in conjunction with most descriptions of action. I want to know whether you posted my letter and I don't much care whether you did so by mistake, by accident, in error or inadvertently: I just want to know where the damn thing is. If that is the case and you say 'I posted it by mistake' rather than simply 'I posted it', then this is an attempt to *make* me care more about the genesis of the current state of affairs; it is an attempt to change the wants of one's audience. Similarly, if I merely want to know whether you attended the meeting, I shall have no interest in how many of the possible aspects of action outlined in section 2 your act exemplified. It will be an infringement of the principle to tell me that you attended it after prior deliberation and paying attention to what you were doing, etc.

It seems to me quite likely that Austin has something like this in mind when he speaks of the natural economy of language. He says, for instance, that when I sit in my chair 'in the usual way ... it *will not do to say* either that I sat in it intentionally or that I did not sit in it intentionally' (PP, p. 190; italics added). This is much more naturally taken as an expression of my second principle than a rejection of the law of excluded middle. More positively in the vein of my own remarks is the claim: 'Only when there is some suggestion that it might have been unintentional does it make *non-misleading* sense to *say*, for example, "I ate my dinner intentionally" ' (PP, p. 284; italics added). But if I have interpreted Austin correctly, this confirms my suggestion that his thesis is one about speech. My principles govern acts of communication, and, as is shown by the examples used to illustrate them, there is a distinction between *what can be said* within the restrictions they impose and *what is true*. It is, after all, true that you have two eyes, one on each side of your nose. Similarly in Austin's example, even if it will not do to say it, yet it may be true that I ate my dinner intentionally. But then Austin cannot hope to establish by *this* claim that it is not possible to attach an excuse- or an aggravation-term to most descriptions of action. Given the possibility of extending the wants of one's audience, the adding of some modifier to most or even all action-descriptions cannot be ruled out. General problems about responsibility are, therefore, not so easily brushed aside.[1]

My second objection was that Austin illicitly moves from the structure of language to a conclusion about the structure of the world. This is a separate defect, and does not rest on the fact that Austin's thesis is at best true only of speech. For suppose not only that it were conversationally inept to modify an action-description most of the time, but also that no term of excuse or aggravation could truthfully be applied. It would still not follow that most actions were 'simple' in the way Austin requires that they should be, for what we are implicitly supposing — all we can fairly suppose — is that no *existing* term of these types could be applied. But we might yet discover something about the nature of actions which causes us to *construct* such a modifying term which we feel does apply to most or even all actions. This may seem a very remote and academic possibility, but consider how the situation has changed since Freud. It might be argued (I do not say that this is correct) that 'unconsciously motivated' is a modifier which actually does apply to most or all actions. Of course, someone might argue that it is problematic just what consequences this would have, if true, for freedom and responsibility, but I have in any case already expressed misgivings about Austin's assumption that we can just unpack these notions into the various modifying expressions. My point now is that the list of modifiers is not something which is given once for all time. If the revolution in our thought about ourselves which Freud prompted can alter the list (and Austin himself recognizes that 'compulsive' is a recent addition, PP, p. 204), then so might some future revolution which we are not yet in a position to describe. Only by making the wholly unjustified conservative assumption that our current vocabulary already takes note of any important features of action can we reach the conclusion that most actions are 'simple' in the required sense. Austin's methods, therefore, will not be capable of dealing with the problems originally outlined, no matter how far their employment is projected from his own introductory and programmatic remarks.

5. Determinism and action

One specific complaint may be levelled against the preceding discussion. It may seem that I have rescued certain possibilities which Austin's assumptions would exclude, but have given no very substantial reason for taking these possibilities seriously. In particular, I have stressed several times the possibility of entertaining comprehensive doubts about the applicability of the concepts of freedom and responsibility, but have provided little by way of positive grounds for doing so.

Now in fact there is more than one direction from which these comprehensive doubts may stem, but one which I mentioned briefly in section 1 is the assumption of causal determinism. The argument which begins from this assumption and ends in scepticism about freedom and responsibility can be set out in a series of steps. First, the enormously impressive record of modern science in detecting and accounting for causal connexions between events in the world gives some ground for taking seriously the assumption of causal determinism, *viz.*

(1) Everything which happens is caused.

But when an event is caused to happen, it cannot but happen, its occurrence becomes inevitable. Given a specific cause — say, the administration of a large dose of arsenic — then there is no possibility of any event occurring other than the appropriate effect, the demise of the victim. Hence,

(2) Everything which happens must happen.

But if all events occur inevitably, then alternative outcomes are ruled out. so

(3) Nothing can happen except what does happen.

Further, if human actions are themselves events subject to causal determination then

(4) No one can ever do anything except what he does do.

Translating this into the past tense, since it is often actions already performed which come under review,

(5) No one could ever have done anything except what he did.

But we recall from section 1 that the picture we have of a free agent is that of a being confronting open possibilities and realizing one rather than another. If that is not so, then

(6) No one ever acts freely.

Moreover, if the performance of an action has its determinants elsewhere than in the agent's free choice, then

(7) No one is ever responsible for what he has done.

And if that is true, then equally

(8) No one can ever reasonably be blamed for what he has done.

This is the most skeletal possible form of an argument which can be developed with a great deal of plausibility.[2] With much of the resulting debate we shall not be concerned, vital though this is for a full answer to the difficulties raised by the argument. Indeed, we shall not be especially concerned with that part of the argument which relates determinism to responsibility. For the fact is that we have enough on our hands even if the argument is allowed only to reach premise (4). On the face of it, if (1)–(4) are true then this necessitates some radical readjustments to our conception of the world and our relation to it. Deeply rooted in our thinking is the assumption that there are unrealized possibilities — people spend their middle age lamenting what might have been.

Moreover, I indicated earlier the centrality of capacities in our conception of a human being, the idea of having the power to perform certain actions even at times when one is not actually performing them. All of this, it seems, will need revision if the argument can be made to stick.

It is with one aspect of these earlier stages of the argument that Austin is concerned in 'Ifs and Cans'. His target is the view that the fears expressed in the argument are ill-founded and that, broadly, causal determinism and the conceptions we have of human agency and human powers in general simply pass each other by. Such is the view expressed by Moore (1912). Moore's claims are made with the utmost tentativeness (and couched in the most tortured prose), but his overall strategy is clear enough. In a nutshell, he argues that the claim made in (4) is ambiguous. If causal determinism is true it will follow that, *in one sense*, no one can do otherwise than he does; but there is a second sense in which people very often can act otherwise than they do, a sense which is unaffected by the truth of determinism and which is also the sense relevant to freedom and responsibility.

Moore supports his position in the following way. First, we often make a distinction between two actions, neither of which was actually performed, in terms of their respective possibility. It may be that I neither walked a mile in twenty minutes this morning nor ran two miles in five minutes; but the first of these actions is·a possibility in a way in which the second is not, and there is no more natural way of expressing this than saying that (in some sense) I could have performed the first but not the second. And Moore is insistent that this is not merely something which we do say but something we are entitled to say (*op. cit.* p. 107). The next task is for him to give an analysis of the sense in question, in order to show that the distinction is a legitimate one and that it survives the truth of causal determinism. Moore suggests that it is indisputably true that I could have walked a mile in twenty minutes in the sense that I could have done so *if* I had chosen, or (as he immediately modifies his analysis) that I *should* have done so if I had chosen (*op. cit.,* p. 110). Moreover, this is not something which a clear-headed causal determinist need disagree with, for his doctrine does not require him to believe that my action would have been just as it was even if my *choice* of action had itself been different. On the contrary, that would itself constitute a difference in the causal antecedents of the action, and in that case we should expect that the action might turn out differently (*op. cit.,* p. 111). Now suppose that we accept this analysis and agree that it legitimates the earlier distinction: it is still not enough to eradicate all worries about freedom and responsibility. Perhaps it is true that I should have acted differently if I had chosen to — but if my choice is itself causally determined, that hardly gives me great autonomy in my actions, or the resulting responsibility. Moore agrees, and he argues that for me to 'have Free Will' it is necessary not only that I could have acted otherwise, where this is construed in the sense just explained, but also that I could have *chosen* to act otherwise, where this is construed on exactly the same pattern, i.e. that I should have chosen to act otherwise if I had chosen to make the choice. (The formulation is Moore's, *op. cit.,* p. 114.) He adds to these conditions a third — that no one should be able to tell in advance what choice I am going to make — argues that all three conditions are often true, that they are probably jointly sufficient for an agent's being free, and that they are certainly compatible with causal determinism (*op. cit.,* p. 115).

In these remarks we have a theory about what it is to have the power to act, how we find out what powers an agent has, and how these matters are affected (or rather, if Moore is right, how they are unaffected) by the truth of determinism. Moore offers a modern version of the view put forward by a long succession of philosophers, including Hobbes, Hume and Mill, that determinism does not have any worrying consequences for human action.

Austin rejects all of Moore's major contentions, but he states that his concern is not with the problem of free will but only with the question 'whether it is ever true, and if so in what sense, that a man could have done something other than what he did actually do' (PP, p. 206). His chief preoccupation, in other words, is with the truth and the analysis of statements such as (4) in the original determinist argument ('no one can ever do anything except what he does do'). His discussion is difficult and at times very rarified: I hope I have said enough about the serious questions lying behind it to show why it is worthwhile to examine it. These larger questions must temporarily recede into the background while the various analytical possibilities are explored in some detail.

In the early stages of his argument Moore had stressed the distinction between saying someone 'absolutely' could have acted differently and saying that he could have acted differently *if he had chosen to* (*op. cit.*, pp. 12–13). By focusing on the latter he obviously aims to make easier his job of taking the sting out of the determinist argument. If a claim about unrealized possibilities is only a hypothetical claim about what the agent's powers would have been if things had been different in a certain definite respect, then this is something the determinist need not dispute. But are Moore's assumptions here correct? Austin suggests that, superficial grammatical form notwithstanding, the statement 'I could have done otherwise if I had chosen to' does not express a hypothetical claim. He proposes two tests which must be passed for a statement 'if p, then q' to be genuinely conditional (PP, pp. 209–10):

(*i*) From 'if p, then q' we can infer 'if not-q, then not-p'. For example, from 'if I ran then I panted', we can infer 'if I did not pant I did not run'.

(*ii*) From 'if p, then q' we can *not* infer 'q, whether or not p'. For example, from 'if I ran then I panted' we can *not* infer 'I panted, whether or not I ran'.

Austin objects that 'I can if I choose' fails both tests. We cannot draw from this the inference 'if I cannot I do not choose to'; and we *can* infer 'I can, whether I choose to or not'. How, then, should we construe the structure of 'I can if I choose'? Austin suggests that the 'if' signifies not conditionality but doubt or hesitation, and he offers a large number of alternative interpretations of the statement, depending upon context (PP, p. 212). What they have in common is that 'the *assertion*, positive and complete, that "I can", is linked to the *raising of the question* whether I choose to, which may be relevant in a variety of ways' (*ibid.*; Austin's italics).

There is another way of putting Austin's point which helps to make clear its relevance to the problem of free will. When we say, with reference to the past, that someone *could have* done something, this one verbal form masks two possible claims: that it *was* within his power, or that it *would have been* within his power (cf. PP, p. 215). The idea that something would have been within an agent's power is incomplete and does indeed need a specification of the condition upon which it would have been within his power. But Austin's point is that the 'could have' in 'I could have done it if I had chosen' is not of this but of the first type. The addition 'if I had chosen' does not serve to give the condition upon which it would have been within my power, but rather has the role which Austin ascribes to it. And then if 'I could have done otherwise if I had chosen' expresses categorically that something *was* within my power, it is not so clear that a determinist will readily agree that this is often true.

If Austin's arguments are cogent it is a serious matter for Moore's strategy. But are they cogent? It is certainly possible to disagree with him over how 'I could have if I had chosen' fares in his two tests for conditionality, and thereby to disagree with his understanding of what it is to be able to do something if one chooses. It is not obvious to me that we can *infer* 'I can' from 'I can if I choose to' (to use the more straightforward present-tense version). That is, it is not obvious to me that my choices have no influence on what my powers are — and Austin offers no argument to the contrary, he merely assumes this to be so. This assumption, that my choices make a difference to what I do but not to what I *can* do, is something which could be fully justified only after giving an account of what it is in general to have the power to perform some action, but one point which is relevant to our deciding the question may be mentioned now. There is a distinction, which will crop up again in section 6, between (*a*) having the power to perform some particular action at some particular moment and (*b*) having the power to perform actions of some general type. Matching this is the distinction between (*a*) the alternatives which are open to an agent in one circumscribed situation, and (*b*) his repertoire of general skills, capacities, etc. Now it is in relation to (*b*) that Austin's claim is plausible: it does not seem likely that my choice at one given moment has an influence on what I can do in general. But it is arguable that exactly the reverse is true in (*a*). What I can do in *this* situation does indeed depend on what choice I make. If so, then we need a more elaborate account of powers than Austin provides at this stage before we can make any confident pronouncements on what it means to be able to do something if one chooses. Only then can we trace back the path from this question to the questions about freedom and determinism.

Whatever we decide about the status of being able to act if one chooses, we need an account of being able to act *simpliciter* if our interest is in the question whether it is ever true that a person could have done something which he did not do. Moore may have been alive to this. It is obviously circular to give an analysis of what a man could have done in terms of what he could have done if he had chosen, and this may be the 'possible complication' which Moore mentions (*op. cit.*, p. 110) and which leads him immediately to modify his suggestion. In its place he proposes that what a man could have done is what he *would* have done if he had chosen. Here we do not attempt to explain 'could' by using that very term in our explanation. This, then, is the proposed analysis of having it in one's power to act in a certain way. And, as Austin points out (PP, pp. 214, 217–18), even if the comment 'he could have acted otherwise' is not itself conditional, it is a separate question whether it should be given an *analysis* which is conditional in form. This leaves us with two questions: whether the concept of having the power to act should be given a conditional analysis, and whether the particular analysis which Moore gives is acceptable. For there are other possible analyses of the same type. There is the suggestion, for example, that what I could have done is a matter of what I should have done if I had *tried* to, and a more complicated analysis which Austin also considers (PP, pp. 219ff.).

With regard to Moore's own analysis, Austin objects that 'I shall if I choose' does not express a conditional claim, any more than 'I can if I choose' does; rather, it asserts something 'categorical' about me (PP, p. 214; Austin's scare-quotes). Once again, if Austin's claim is correct that 'I shall if I choose' does not state that the action will be a causal consequence of my choosing, this is likely to have repercussions for Moore's attempt to take the sting out of determinism. To support his claim, Austin contrasts 'I shall if I choose' with something like 'I shall ruin him if I am extravagant', which he says does express a connexion between action and causal condition, on the grounds that it 'makes good sense in general to stress the "shall" ' in the former but not the latter (*ibid.*). By way of more positive comment on the proposed analysis, he suggests that ' "I shall" is not an assertion of *fact* but an expression of *intention*, verging towards the giving of some undertaking: and the *if*, consequently, is the *if* not of condition but of *stipulation*' (PP, pp. 213–14; Austin's italics). Clearly, if all this is correct Moore's analysis is completely misguided. To say merely that I *can* do something is far removed from expressing any kind of intention to do it, and in that case it will not be possible to analyse the first by means of the second.

But how secure are Austin's own claims? It is evident that his attention is here directed exclusively to speech acts, and to the circumstances associated with the actual utterance of a string of words — only in that way is it possible for him to talk of whether I can stress the 'shall'. Moreover, he adds a further limitation by concentrating on the first-person speech act. Even if 'I shall if I choose' were an expression of intention, 'he will if he chooses' is not, and is probably not related to intention in any other way. The upshot is that if what he says is correct at all it must be construed as a claim about what utterance-acts are possible, given the conventions governing verbal pronouncements, not as a claim to do with the contents of certain utterances and the relations which obtain between them. Of course it looks perverse to draw from 'I shall marry him if I choose' the inference 'if I shall not marry him I do not choose', because it is not easy to imagine circumstances in which I should actually *say* this. But the perspective changes if we concentrate on the statement-content, the core meaning of what I say. We shall then remember that you and I are, in that sense, making the same statement if I say 'I shall if I choose' and you say of me 'he will if he chooses.' If we also remember that conversational oddity does not enter into the relevant questions about statement-contents then we shall see that there really is no problem about the inference here.

On the other hand, it can fairly be said that although we may in this way establish that 'I shall if I choose' is genuinely conditional, we have not done anything to show that it has the least plausibility as an analysis of 'I can'. Now Austin points out that if we are bent on seeking a conditional analysis, this particular one is not the most plausible, and he suggests that it would be more plausible to analyse 'I can' as 'I shall if I try' (PP, p. 218). I think there are at least two reasons for agreeing with Austin about this. First, the connexion between trying to do something and doing it is different from the connexion between choosing to do something and doing it, and it is the first connexion which is more appropriate for the purpose of analysing the power to act. A man may choose to do something but then subsequently rescind his choice or else, for a variety of reasons, fail to follow it through. In that case it may be true that he can do something but not necessarily true that he would if he chose to — perhaps because he vacillates. In contrast, trying to do something is more intimately connected with performance. For one thing, the temporal relations are different here: I can choose now to do something tomorrow, but if I try now to do something then now is also the time for my doing it. To try is already to be launched into the action, as it were. Connected with this is the second point. Austin argues that whereas what a man *can* do depends on his abilities and opportunities, what he *would* do depends also upon his motives (PP, p. 224). We shall therefore need to build into the 'if ... ' part of our analysis a factor which will take care of this, and we may feel that trying is a factor of the appropriate kind (PP, p. 228n.).

All the same, the conditional analysis involving the notion of trying is one to which Austin grants 'plausibility, but no more' (PP, p. 218n.):

'Consider the case where I miss a very short putt and kick myself because I could have holed it. It is not that I should have holed it if I had tried: I did try, and missed. It is not that I should have holed it if conditions had been different: that might of course be so, but I am talking about conditions as they precisely were, and asserting that I could have holed it. There is the rub. Nor does "I can hole it this time" mean that I shall hole it this time if I try or if anything else: for I may try and miss, and yet not be convinced that I could not have done it; indeed, further experiments may confirm my belief that I could have done it that time although I did not.'

(*ibid.*)

In fact, Austin offers no other arguments against the proposed analysis, and this one is not in all respects satisfactory. It raises many questions about the connexion between power and action, some of which I shall comment on later, but here its force consists in offering an example where what is expressed in the analysis is not true but where we should still want to say that I could have performed the action in question. Construed in this way, it is open to the rejoinder that perhaps we ought *not* to say in such circumstances that I could have performed that action. If the analysis turned out to be plausible, informative and effective in a wide variety of contexts, then this might provide a reason for changing what we might otherwise want to say in this case. Austin does indeed consider one argument for doubting whether we should say that I could have performed the action in this case, and it is an argument from a determinist standpoint. Surely, if I tried and missed then something must have caused me to miss, so that I could not, after all, have done it? Austin does not actually say this argument will not do; but he points out that it conflicts with 'the traditional beliefs enshrined in the word *can*' (*ibid.*), and it is fairly obvious which side he will be on in a dispute between the conclusions of modern science and the beliefs embodied in a time-tested concept. But when we recall that the avowed purpose of his discussion is to decide *whether it is ever true*, and if so in what sense, that a man could have done something which he did not do (cf. PP, p. 206), we cannot but regard his argument here as question-begging.

Still, these deficiencies are not crucial for testing the adequacy of the analysis, for other arguments of a more general kind are available which show that it ought to be rejected. First, there is the difficulty parallel to the one considered by Moore in putting forward his original analysis. Surely, for it to be true that I can do something it must be true not only that I should do it if I tried, but also that I can *try* to do it? It might be true of a man bound hand-and-foot that he would light a cigarette *if* he tried; but since he is prevented from trying, it is not true that he can do it. If we followed Moore's own strategy at this point we should supplement our analysis in the same way: for a man to be able to do something it must be true both that he would do it if he tried and that he can try to do it, where this is taken to mean that he would try to do it if he tried to try. Now it might be objected that 'trying to try' is an incoherent notion. But a sufficiently tenacious proponent of the analysis might deny this; he might say that 'trying' denotes something like opening a matchbox and 'trying to try' denotes something like moving an arm muscle. Let us not object to this: his difficulties are still not at an end. We may now raise the same form of objection all over again, and point out that it is also necessary that the agent should *be able* to try to try, not just that something would follow *if* he tried to try. If the proponent repeats his previous move at this stage he is in a fix; for, granting for the sake of argument that 'trying to try to try' makes sense, he will by the same principle need to add that the agent *can* try to try to try, and so *ad infinitum*. It will then follow that his analysis of having the power to perform an action consists of an infinite number of conditions and thus can never be completed. The analysis should therefore be rejected. (For further discussion, cf. Graham 1973.)

6. The analysis of ability
Let us review the situation. The determinist argument sketched at the beginning of the previous section cast doubt on the belief that we are at least sometimes free agents, capable of initiating one out of several possible courses of action. Whether this belief was correct, it seemed, would depend partly on whether it is true that everything which happens is caused and partly on what it means to say that an agent can perform one action or another. Moore proposed an analysis of the idea of having it within one's power to act which would allow us to keep our beliefs about agency *whether or not* universal causation obtains. We have agreed with

Austin, however, in rejecting Moore's analysis (even if Austin's own reasons for doing so are dubious). This still leaves us with the question what to put in its place.

Austin himself does not offer any alternative analysis, but he does make two remarks which carry implications about the structure of the concept of having the power to act.

> 'We are tempted to say that "He can" sometimes mean just that he has the ability, with *nothing said* about opportunity, sometimes *just* that he has the chance, with nothing said about ability, sometimes, however, that he really actually *fully can* here and now, having both ability and opportunity.'
>
> (PP, p. 230; Austin's italics)

He then goes on, perhaps partly retracting what he had just suggested:

> 'The only point of which I feel certain is that such verbs as *can* and *know* have each an all-in paradigm use, around which cluster and from which divagate, little by little and along different paths, a whole series of other uses, for many of which, though perhaps not for all, a synonymous expression ("opportunity", "realize" and so on) can be found.'
>
> (*ibid.*)

Although he expresses misgivings about whether talking of 'senses' and so on will be adequate for dealing with the matter, Austin is here doing something very close to multiplying senses of 'can', and in this he has been followed by many other philosophers. In opposition to this, and in line with the theoretical economy associated with a narrow theory of meaning, I shall put forward a simpler interpretation of the structure of abilities, but one which is adequate for the work which the concept of ability can legitimately be expected to do. I shall give an analysis of ability which is an alternative to the type I agree with Austin in rejecting, or at least sufficient of an analysis to enable us to see some of the implications it holds for problems of freedom. The analysis is also an alternative in *style* to those typically offered by Austin. This shows itself most clearly in the fact that I am prepared to treat as roughly synonymous a number of terms such as 'capacity', 'ability', 'power', and so on. There may be differences between these terms, but they are not germane to the present purpose, and I reject Austin's suggestion that all such terms must be dealt with before we get to grips with 'can' (PP, p. 229n.).[3] Related to this, although I *begin* from a consideration of the things we say about an agent's powers and the circumstances in which we say them, some of this is not left intact by the analysis. My aim is to produce an informative, systematic and acceptable account of an idea which may in practice be applied in an inconsistent and obscure way, and possibly not uniformly by all users.

There are two different contexts where we need to talk of what an agent can do: those where he has the power to perform some particular action in a particular historical situation (what I shall call a *situational power*), and those where he has the power to perform actions of some general type (what I shall call a *general power*). The difference is captured in the difference between the following two statements:

(*1*) John can break that stick here and now (situational power)

(*2*) John can break sticks (general power).

Both situational and general powers can be described in a highly specific or a very unspecific way ('John can break walking sticks into two equal parts with his bare hands', 'John can walk here and now'), but the main distinction between them is that a situational power is possessed by an agent at a moment in time (more or less), whereas a general power is possessed over a *span* of time. This relates to the fact that the most obvious way to isolate a particular action is by means of a spatio-temporal indicator ('John can break *that* stick *here and now*'), whereas a *type* of action can be specified entirely in general terms in such a way that the type can be exemplified on more than one occasion. From this we can draw the idea of *matching* situational and general powers: a situational and general power are matching when the action or type of action they qualify is described by the same terms, the only difference being in the addition of the necessary 'uniqueness-indicators' in the situational power. Thus, (*1*) and (*2*) involve the ascription of a matching pair of situational and general powers.

One reason we have for making the distinction between these two kinds of power is that it can put us on our guard against a certain confusion. It is clear enough from (*1*) and (*2*) that the verbal form of two statements ascribing matching situational and general abilities is very similar; but having a certain situational ability is compatible with *not* having the matching general ability, and vice versa. It is perhaps the latter which is more easily seen. It may be that it is within my power in general to balance ten cups on top of each other but not within my power to do so here and now, either because ten cups are not available or because I suffer from a momentary flush of embarrassment which prevents me from doing so. Being able to perform actions of a general type over a period of time does not entail being able to perform a particular action of that type at any given moment within that span. The reverse, though less obvious, is also true. People often manage to do things by fluke; that is, they perform an action which is of a type which, in general, they are unable to perform. Now a man's performing a particular, token action is sufficient to prove that he *can* perform it, i.e. that he has the relevant situational power, but if he is able to do so only by fluke then he lacks the matching general power.

My emphasis on the two kinds of power, and my insistence on the disconnexion between them, may seem to suggest that I am myself multiplying senses of 'can' and have merely reduced the number of senses to two from Austin's three. This is not necessarily so. My distinction arises from a perfectly general need we have to talk of action in two different ways, both of particular actions and of action-types, and so far this has nothing especially to do with powers.[4] We could equally distinguish between wanting to eat cream buns and wanting to eat that cream bun now, but that would not show that 'want' has two different senses. Whether we talk of different senses in the case of abilities depends on whether the analysis of 'can' differs significantly as between expressing situational and general powers. I shall argue now that it does not. The analysis which I propose in both contexts is essentially causal, and it will therefore obviously have repercussions for the questions of freedom and responsibility. But it is far from obvious just *what* the repercussions are. In any case, we should test the adequacy of any proposed analysis on its own feet and only then see what follows about these other matters, rather than constantly looking over our shoulders in order to arrive at an analysis which allows us to keep our prejudices about freedom and responsibility intact.

It is convenient to begin with the idea of *not* possessing some situational power. Where we are prepared to assert that someone cannot perform a particular action in a circumscribed situation, e.g. 'John cannot light a cigarette now', we are generally prepared to cite some feature either of the agent or of his circumstances which prevents him from performing that action — there are no matches around, there are matches but they are damp, John has atrophied arms, John is unconscious, and so on. I suggest that the presence of such different factors, or different kinds of factor, has no bearing on the *sense* of the statement that the agent cannot perform the action. The most economical view to take over the analysis of that is that it does not involve a description or naming of the factor which functions as an obstacle or impediment to action; rather, it merely involves the idea that *there is* such a factor. To name it or describe it is then to give the grounds for making that statement. In other words, you can understand the content of what I say here, even if you have no idea what my reasons are for saying it. More than this, suppose that I say 'John cannot enter the room' and that my claim is grounded in a theory of phobia which I hold, believing that a certain mental state can function as a factor of the appropriate kind. Then you may well understand and indeed accept what I say, even if you have no acquaintance at all with the theory to which I subscribe. This explains how the development of new theories of human behaviour can alter our view of the range of someone's situational powers, without our having to suppose that each time this happens a new sense of 'power' or 'can' is called into existence.

I said that this analysis was essentially causal, and this should now be made explicit. Normally, an obstacle is something which may be got round or through or over, but I am here using 'obstacle' in a stronger, technical sense, to signify a factor which is causally sufficient for the non-performance of the action. When an agent cannot perform a particular action, there is a factor which causally *rules out* the action. Two further points. Given the causal complexity of different situations, the question whether a certain feature constitutes an obstacle will depend upon context. A headache or a 25 m.p.h. head-wind may be causally sufficient for the non-achievement of a four-minute mile in one situation but not in another, or for one agent but not for another. It will not usually be possible to say that a given feature is, just in general, an obstacle to the performance of a given action. Secondly, and related to this, a feature may exist over a period of time under some general description and only at a later moment qualify as an obstacle. But it is existence at the appropriate moment which is crucial. If it is true that you cannot crack that nut at time *t* then the factor which causally excludes this action may have been in existence long before time t, but it must exist *at* time t.

The analysis can now be extended to the idea of having (rather than not having) a situational power. For it to be true that I can perform an action, it must be true that there is *no* feature the existence of which would causally rule out my performance of the action. Every factor which, in that situation, would causally exclude the action is in fact absent. That is what I suggest it means to say that I have a situational power.

It is here that my disagreement with Austin's remarks is most apparent. He had said that sometimes 'he can' means just that an agent has an opportunity, with nothing said about ability, and that there is a whole series of uses of 'can' besides the 'all-in, paradigm use' (PP, p. 230). But the disagreement is not just a particular one about the analysis of the power to act: it also raises some of the more general issues about method and meaning discussed in chapters II and III. I do not necessarily deny Austin the datum that we probably say 'he can' when the stringent conditions of my analysis are not fulfilled, but there can be more than one explanation for this. Suppose that I say to someone, 'It's ten o'clock, so you can hear the news'. When I say this I may very well *take for granted* that a certain range of possible obstacles is absent, that the person I am speaking to has normal hearing and so on, and intend to focus on a different range in order to make a point not about the agent but about the external circumstances. In this way I can hope to convey a message only about the agent's opportunity. But this can be explained by reference to the general distinction between what *I* mean and what my statement means, instead of invoking different senses of the particular verb 'can'. I use a statement which has one unequivocal meaning in order to convey a more limited message than that contained in the statement itself. Connected with this is the further point that what is for Austin, given his views on current usage, a hard unalterable datum is for me something which goes into the melting-pot of analysis and may become transformed or evaporate in the process. If the person I speak to is, in fact, deaf then whereas Austin would say that he still can in one sense hear the news, I should say that we must withdraw the claim that he can: an obstacle exists in an area which we had (wrongly, as it happens) discounted. In the same way, if I have two broken arms and know nothing about computers then it is not that I cannot, in two different senses, programme this computer; rather, I cannot, unequivocally, but for two different reasons. In short, analysis does not leave everything as it is, so far as our descriptions of the world are concerned. The investigation into what we say and the rationale behind our utterances should lead us to classify and order them, accord priority to some rather than others, and, depending on the content of the rationale, be prepared to withdraw the application of a concept in a certain kind of situation. Another example of the same would be what Austin refers to in passing as 'the *can* ... of legal or other *right*' (PP, p. 213; Austin's italics). We often say things like 'I cannot meet you tonight because I promised to stay at home'. There is a far stronger case here for arguing that this involves a different sense of 'can' from the one in my analysis, but there is also some plausibility in treating it as an off-centre or metaphorical use, or even a misuse, of the *same* sense of 'can'. It would then be a matter, perhaps, of giving an explanation rather than a good rationale for this use. Nor would this be difficult: it is no doubt a psychologically useful prop to regard legal and moral considerations as not merely persuasive but actually causally effective.

A doubt may persist that I am making much out of nothing here. Surely, in a sense, we all agree about the facts in the cases under discussion? Why does it matter that we should decide to apply or withhold particular words such as 'can' or 'is able to' in connexion with them? Is this not, at bottom, a merely verbal and barren dispute? The context in which the analysis is conducted should make it clear why this is not so. The descriptions which we decide upon for the various cases matter because of the inferences which we then go on to make about them, and the consequences this has for our attitudes and reactions. For example, we saw in the original determinist argument that intimately bound up with the idea of an agent's being able to embark on a course of action is the idea that the agent possesses freedom in that respect. This provides us with a clear example of how an apparently academic question of analysis can have extraneous importance. If it is allowed that there is a sense of 'can' which relates *only* to the state of the agent and not at all to his opportunities, then a whole cluster of spurious freedoms may thereby be generated. On that view, we shall be able to say that a penniless but able-bodied beggar has the freedom to go and dine at the Ritz. But the whole point of terms like 'can' is to express what is *possible*: if they come to be used in contexts where a course of action is, for whatever reason, *not* possible, then the purpose in employing such terms is frustrated. That is one reason why I insist on the unrestricted scope of obstacles in my analysis of situational ability. If we sometimes say 'he can' to mean only that it is nothing about *him* which prevents him, then we ought to stop saying it.

Before considering further the practical implications of the analysis I need to say something about *general* powers of action. General powers, I suggested, exist over a period of time, whether long or short, and although when we talk of such powers we may not explicitly assign them to a particular period of time, it must be possible to do so. I used to be able to turn a handspring, say, from the time I learnt until around the age of eighteen, or the doctor tells me after a successful operation that I shall now be able to walk unaided, implicitly indefinitely into the future. I suggest that what is required for me to possess any given general power is that within the implicit time-span there must be a variety of circumstances in which

I possess the matching situational power. 'Variety' here covers two things. It relates, first, to number. If my performing actions of a given type is causally excluded on every occasion but one within some time-span, then I do not possess the ability in general to perform actions of that type. But it relates also to the qualitative nature of those occasions. Suppose that my walking a tightrope is causally excluded on all occasions except those where freak weather conditions occur. Then it would again be false to say that I was able, in general, to walk a tightrope. That would require more than the absence of obstacles in particular, and particularly special, circumstances. (What I do possess here is a different general capacity, specified by a different action-description, *viz*. I can, in general, walk-a-tightrope-in-freak-weather-condit-ions.)

If this account is correct, then the need to multiply senses of 'can' will be avoided. We have accepted the need to talk of both situational and general powers, but the same kind of conditions govern the possession of either type of power, and the variation in those conditions arises from the difference between action-types and particular actions; and I have already said that that is a general distinction which it will in any case be necessary to make in several other contexts.

What can we now say about the determinist argument laid out at the beginning of section 5, in the light of this account of abilities? Since my analysis is essentially causal, it may seem that I am committed to allowing the argument to go through unscathed. Things are not quite as clear-cut as this, however. In the first place, and this is no trivial matter, what we are able to say about an agent's *general* powers will in one way be unaffected by the truth of causal determinism. It is obvious, and a determinist has no reason to deny, that the complex of causal circumstances in which agents find themselves is constantly changing. Hence, even if at any given moment the causal circumstances make some particular action inevitable, nevertheless it is perfectly possible that over a period of time there will be *other* sets of circumstances which causally allow *other* actions. Consequently, although at some moment it may be that it is causally impossible for me to perform some action A, this will not necessarily disbar anyone from ascribing to me the general capacity to perform A-type actions. This is important because, as I have already indicated, central to our idea of a human being is the notion of a being which not only possesses properties which are 'there', so to speak, but also latent properties, a repertoire of capacities and general skills. If my arguments have been correct then the truth of determinism will not force us to rebuild a picture of human beings which leaves this dimension out altogether.

But what about situational powers? Here the problems are thrown into sharp relief by reconsidering the case Austin discusses, where a man fails in his attempt to perform some particular action, such as holing a short putt, but remains convinced that he could have performed it (PP, p. 218n.). Now it follows from what has just been said that the agent may be justified in claiming the general ability to perform action *of that type*, whatever the causal antecedents of his behaviour on this occasion. But Austin insists on more than this: he insists that the agent is entitled to say that he could have performed *that* action *then*. The difficulty is that he provides no analysis of powers which would show *why* the agent may claim this, despite his failure. Moreover, he has only unsupported counter-assertion to offer in answer to the suggestion that if the agent tried and failed, then there must have been something which caused him to fail, so that he was incapable of succeeding. 'Abilities' he replies, 'sometimes fail for no reason' (*ibid.*). But I suspect that this reply is both contrary to fact and contrary to reason. That is, it is not just the causal regularity of the actual world which would lead us to search for a reason for the man's failure: it also seems reasonable *a priori* to suppose that if an agent fails to perform some action then there must have been something in the circumstances, or in the agent's chosen means to his end, which were inadequate or inappropriate for succeeding. We may not know *what* factor is responsible, but it is reasonable to look for one. The implication of this is that in the kind of case under discussion we may very well *not* be justified in ascribing to the agent a situational ability to perform that action which he failed to perform. Given *that* situation, and given how he behaved, it may be that he could not have holed the putt.

Failure in the sense of frustrated attempt is something different from mere non-performance, however. If an agent merely *did* not do something, there is not the same case for thinking *a priori* that there must have been some factor which prevented him. On the contrary, this depends precisely on the contingent question whether all events, including human actions, are causally determined to be just as they are. We thus see that my analysis *on its own* does not tell us how far the determinist argument can go. What we can say, however, is that *if* all human actions are causally determined then it follows, in the light of my analysis, that it is always mistaken to ascribe to an agent the situational ability to have acted differently. It will always be wrong to say that someone could have performed some particular action except, vacuously and uninformatively, in those cases where the action *was* performed. For, if all actions were causally determined, it will be false to say that there was no causal obstacle to the agent's acting differently there and then.

It would take several further books to consider in full the proper impact of determinism on our conception of ourselves. I have merely tried to show that it would imply the falsity of one firmly-held belief about our status as agents, on a plausible analysis of what it is to have the power to act in a certain way. In contrast, Austin simply re-asserts the firmly-held belief and implicitly casts doubt thereby on the truth of determinism. But he produces no analysis to justify the move. What we ordinarily say and what we ordinarily believe remain unclarified and unchallenged.

7. Conclusion

Though my criticisms of Austin have been severe, it would be wrong to leave the reader with the impression that I think there is no value in his work, either in the philosophy of action or in general. Where he takes language as his subject matter there are the theories of performatives and illocution, which whatever their limitations, contain important insights into the difference which language makes to the world. Indeed, there are major and minor insights scattered throughout his work, into the nature and structure of language. In the present context, Austin's discussion threw into sharp relief many of the problems associated with the language we use to talk about people's abilities, and made it clear that these were an important part of the traditional problem of free will. If my claim in Chapter II was correct, that our language is a mediating influence on our interpretation of the world, then it would be foolish not to welcome information about it, and such information Austin frequently provides. What one has to be on one's guard against, however, is the repeated tendency to suppose that an insight into a particular form of language is really an insight into the nature of things, how the world is or how people are. In the early part of this chapter I tried to show how Austin makes this unjustified transition with regard to the nature of action and an agent's knowledge of his own actions. A similar shift occurs in his discussion of powers of action. He raises the question whether his arguments might not as easily be assigned to grammar as to philosophy (PP, p. 231), and, as we saw, pits against the plausibility of determinism the fact that it conflicts with the traditional beliefs enshrined in the word 'can'. Now of course this is a transition which would not be at all unjustified if certain of Austin's other assumptions were acceptable. If we could suppose that our existing language contained all the wisdom necessary for understanding the world and presented a structurally clear and complete picture of it, there would be no problem. We could then regard the information which Austin provides as, indifferently, information about language or information about the world. But these are suppositions to which we are not entitled, suppositions which we have good reason for rejecting.

In the philosophy of action as elsewhere, it is Austin's conservatism which finally asserts itself as the strongest force in his investigations. Twice in his discussions of action he makes concessions which appear to contradict this, warning us against ignoring the contribution which psychology can make in providing perspectives not captured in existing ordinary language (PP, pp. 189, 203-4). But the concessions are nominal, being followed in each case by the suggestion that if the perspectives were of practical importance they probably would already have found a place in our language. There is little enough to be said at any time for attempting to stifle possible change in this way, but there is the added disincentive in the present context that an insistence on preserving what we do already say may involve preserving an inconsistency. It is quite possible that considerations from one area should lead us to ascribe a certain kind of freedom to an agent, and considerations from another area lead us to say the opposite. Now we have seen places where Austin exhibits a lack of concern when faced with such a possibility. He recognizes that in dealing with a hybrid language like English we are likely to find different, disparate and even conflicting ways of thought encapsulated, and he asks rhetorically why we should not simply accept that situation (PP, p. 203n. Cf. PP, p. 184). The short answer is that in this area the different possible conceptions of agency and of the freedom (or otherwise) which an agent has are likely to lead to different *treatment* of agents. Where we are talking of ways of looking at things which lead to action, we are forced to make a choice between conflicting ways. It is the specific virtue of philosophy, when it is done properly, to help us with these choices, by making us conscious of the implications of the conceptions with which we operate and probing their inadequacies. A philosophy like Austin's, which is essentially uncritical of current ways of looking at things, is almost bound to be deficient in delivering up these benefits.

There is one further point, which I have tried to exclude from the main part of my discussion, because it may be thought to be a matter of purely personal reaction which is irrelevant to the content or the method of Austin's philosophy. I began this book by comparing Austin's influence to Wittgenstein's, and I suggested that my criticisms of Austin would apply in large measure to many other philosophers, specifically including the later Wittgenstein. In both, for example, there is the excessive premium placed on existing usage and the conservatism associated with this. But there is a marked difference in tone between the two philosophers, and a difference which is not flattering to Austin. With Wittgenstein one has the impression that he was driven to deny that there were any philosophical problems, that ordinary language is perfectly in order and that philosophy leaves everything as it is, because it took him to the verge of madness to suppose otherwise. With Austin one has the impression that ultimately he thought there were no philosophical problems because he was incapable of imagining that the world was anything but a straightforward, unmysterious, unproblematic place. What some would describe as his gentle, ironic humour when he approaches genuinely puzzling and important questions, such as how far an agent can be expected to have the correct view of his own actions or how reliable our perceptions are, seems to me to be nothing less than flippancy. But I hope my discussion has shown that, even if philosophers are not entitled to much respect, philosophical problems are.

Notes

II Philosophy of Language as a Method

[1] And in fact (D) is already an oversimplification of Mackie's final analysis. Cf. *op. cit.*, section 2 and Mackie 1974.

[2] It should be clear that 'creative' is being used here to cover many different uses of language which have in common the negative feature of not correlating with or mapping some part of the world. It might be argued that on this criterion all assertions or judgments are creative, either because they contain particular terms which do not have a mapping function or because they contain an element of *judgment* or *assertion* which does not reflect a pre-existing feature of the world but is, rather, a response to it. In both respects judgments differ from representational pictures, and this is one reason for insisting on the greater complexity of the relation between language and the world than that obtaining between image and thing.

[3] Cf. Hampshire, 1960. This claim has been contested by Urmson and Warnock, 1961, but Austin often argues in a way which seems to commit him to the stronger thesis (e.g. PP, pp. 187, 198, 280–2).

[4] It is sometimes said that it is wrong to accuse Austin of conservatism and hostility to new terminology, on the grounds that he introduces a great deal himself, for example in *How To Do Things With Words* (cf. Urmson and Warnock, *op. cit.*, p. 47; and Pears, 1962, p. 50). But it is significant that nearly all the new terms Austin introduces are *meta*-terms, terms to talk about the way we talk. In practice he nearly always leaves the ground-level corpus, the things we say in talking about the world, unchanged.

5 This is one respect in which philosophy, even a philosophy of language, differs from the adjacent discipline of theoretical linguistics. The chief preoccupation of the theoretical linguist is not to recommend 'correct' usage but to formulate a theory which is adequate for describing and explaining actual usage. As we should expect, however, there are many points of contact between the two disciplines, and it is a dangerous error to suppose that neither has anything to learn from the other.

6 This is well brought out when he discusses his method in French, a language which forces the descriptive/normative ambiguity into the open by having different verb forms for each. Austin says that his question is 'qu'est-ce qu'on *dirait* quand ... ?' (CR, pp. 33–4) — a descriptive question.

III Philosophy of Language as a Subject: Performatives

1 It may, of course, be in a different way in each of these cases. It may also, for reasons already given in Chapter II, section 3, be misleading to use the metaphor of mapping here. But by whatever name we call it, there can be no doubt that the capacity to which I am gesturing is a central one in human nature.

2 Austin also argues that constatives themselves are assessable in terms of felicity (W, pp. 135–8, PP, pp. 248–9). But his argument here is obscure. He certainly shows that a constative utterance can 'go wrong' in some way other than simply failing to be true, as for example when I say 'The cat is on the mat, but I don't believe it is.' It is less clear whether he shows that the defect in such a case has to do with infringement of the same kind of felicity-conditions as in performatives. Cf. Graham, 1974.

3 Minor attempts include, for example, the suggestion that performatives might be characterised in terms of the vocabulary they are composed of (W, p. 59) — a suggestion which looks hopeless from the start.

4 I cannot claim much originality for this account. I have learnt most from Lemmon, 1962; Hedenius, 1963, and Hartnack, 1963.

5 Or, indeed, at any other stage. See Chapter VII, where I also do not offer an analysis of truth.

[6] This is an only slightly amended example provided by my school-mate Charles Grafton. I am grateful to him, though the teacher on the receiving-end of his statement was not.

[7] For the notion of an INUS-condition, cf. Chapter II, section 6 and Mackie 1965.

[8] Two qualifications are necessary here. First, the contrast I claim between the meaning of 'state' and the meaning of 'promise' depends on our distinguishing a 'core' meaning in an utterance and keeping this as general as possible, a position which I defend more fully in Chapter IV, section 3. But secondly, someone might argue that even if this is conceded, there is not a sharp contrast but only a difference of degree between statements like 'I promise' and 'I state', i.e. that there is a continuum running from cases where the required social convention is highly indispensable to cases where it is arguable that self-verification rests wholly on meaning and not at all on (changeable) convention. The shortest way of dealing with this second point is to say that it suggests a result which I should find neither surprising nor worrying. For even if all of Austin's self-verifying examples such as 'I state', 'I maintain', etc., form a continuum with the original performatives, there is still the distinction between them and statements which are not and cannot be self-verifying. To that extent, the idea of a performative would still stand.

IV Philosophy of Language as a Subject: Illocution

[1] I was gratified to discover not only advocacy of a narrow theory but also some of the same arguments in support of it in Wertheimer 1972, Chapter 2. This book should be compulsory reading for all those philosophers in the habit of beginning sentences 'There is a sense in which ... ' For a sensitive discussion of the practical difficulties of realising the aims of a narrow theory, see also Wiggins, *op. cit.*, section 2.

[2] Cf. Dummett, 1973, pp. 93ff., 103ff. As regards sentences, there is one further important respect in which they are crucially different from names. For much of the time we employ entirely original sentences, which have never before been used by anyone else. What matters for my point is that in framing these sentences we make use of a stock of words which are essentially re-applicable.

[3] Skinner, 1970 would say of such cases that they depend on the existence of a mutually recognized convention such that what

I say will be acceptable as a threat (p. 131). This looks to me too like a re-statement of the claim that convention is involved, not an explanation.

4 Austin, for example, makes a provisional division of illocutionary acts into five classes (W, pp. 150ff.), yet even within each of these there is more diversity than would allow a simple summing up of illocution as 'dependent on convention' or whatever.

V Philosophical Problems: Knowledge

1 One could, and philosophers do, spend a great deal of time teasing out the differences between 'adequate evidence', 'good reasons', etc. Such distinctions may be valid, but they are not germane to my purpose and I ignore them.

2 If the further analysis of capacities which I suggest in Chapter VIII, section 6 is anything like correct, then this analysis of knowledge will in any case not be totally distinct from a causal analysis.

3 And my reasons for doing so need not be dubious. I may decide that it is morally more important to perform some action other than the one I promised to.

4 In making this point I should mention that the paper 'Other Minds' was delivered six years before the lectures on which *How To Do Things With Words* is based. 'Know' in fact appears on Austin's list of illocutionary acts with a question mark beside it (W, p. 161). But these considerations do not save Austin from my point: it is not as though he had accepted the distinct nature of the two theories by the later date.

VI Philosophical Problems: Perception

1 There is reason to suppose that when the term 'sense-datum' was originally introduced into philosophical discussion it did not have the meaning given here but was rather used in a non-committal way to mean 'whatever kind of thing it is which is perceived' (cf. Locke, 1967, pp. 21-3). However, it is now most commonly used with the meaning I give in the text, and I shall always use it myself in that way.

2 Most of the arguments which I have introduced in this section are deployed by Ayer, 1940, the main target of Austin's attack. I have not stuck closely to Ayer's version of them and I

shall not do so in succeeding sections. Nor am I particularly concerned to determine whether Austin's criticisms are fairly directed against Ayer, though there is some reason to think that they are not (cf. Hirst 1963; Ayer 1967). My aim is to decide what there is of enduring merit in the arguments and in Austin's attitude towards them. Accordingly, I shall refer to Ayer's discussion only where it will facilitate my own.

[3] I deal with Austin's arguments in a highly selective way. Ayer does not, in my view, put forward a very strong case for multiplying senses of 'see' and Austin makes some valid points against him. I shall not consider these points (or indeed Ayer's own arguments), and it may therefore look as though I effect an easy demolition of Austin by noticing only what is indefensible in his discussion. My aim once again, however, is to assess Austin's contribution to this problem on its own feet, rather than his success in a polemic against a particular view, and this is my reason for proceeding as I do.

[4] Nor is this merely an *ad hoc* invention to deal with this particular example. When the boring military strategist moves the salt and pepper pots around the table, saying 'These are our two battalions', the same sense is in play. Indeed, though I shall not pursue the matter here, 'is' is a very clear example of a term which cries out not just for dual but for multiple analysis, in defiance of the general injunction to avoid multiplying senses. Philosophers have long been aware of this, though there is disagreement as to just how many distinct senses 'is' has.

[5] In fairness to Austin, it is not clear from his remark whether he would want to use it in the way I have suggested. I have already noted his tendency simply to present the mass of cases where we use some expression, his tendency not to try very hard to systematise them, and this is evident in the present instance. Austin simply presents the case cited as one to be considered with the others. But then it is precisely the failure to understand the systematisation which is involved in analysis that vitiates this kind of objection.

VII Philosophical Problems: Truth

[1] It is sometimes argued that Austin makes statement-contents rather than statement-acts the primary truth-bearers (cf. Furberg, 1971, p. 124; Forguson, 1973, pp. 182–5). Evidence which may be cited in support of this is Austin's remark that the same sentence may be used by two different people to

make the same statement (PP, p. 120). Surely, if he talks of two people making the same statement he cannot be referring to a statement-act, which is a unique occurrence?

When I originally introduced the statement-act/content distinction in Chapter III, section 5, I noted that it is a distinction which Austin may not have been fully alive to, and this certainly makes interpretation of his position more hazardous. But I do not think it is right to suppose he thought of statement-contents as the primary truth-bearers. First, we need to observe a further distinction, different from the act/content distinction, viz. that between statement-tokens and statement-types. I may think of a statement-act *merely* as a unique historical occurrence, a token, or as a concrete occurrence *of a general type*, possibly exemplified on more than one occasion. I might, for example, go to two successive performances of *Hamlet* and say that the famous soliloquy was too soft in the first and too loud in the second. Now it is clear here that my comments are about statement-acts (a statement-content cannot be loud or soft), but I am able to abstract from those unique occurrences and talk of *the* soliloquy, one statement-act of a general type which can be performed more than once. When we put together all of Austin's remarks – about 'statement' referring to the historic use of a sentence, as well as its being possible for two people to make the same statement — the most reasonable interpretation is that he regarded statement-acts as primary truth-bearers *by virtue of their being acts which were particular tokens of some general type of statement-act*. And that is still to ascribe truth to concrete statement-acts.

² Curiously, the same is *not* true of the paper 'Truth' itself. I suggest a reason why in section 5.

³ Of course, if I promise in saying 'I promise' then the fact that I promise is also part of the world. The distinction between dependent and independent truth is not meant to imply a distinction between facts which are not in the world and facts which are. That is why I claim only that my distinction should *make it easier to see* that facts are part of the world.

⁴ In his earlier paper (1950b) it is not even clear whether Strawson really wishes to hold that facts and true statements are one and the same. On the one hand he says, 'If you prize the statements off the world you prize the facts off it too' (p. 39), yet on the other hand, 'It would indeed be wrong ... to identify "fact" and "true statement"; for these expressions have different roles in our language' (p. 38). What is clear,

however, is that in his later paper (1965) he puts forward objections similar to those which I go on to make in the text.

5 There may be an extraneous explanation for this. A contemporary of Austin's has suggested to me that he may have written 'Truth' with his tongue in his cheek, in order to teach a lesson to anyone who thought that an Austinian illocutionary analysis could be adopted wherever one wished. But if Austin did have his tongue in his cheek when he wrote 'Truth' he must have wished that he had bitten it off instead by the time he had to write the infinitely inferior 'Unfair to Facts'. It should perhaps be stressed that he did not choose to publish the latter in his lifetime.

6 Nor is this implicit parallel confined to one time or place. The Emperor Vespasian is reputed to have drawn it when placing a tax on public lavatories, and it is present in an early Portuguese anarchist poster bearing the slogan 'Cuando merda tiver valer, pobre nasce sem cu'. See also Melly, 1965, p. 187.

7 It should be emphasised that this is the only place where the view I describe can be attributed to Austin. Elsewhere, not only in his discussion of particular truths but also in remarks about the nature of truth itself, Austin concentrates on the creative aspect of truth-claims. Cf. Chapter IV, section 5, and Strawson 1973.

VIII Philosophical Problems: Action

1 My interpretation of the 'natural economy of language' derives from some unpublished suggestions of H. P. Grice. Cf. Searle, 1969, pp. 141ff.

2 On the other side, it is an argument which can be questioned at every single stage, including the assumption of premise (1). It may be argued that the scope of (1) is so wide that we could never know it to be true, or that the evidence of quantum physics shows that (1) is in fact false. Or it may be said that (2) does not follow since causation does not, on a proper understanding, include the idea of inevitability but only of regular occurrence. A common way of attempting to undermine the argument at another point is to object that human actions are not, in the required sense, events, and that it is a conceptual error to suppose that their occurrence can be explained by reference to causes, as opposed to people's reasons and purposes. None of these strategies seems to me very impressive, but I cannot pursue this here.

3 One qualification. In discussing the concept of capacities with others, I have come to the conclusion that though we talk of an agent's abilities as short-hand for what things the agent can do, we also speak of someone's *having the ability* to do something even if he *cannot* do it. For example, we might say that someone had the ability to win a race but could not because he was not allowed to enter. This may seems precisely to support Austin's claim about the need to observe fine distinctions, and to reveal the inadequacy of my alternative procedure. But it does not. The difference in idiom here is worth noting not because we happen to speak in this way but because our so speaking marks a distinction which there are, independently, good reasons for recovering. A human agent occupies a continuous stretch of space-time, although moving around in constantly changing circumstances. In the person of the agent, therefore, we have a clearly definable, circumscribed area within which there may be obstacles to the performance of certain actions. Our interest in knowing of the presence of obstacles, and the existence of an easily defined area where they may occur, explains and justifies the use of a separate but related form of expression in connexion with that area. In this sense, to say that an agent has the ability to do something is to say that *so far as concerns the agent himself* (as opposed to the circumstances in which he finds himself) there is no obstacle to his acting.

This idea of *agent-ability* I ignore in the sketch of an analysis which I go on to give. In any fully developed analysis it would occupy an essential place.

4 The distinction has great importance in moral contexts. Cf. Graham, 1975, section III.

Bibliography

1. Articles

Anscombe, G. E. M. (1965), 'The Intentionality of Sensation: A Grammatical Feature', in *Analytical Philosophy*, second series, ed. R. J. Butler, Blackwell, Oxford.

Ayer, A. J. (1967), 'Has Austin Refuted Sense-data?', *Synthese* 17. Reprinted in Fann (below).

Bennett, J. (1966), 'Real', *Mind* 75. Reprinted in Fann (below).

Cohen, L. J. (1964), 'Do Illocutionary Forces Exist?', *Philosophical Quarterly* 14. Reprinted in Fann (below).

Coval, S. and Forrest, T. (1967), 'Which Word Wears the Trousers?', *Mind* 76.

Edgley, R. (1975), 'Freedom of Speech and Academic Freedom', *Radical Philosophy* 10.

Fodor, J. A. (1964), 'On Knowing What We Would Say', *Philosophical Review* 73.

Fodor, J. A. and Katz, J. J. (1963), 'The Availability of What We Say', *Philosophical Review* 72.

Forguson, L. W. (1973), 'Locutionary and Illocutionary Acts', in Berlin (below).

Forrest, T. See S. Coval.

Goldman, A. I. (1967), 'A Causal Theory of Knowing', *Journal of Philosophy* 64.

Graham, K. (1973), 'Ifs, Cans and Dispositions', *Ratio* 14.

Graham, K. (1974), 'Belief and the Limits of Irrationality', *Inquiry* 17.

Graham, K. (1975), 'Moral Notions and Moral Misconceptions', *Analysis* 35.

Grice, H. P. (1957), 'Meaning', *Philosophical Review* 66.

Grice, H. P. (1961), 'The Causal Theory of Perception', *Proceedings of the Aristotelian Society*, supplementary volume 35.

Grice, H. P. (1968), 'Utterer's Meaning, Sentence-meaning and Word-meaning', *Foundations of Language* 4.

Grice, H. P. (1969), 'Utterer's Meaning and Intention', *Philosophical*

Review 78.

Hampshire, S. (1960), 'J. L. Austin, 1911–60', *Proceedings of the Aristotelian Society* 60.

Hartnack, J. (1963), 'The Performatory Use of Sentences', *Theoria* 29.

Hedenius, I. (1963), 'Performatives', *Theoria* 29.

Hirst, R. J. (1963), 'A Critical Study of *Sense and Sensibilia*', *Philosophical Quarterly* 13. Reprinted in Fann (below).

Katz, J. J. See J. A. Fodor.

Lemmon, E. J. (1962), 'On Sentences Verifiable by their Use', *Analysis* 22.

Lemmon, E. J. (1966), 'Sentences, Statements and Propositions', in *British Analytical Philosophy*, eds. B. Williams and A. Montefiore, Routledge & Kegan Paul, London.

Mackie, J. L. (1965), 'Causes and Conditions', *American Philosophical Quarterly* 2.

Mackie, J. L. (1970), 'Simple Truth', *Philosophical Quarterly* 20.

Mates, B. (1958), 'On the Verification of Statements about Ordinary Language', *Inquiry* 1.

Moore, G. E. (1942), 'An Autobiography', in *The Philosophy of G. E. Moore*, ed. P. A. Schilpp, Northwestern University, Evanston.

Pears, D. F. (1962), 'An Original Philosopher', *Times Literary Supplement* 9th February 1962. Reprinted in Fann (below).

Scriven, M. (1956), 'Randomness and the Causal Order', *Analysis* 17.

Searle, J. R. (1968), 'Austin on Locutionary and Illocutionary Acts', *Philosophical Review* 77. Reprinted in Berlin (below).

Skinner, Q. (1970), 'Conventions and the Understanding of Speech Acts', *Philosophical Quarterly* 20.

Skinner, Q. (1972), ' "Social Meaning" and the Explanation of Social Actions', in *Philosophy, Politics and Society*, fourth series, eds. P. Laslett, W.G. Runciman and Q. Skinner, Blackwell, Oxford.

Strawson, P. F. (1949), 'Truth', *Analysis* 9.

Strawson, P. F. (1950a), 'On Referring', *Mind* 59.

Strawson, P. F. (1950b), 'Truth', *Proceedings of the Aristotelian Society*, supplementary volume 24. Reprinted in *Truth*, ed. G. Pitcher, Prentice-Hall, Englewood Cliffs, New Jersey, 1964.

Strawson, P. F. (1964), 'Intention and Convention in Speech Acts', *Philosophical Review* 73. Reprinted in Fann (below).

Strawson, P. F. (1965), 'Truth: A Reconsideration of Austin's Views', *Philosophical Quarterly* 15.

Strawson, P. F. (1973), 'Austin and "Locutionary Meaning" ', in Berlin (below).

Urmson, J. O. and Warnock, G. J. (1960), 'J. L. Austin', *Mind* 70. Reprinted in Fann (below).

Warnock, G. J. (1964), 'Truth and Correspondence', in *Knowledge and Experience*, ed. C. D. Rollins, University of Pittsburgh Press.

Watling, J. L. (1955), 'Inference from the Known to the Unknown', *Proceedings of the Aristotelian Society* 55.

Wiggins, D. (1971), 'On Sentence-sense, Word-sense and Difference of Word-sense', in *Semantics*, eds. D.D. Steinberg and L. A. Jakobovits, Cambridge University Press.

Wisdom, J. (1946), 'Other Minds', *Proceedings of the Aristotelian Society*, supplementary volume 20.

2. Books

Armstrong, D. M. (1973), *Belief, Truth and Knowledge*, Cambridge University Press.

Ayer, A. J. (1940), *The Foundations of Empirical Knowledge*, Macmillan, London.

Ayer, A. J. (1956), *The Problem of Knowledge*, Penguin, Harmondsworth.

Berlin, I. Ed. (1973), *Essays on J. L. Austin*, Clarendon Press, Oxford.

Black, M. See P. T. Geach.

Chisholm, R. M. (1966), *Theory of Knowledge*, Prentice-Hall, Englewood Cliffs, New Jersey.

Dretske, F. (1969), *Seeing and Knowing*, Routledge & Kegan Paul, London.

Dummett, M. (1973), *Frege*, Duckworth, London.

Fann, K. T. ed. (1969), *Symposium on J. L. Austin*, Routledge & Kegan Paul, London.

Furberg, M. (1971), *Saying and Meaning*, Blackwell, Oxford.

Geach, P. T. and Black, M. eds. (1952), *Translations from the Philosophical Writings of Gottlob Frege*, Blackwell, Oxford.

Locke, D. (1967), *Perception and Our Knowledge of the External World*, George Allen & Unwin Ltd., London.

Mackie, J.L. (1973), *Truth, Probability and Paradox*, Clarendon Press, Oxford.

Mackie, J. L. (1974), *The Cement of the Universe*, Clarendon Press, Oxford.

Melly, G. (1965), *Owning Up*, Weidenfeld and Nicholson, London.

Moore, G. E. (1912), *Ethics*, second edition, Oxford University Press (1966).

Quine, W. V. O. (1953), *From a Logical Point of View*, Harvard University Press.

Ryle, G. (1949), *The Concept of Mind*, Hutchinson, London.

Searle, J. R. (1969), *Speech Acts*, Cambridge University Press.

Wertheimer, R. (1972), *The Significance of Sense*, Cornell University Press, Ithaca and London.

Wiggins, D. (1967), *Identity and Spatio-temporal Continuity*, Blackwell, Oxford.

Index

277